PELICAN BOOKS

THE SUEZ AFFAIR

Hugh Thomas was born in 1931 and educated at Sherborne, Dorset, and Queens' College, Cambridge, where he was president of the Union. After a year at the Sorbonne, he joined the Foreign Office, but left it in 1957. He was for a time a Labour parliamentary candidate and a lecturer at the Royal Military Academy, Sandhurst. Afterwards he was an adviser on disarmament to the United Nations Association, and since 1966 has been Professor of History at the University of Reading. He has written two novels, *The World's Game* and *The Oxygen Age*, and edited the anthology *The Establishment*. In 1961 he published *The Spanish Civil War* (available as a Pelican book). He has just completed his second study of a Hispanic revolution, *Cuba or The Pursuit of Freedom*, to be published in autumn 1970.

Ann Smallbom
25. 2. 71.

HUGH THOMAS

The Suez Affair

PENGUIN BOOKS

Penguin Books Ltd, Harmondsworth, Middlesex, England
Penguin Books Australia Ltd, Ringwood, Victoria, Australia

—

First published by Weidenfeld and Nicolson 1967
Substantially revised edition published in Pelican Books 1970
Copyright © Hugh Thomas, 1966, 1967

—

Some of the material in this book was originally
published in the *Sunday Times*

—

Made and printed in Great Britain
by Hazell Watson & Viney Ltd,
Aylesbury, Bucks
Set in Linotype Times

CONTENTS

MAPS

(drawn by Ted Powers)

PREFACE TO THE FIRST EDITION

IN this inquiry I try and tell the story of the 'great expedition' to Suez set on foot in 1956 by the British and French Governments of the time, taking into account such material as has since then been published and such personal recollections as I have been able to gather during the course of a summer ten years later. Could it fairly be said that, as one senior adviser of the Government put it, Suez represented 'a complete breakdown of cabinet government', or, as another put it, that it could be called a 'collective aberration'? Could Dulles be saddled with all the blame? Did illness play a decisive part in disturbing the judgement of the Prime Minister of the time? Could the expedition ever have been a success? Was there a military failure or only a political one? And what about the Israelis; and was Nasser really angry about the Aswan Dam? All these seemed interesting questions about which I, like others, had jumped to conclusions at the time and which I had not explored since.

If Suez had led to a great triumph for any of the countries concerned, some of these problems might have been smoothed away; but, looking back on it, no one can be quite happy. The ignominy may have been greatest for Britain and France; but even Egypt (whose army was smashed) and Israel (whose victory depended rather more than was admitted at the time on Anglo-French help) find Suez historically a little unsettling; for the USA, Suez was a diplomatic failure. Victory brings autobiographies, official histories, not to speak of memorial banquets; defeat is not only an orphan, as President Kennedy put it, but also inarticulate.

Suez is thus left in a curious no man's land of time; too painful, too close to be reached effectively by the heavy artillery of history; but also a little too far for the snipers of contemporary politics and journalism. The account which follows thus resembles a journey to one of those accidentally preserved châteaux between the lines which crop up in plays about the First World War. For Britain, of course, this journey is peculiarly poignant. In 1956 much of the British Empire seemed to survive; Europe had not recovered, Africa was not free. The British standard of living was still higher than any on the Continent. For the USA, Suez was one more crisis between Korea and Castro; for us, it is an event already in another world, a world certain to disintegrate, Suez or no Suez, a world already based more on prestige than on power, but one to which the previous two or three centuries of imperial history had accustomed us. To remember Suez is to remember a time when the Chancellor of the Exchequer could think of nothing more terrible than to 'sink' to the status of a 'new Netherlands'.

In order to investigate the truth, I approached the surviving protagonists of that time. To some, of course, the memory was too painful to be revived. Some cloaked their pain by that curious statute, the Official Secrets Act, others by more elaborate devices. Many were helpful, and to them I express my gratitude, even though, since this is a work from no man's land, I cannot do so by name.

This method of work, of course, has special limitations. Memories are not reliable. With the best will in the world, everyone forgets, particularly disagreeable facts. One of the curious aspects of this affair, however, and one which seemed to give the search for oral testimony extra point, was the fact that on one interesting aspect of it official papers not only were not available to me but may never be to anyone; for if they existed, they seem to have been destroyed at the time, or soon after. It also seemed likely that unless some effort was made to collect the recollections of some of the British participants in the affair, such case as Britain had would go by default on every instance; thus the machinery of American historiography is already grinding over the age of Eisenhower, based on the papers of the President and his Secretary of State, and though those statesmen, of course, had a point of view it would be absurd to think that their version is always right: Mr Eisenhower's memory sometimes falters, his Secretary of State occasionally deluded himself.

Most of my informants were British; but there were some critical exceptions. I have usually preferred the evidence of my informants to any secondary authorities, though sometimes the statements or allegations made by these are used or examined. I cannot pretend that this book gives the full story of Suez. It is an interim Report.

The number of veiled source references may perhaps seem excessively discreet. This illustrates one of the problems of writing contemporary history. Since many of those who spoke to me did so strictly 'off the record', this sort of discretion is inevitable.

I must thank the *Sunday Times* for urging on me this task and Mr Mark Boxer of that paper for his patient assistance. This book is an expanded version of the articles published in the *Sunday Times*; but rather less than a third of the material has been published before. I am also grateful to Mr D. C. Watt of the London School of Economics for reading the proofs and for a good deal of other invaluable assistance.

21 October 1966   HUGH THOMAS

PREFACE TO THE PELICAN EDITION

THIS second edition of *The Suez Affair* has been substantially revised, and takes into account relevant works published since the first edition of April 1967. Of these the most important were Anthony Nutting's *No End of a Lesson*, General Paul Ely's *Mémoires*, volume II (*Suez ... le 13 mai*), General Maurice Challe's *Notre Révolte* and General André Beaufre's *L'Expédition de Suez*. The only important change of substance rendered necessary relates to the timing of the proposal whereby Britain joined France and Israel in a political alliance in October 1956. This is discussed in the text on pages 96–8.

The attributions to anonymous individuals rendered necessary by the confidentiality of their evidence have continued, despite the understandable irritation caused to some readers. However, with the deaths since 1967 of Lords Kilmuir and Tenby (Gwilym Lloyd George) I have felt it possible to identify these gentlemen among my sources (they were in the first edition described as a 'senior Minister' and a 'well-placed Minister'). For the rest I can only assure sceptical readers that all the other sources are what they are described to be.

The dramatic occurrences of July–November 1956 are now no longer a matter of the first political importance in either England or France and hence can perhaps be considered a subject for at least preliminary historical inquiry. The events themselves have been overshadowed in the Middle East by the June War of 1967, a conflict which indeed overnight relegated the happenings of eleven years before to a problem of history, particularly in the region of actual combat. Nevertheless history itself often acts upon current political controversy : could or would the Egyptian President have argued in 1967 that Britain and the USA were in secret alliance with Israel had there not been secret relationships in 1956? Perhaps, contrariwise, before the war of 1967, the belief that Israel was alone, whereas in 1956 she had relied on France and Britain to provide aerial assistance, was one reason why Colonel Nasser was tempted into a policy of adventure, somewhat against his better judgement. I hope therefore that this new edition of *The Suez Affair* will further soothe old anxieties.

1 February 1970 HUGH THOMAS

MAP 1
SUEZ AT THE CENTRE OF THE WORLD

── Oil Pipeline ■ British Bases ▲ Oil Wells

500 miles   1,000 miles

French Empire

Libya

Algeria

Tunisia

Morocco

Agadir

Gibraltar

Algiers

Alexandria
Cairo
Suez
Port Said

■ Malta

Brindisi

Marseilles

Paris

Southampton
London

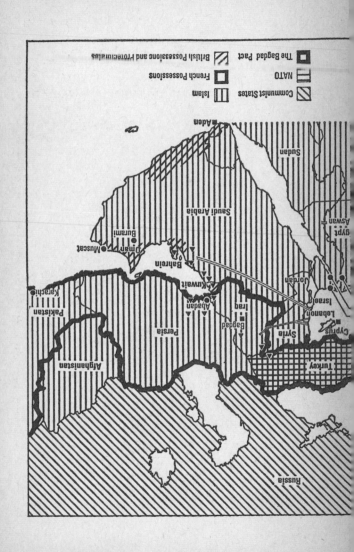

1

APPEASEMENT

28 November [1893]. On board the Hydaspes.

The only fellow passengers I have made acquaintance with
are Lady Waterford and Sir John Stokes, the latter on his
way to the Suez Canal of which he is a Director, to open the
new railroad from Port Said to Ismailia. With Stokes I have
had much talk about the Suez Canal, British trade and the
Mediterranean route in time of war. He tells me three-
quarters of the tonnage passing through the Canal is British,
of which perhaps half is for English ports, the rest for other
ports in Europe. In time of war with France this could not
continue. The Red Sea was quite safe but the whole line of
the Mediterranean would be blocked and this would continue until the British had broken up the enemy's forces and
confined them to their ports, then convoys could be arranged
and trade resumed. ... He considers that the Canal will
eventually be internationalized, though by the terms of the
concession it will revert to Egypt in 1959 [*sic*] but 'nobody
looks so far as that ahead'.

From The Diaries of Wilfred Scawen Blunt

ONE spring day in April 1955 a crowd gathered in front of the
Prime Minister's house in Downing Street to watch the immortal Churchill leave for Buckingham Palace to give up the
seals of office. As the day wore on, and Churchill's departure
was delayed, the people drifted little by little away towards the
small door in the Foreign Office on Horseguards Parade from
which Sir Anthony Eden, the Foreign Secretary, would ultimately come out in answer to the Queen's summons. The scene
was reminiscent of one in Saint-Simon's memoirs where, when
it becomes clear that the Great King, Louis XIV, is dead, the
courtiers and royal bastards scurry across to the apartments of
the Regent Orleans. A new age was beginning, though Eden
was not intended to be a regent.

Churchill had given up power at that time since his party
wanted an election at the then favourable moment which might

not recur. It was desirable to fight with the new leader, if there were to be one; and it had become clear that Churchill could not linger on much more, though the old Prime Minister himself had sought to postpone his departure, partly perhaps because at the last he had had doubts about the successor whom he himself had named. But the new leader had to be Eden: Churchill had made him his heir in the middle of the war. Eden had thus had a long time as dauphin.

Having been for so long Foreign Secretary, Eden knew of all the troubles abroad likely to beset him as Prime Minister: had Russia really changed since Stalin's death two years before? The matter would soon be put to the test at the much-heralded Summit Conference, ironically an idea pressed by Churchill since 1953 rather against Eden's inclination. There was a chance of war between Communist China and Chiang Kai-shek over the Chinese off-shore islands. The settlement of the French war in Vietnam, achieved after much work at Geneva by Eden himself, was still not a year old; it was unclear whether it would last. The long struggle for German rearmament which had so debilitated the French parliament was admittedly about to end with Germany's entry into NATO. But Churchill's last major decision had been to approve a project to build a British hydrogen bomb: a scheme fraught with uncertainties since it offered a poor example to the rest of the world as to what might be expected from a Great Power of less than the top rank.

More dangerous still, the Middle East was a cauldron of enmities: enmity between Britain, still the paramount power, her commercial interests preserved by treaties and troops, and Arab nationalism; enmity between the traditional Arab leaders in Iraq and Saudi Arabia and Nasser in Egypt; old enmities between Iraq and Egypt as to who would be the decisive magnet of Arab unity; enmity between Iraq and Syria over the traditional desire of the Iraqi royal house to establish themselves as monarchs of the Fertile Crescent, that is, Syria and Iraq unified; rivalry between Britain and France who, till the Second World War, had a dependency in Syria and Lebanon from which during the Vichy era she had been expelled by British troops; enmity between France and all the Arab countries, since in the French civil war with revolutionary Algeria (the war had begun the previous autumn), Nasser appeared to French politicians to be the patron of the rebels; barely concealed rivalry between Britain and the USA who, with no traditional interests, thought chiefly of commerce with Arab nationalism with which they believed, owing to their own long-lost colonial past, they could get on terms (Britain hoped to renew something of her position in the Middle East with a new Defence Pact; the USA wanted an alliance formed by a ring of states against the Russian border); and, most important of all, enmity between the new small state of Israel, with a population still under two million, and her Arab neighbours, who, forty million strong, smarted from defeat by Israel in the formally unfinished war following Britain's abandonment of her mandate in Palestine. There was also Arab suspicion that US policy towards the Middle East was directed by Zionists.

British concern for the Middle East derived of course from her long association with it during the slow collapse of the Turkish Empire, culminating in the victories there in the World Wars. The British Empire had defended Egypt twice. The achievements of travellers and adventurers such as Gordon, Doughty and Lawrence exercised a powerful hold over patriotic emotions. Cromer, Milner, Allenby, Kitchener and Lloyd still guarded the conservative imagination. The Middle East also provided most of the oil used by Britain and half that used by West Europe. British commercial interests also included the Suez Canal Company, a great international enterprise, technically of Egyptian nationality, which, having been for two generations the path to empire, had become even more important as the path to petrol.

Britain in 1956 still ruled half Africa. The word 'Empire' was scarcely anachronistic. The continuing political weakness of France and of Europe, combined with the unpopular dogmatism of US diplomacy under the inspiration of John Foster Dulles, gave Britain the illusion of greater power than she actually possessed.

The great controversy during Churchill's second administration had concerned Egypt, where British troops had been since 1882, partly to guarantee the safe working of the Suez Canal, partly to maintain other Middle Eastern interests. Britain had withdrawn troops from Cairo in 1947 and from Palestine in 1948. After the officers' revolution of 1952 (which eventually brought Nasser to be President of Egypt), Britain agreed, by the Treaty of 1954, to withdraw from the Canal Zone, leaving behind the large base at Ismailia to which she could theoretically return in the event of an attack on any members of the Arab League, or on Turkey (though not if the attack were by Israel). This withdrawal had been agreed without, as Britain (and the USA) had previously hoped, the previous establishment of a new Middle East Defence Organization, and only after much terrorist activity against British forces in the Canal Zone, culminating in a famous night of bloodshed in Cairo in 1952. Churchill had disliked this 'scuttle' from Egypt and, though reluctantly supporting his Foreign Secretary, Eden, had given encouragement to Conservatives of the imperialist Right such as Captain Charles Waterhouse and the young Julian Amery.[1] By the time that Eden became Prime Minister, the first withdrawals of troops from Egypt were beginning. It was planned that British civilian technicians would keep up the base after the soldiers had left.

For the 'Suez group' (of which Amery was secretary and Waterhouse leader) the rot in the British position in the Middle East had begun with the withdrawal from Palestine:

We should have held Haifa and the Holy Places and from there guaranteed Israeli and Arab frontiers. The abandonment of Palestine forced us to build up in Egypt. Then the abandonment of Abadan showed the Pashas the way. The next withdrawal – from Egypt – led to the collapse of the old idea of the Commonwealth. Hadn't the withdrawal from India been based on the assumption we would stay in Egypt?[2]

1. cf. Lord Moran, *Churchill, The Struggle for Survival*, pp. 478 ff. Churchill's private secretary telephoned Amery to congratulate him on a speech which he had made criticizing the withdrawal from Suez (evidence of Julian Amery).
2. Amery to the author.

Thus Amery recalled in 1966; such views were in 1956 held by a powerful minority; even Sir Robert Boothby (on the liberal though pro-Israeli wing of the Conservative Party) thought that Britain should establish a base at Haifa; and Churchill's ideas were close to those of Amery.

The US on the other hand desired a general Middle East defence agreement, which would include Egypt, though only after the British had left it, so as to avoid any taint of 'colonialism'. US diplomats had brought pressure on the British to withdraw from Egypt and immediately after having achieved this offered Nasser a grant-aid agreement so that he could buy arms. Nasser rejected this because he feared that he would be accused of 'selling his country out to another big power before the British even got out of the place'.[3] But the US pressed on with their defence plan, hoping to include in it Pakistan, Turkey, Iraq and others. Britain seized on this as a possible way of prolonging her rights in Iraq which were due shortly to expire – but this idea offended both Egypt and the US. Nasser argued to Eden in Cairo in February 1955 that security in the Middle East was to be gained not by bases but by economic and social advance. Egypt also considered this new plan treacherous to Arab interests since Turkey had recognized Israel.

This conversation between Eden and Nasser was a curious occasion: Eden, passing through Cairo on his way to the Far East, had summoned Nasser, already Prime Minister, to the British Embassy and had lectured him on foreign policy, without allowing him much time to talk. Nasser felt that Eden treated him as 'a junior official who could not be expected to understand politics'.[4] Eden on the other hand left thinking Nasser 'a fine man physically',[5] and on return to London told

3. A comment by Henry Byroade, Assistant Secretary of State for Near Eastern Affairs. Dulles's evidence in the hearings on the Eisenhower Doctrine makes clear the US pressure on Britain.

4. See Nasser's interview in the *Sunday Times*, 24 June 1962; Nasser later said the same to Woodrow Wyatt who reported the conversation to the author. Eden (*Full Circle*, p. 221) suggests that he was quite unaware of any such tension.

5. Eden, p. 221.

the Conservative Party's 1922 Committee that Nasser was the best sort of Egyptian and a great improvement on the Pashas of the past.[6] By then, however, Nasser and his brother officers had decided to embark upon a diplomacy of 'non-alignment' with either the Soviet bloc or the West.

British relations were ambiguous with Egypt; they were worse with Israel. Even when British troops were still in the Canal Zone, Egypt had with impunity prevented ships bound to and from Israel from using the Suez Canal. In justification Egypt claimed to be still at war with Israel and, so the British law officers (of the Labour administration) had argued, Israel had no case to force Egypt to open the Canal.[7] Still, Britain had taken the matter to the UN, where a resolution in late 1951 had called on Egypt to lift the ban. But Egypt did not do so, and the Conservatives, who recaptured power in London at that time, did nothing to make her carry out the resolution. Israel was also hampered from using for commerce the eastern side of the Sinai peninsula (on which she had the small port of Eilat) because of Egyptian fortifications on the two little islands at the foot of the Gulf of Akaba.

The Arab-Israeli tension disturbed the rest of the world. Britain, France and the USA had issued a declaration in 1950 saying that they would try and balance the flow of arms to the two sides and take common counsel if either Israel or the Arabs crossed the armistice lines of 1948. This Tripartite Declaration, which the governments concerned frequently announced as the keystone of their policies in the Middle East, had no binding power. When the British finally left the Suez Canal Zone, it would be but one more 'scrap of paper', relying for its credibility on faraway forces unable to act fast. Israel could now never expect the opening of the Suez Canal to her, nor any settlement of the sporadic violence on her borders; and so Israel, like Egypt, moved into a more militant posture.

Ever since the end of the open war between Israel and the Arabs, the latter had never lost hope that one day the state of Israel would be removed. Arab guerrilla raids were made into

6. Evidence of a Conservative MP.
7. Evidence of a Cabinet Minister.

Israel. Israel replied to these by massive reprisals. Her reprisal raid (six weeks after the formation of the Bagdad Pact) on 28 February 1955 caused the Middle East crisis to become again a world one. Thereafter tragedy seemed inevitable; and indeed it came, though not surprisingly, for Israel or for Egypt, but for the two old empires of North-western Europe the emotions of whose leaders as much as the interests of whose people chanced to be so deeply concerned.

Soon after, Nasser requested $27 million worth of arms from the USA. The State Department rightly believed that Nasser had no money and asked for payment in cash[8]; Eisenhower in his memoirs suggests that this financial argument weighed as much with him as his obligation to maintain the balance between Israel and her neighbours. Nasser also refused to accept a US military advisory group of officers to supervise the use of the arms if they were sold and that may have been a more telling point with the Pentagon. Thwarted of arms, in the month that Eden took power in England, April 1955, the Egyptian General Staff set up a special organization in the Gaza strip under their Intelligence Branch to carry out sabotage and terrorism inside Israel. These '*fedayun*' or self-sacrifice guerrilleros of the border apparently numbered about 700. The same month Britain adhered formally to the Bagdad Pact and at the Bandung Conference Nasser asked Chou en-Lai if China would sell arms to Egypt (following the earlier example of Syria who had in March actually received a Russian guarantee).[9] The stakes were beginning to be raised.

In May 1955 Eden called for a general election. He won it by an increased majority, and in July met Eisenhower, Bulganin and Khrushchev and the French Prime Minister at Geneva. Churchill's absence meant that the occasion did not become one of those great brindisis of international good cheer which marked the Second World War. The meetings indeed seemed like a curious parody of those grander times. None of the participants brought any carefully prepared new plan to dis

8. Eisenhower, *Waging Peace*, p. 24.

9. Seale, *The Struggle for Syria*, p. 235; Dayan, *Diary of the Sinai Campaign*, p. 5. The Bandung Conference was also in April 1955.

cuss; but all, except the Russians, thought up some headline-catching idea at the last minute. The consequence was that the Conference did nothing save to create the short-lived feeling of well-being known as the 'Spirit of Geneva'. The British Foreign Secretary, Harold Macmillan, returned to London with the happy comment: 'There ain't gonna be no war.' The hopes so engendered were swiftly dashed by events in the Middle East.

In May Egypt had learned that though China could not help her, Russia would sell her arms in almost any quantity. The next month therefore Nasser made a final appeal for war material to Britain and the USA, and directly threatened to turn to Russia if she were thwarted. This threat was apparently dismissed as bluff. At the same time Israel, who already had friends in the French Ministries of the Interior (which looked after Algeria) and of Defence, received some tanks and other new weapons from France. At the end of June Russo-Egyptian negotiations for arms began. The next month an election in Israel brought a majority of deputies to the Knesset who were eager for strong action. On 26 July secret deliveries of arms began to leave Prague for Cairo. In September Israel carried out another strong counter-raid on an Egyptian frontier post. Egypt immediately tightened her control over the Gulf of Akaba, preventing Israeli civil aeroplanes from flying over it. The adversaries thus seemed to be giving blow for blow in a diplomatic contest whose conclusion could surely only be war.

Until this time Egypt's armed forces had been only equipped with old British armaments. Now she began to order Stalin tanks, MiGs and Ilyushins, as well as Czech rifles. The sums pledged were believed to be over £12 million and even thought to approach £30 million,[10] though payment was to be made in cotton. The US administration dispatched a Middle East expert, George Allen, to try and prevent the Czech arms deal from being confirmed. He failed. The Agreement was announced on 27 September. Dulles consequently told Molotov at the Foreign Ministers' Conference in Geneva in October that the Czech shipment was making war more likely in the Middle East. Israel replied by asking the USA for more arms,

10. Eisenhower, p. 25.

but, Eisenhower has since explained, 'after considerable deliberation . . . we decided against it'.[11]

Israeli anxiety therefore grew. They did not know what and how many weapons Egypt was buying. So far as aircraft were concerned, Israel herself had then only thirty obsolete jet fighters. The Prime Minister, Moshe Sharett, a man of peace, flew to Paris and buttonholed the Foreign Ministers of the Great Powers both there and later in Geneva. Israel received encouragement only from the French Prime Minister, Edgar Faure, who promised to sell her a modern version of the Mystère fighter-bomber, the Mark IV; but the inclination in the Quai d'Orsay was still to try and limit Nasser's help to the Algerian rebels by placating Egypt, rather than to enter upon enmity with her. Shimon Peres, Director-General of the Israeli Ministry of Defence, had been in contact with French politicians and officials in pursuit of arms since 1954, but up till then the Quai d'Orsay had finally decided policy. Israel was then further perturbed by the establishment of a joint Egyptian-Syrian command on 19 October.

These events, as well as spoiling the international climate of Geneva, persuaded some in Israel to contemplate a preventive war against Egypt. Ben Gurion, the father of the Israeli state, had, after several months in the desert at Sde Boker, returned to the Cabinet as Minister of Defence. On 23 October, while the Prime Minister, Sharett, was still in Europe, Ben Gurion instructed the Chief of Staff of the Israeli army, Moshe Dayan, 'among other things . . . to be prepared to capture the Straits of Tiran . . . in order to ensure freedom of shipping through the Gulf of Akaba and the Red Sea'.[12] Ten days later Ben Gurion became Prime Minister again, publicly declared that the Israelis would not let themselves be slaughtered as if they were cattle and immediately proposed in Cabinet a bold thrust west against Egypt. But the Israeli Cabinet rejected the idea and uneasily entered upon diplomatic negotiations to avoid having recourse to war. In these her new Prime Minister and her Chief of Staff had little faith. Dayan wrote to Ben

11. Eisenhower, p. 25; Seale, pp. 235–6.   12. Dayan, p. 12.

Gurion on 5 December that he thought Israel should capture the Straits of Tiran 'within one month'.[13]

Britain, the USA and France continued for some time to hope that they could secure their ends in the Middle East by a policy of conciliation with Nasser. Despite the Czech-Egyptian arms deal, this came easiest to the USA: the US administration still believed Nasser to be a representative of authentic Arab nationalism. The British were worried about 'letting Russia into the Middle East' and hence into Africa, but they thought that this could for the time being at least be best prevented by outbidding the Communists in anything they had to offer. Even France, in late 1955, embarked on a careful appeasement of Nasser, promising further sales of arms, on the condition that Nasser's radio, the Voice of the Arabs, ceased attacks on French policy in Algeria.

In November Eden carried this policy of appeasement a little further in a speech at the Guildhall, with a vague suggestion that, if Israel and the Arabs could reach agreement on their frontiers, Britain and perhaps the USA would guarantee them. In his memoirs Eden admitted that this speech was 'unwise', though he seems not to have realized even then that what he said was regarded by the Israelis as a threat to their own boundaries: they suspected that the Negev might be taken from them, perhaps as a result of some secret treaty. This fear dictated Israeli attitudes towards Britain till even as late as 1958.

The policy of conciliating Nasser, however, reached its peak when the next month, in December 1955, Britain and the USA offered to pay the foreign exchange costs of Nasser's splendid project for a new dam high up the Nile above Aswan. Britain had doubts about the economic value of this project and knew that it would cause difficulties with the Sudan (which would become independent on 1 January 1956) but agreed to support it, as Eden says in his memoirs, specifically in order to keep Russia out of Africa;[14] Russia had hinted that she would be prepared to pay for the dam just before. (Britain continued to

13. Dayan, p. 15.
14. Eden, p. 420. See also J. E. Dougherty's article 'The Aswan Decision in Perspective', *Political Science Quarterly*, March 1959.

suspect that the development of the Nile valley in a less grandiose way would be better than the High Dam.) Dulles, recalling legal experience of loans to Latin America, believed that it was always undesirable to be a creditor nation on this scale, but finally agreed for, it seems, the same motive that impelled the British. The World Bank agreed also to help.[15] A memorandum by Eisenhower as early as April 1953 had in fact argued that help for the Aswan Dam should be specifically compensated for by Egyptian backing for Western policy in the area.[16]

Nasser did not show much enthusiasm for this offer. His technicians preferred working with Western machinery and suppliers but both he and his financial advisers disliked the Western budgetary control that the World Bank regarded as a condition for a loan. If the West had indeed financed the Dam, the Egyptian economy would have been largely directed by Washington for five years.

The British meantime were struggling on with their schemes to extend the Bagdad Pact. Persia had joined it in early October, but Jordan was reluctant. A visit by the British Chief of the Imperial General Staff, General Templer, to Amman in January was counter-productive. Riots, encouraged by anti-British broadcasts from Cairo, broke through the Jordanian capital and three Governments fell in succession. A new Jordanian Prime Minister promised to keep the country out of the Bagdad Pact. This marked a victory for Nasser, and Cairo Radio redoubled its attacks on Iraq, the only Arab nation in the Pact.

In March 1956 new British and French Foreign Ministers, Selwyn Lloyd and Christian Pineau, separately visited the Middle East and each of them called on Nasser. While Lloyd

15. The USA, Britain and the World Bank would pay for the initial costs of tools, materials, etc. from sources outside Egypt, during the first stage of the project (four or five years). Afterwards, there would probably be other commitments. The USA expected that their annual commitment would be $10 million, or $56 million in all over the first five years of construction, while the British would be responsible for $14 million in all. The World Bank would raise a loan of $200 million, at 5 per cent.

16. Memorandum by the President, 23 April 1953.

was dining with Nasser, the news came that King Hussein of Jordan had dismissed General Glubb, Lawrence's heir and commander of the Arab Legion, the British-trained force which made Jordan the strongest Arab country, militarily, after Egypt.[17] Glubb was the last symbol of the old British paternalist hegemony in the Middle East, based on friendship with that 'world of camels and childlike bedouin with flowing cloaks' of which Nasser explicitly was so ashamed. Nasser heard this news on getting home, and thought it (he afterwards remarked) a clever move by Britain, and next morning congratulated Lloyd. Lloyd thought this a bad joke. The ensuing conversation was clearly as misunderstood by the two parties to it as was that between Eden and Nasser eighteen months previously. For Lloyd believed that in the course of it Nasser promised to cease anti-British propaganda on Cairo Radio; it was the breach of this promise (rather than, as was sometimes said, the belief that Hussein's act had been engineered to coincide with his dinner) that caused Lloyd to believe that Nasser had deceived him. On the other hand, Nasser found Lloyd 'far more receptive' than Eden had been, though he later refused to admit any obligation to him. Nasser also made quite clear to Lloyd that he was irretrievably opposed to the Bagdad Pact and that was that.[18] Lloyd also encountered other personal challenges in the Middle East: among them during his visit to Bahrein a demonstration against Sir Charles Belgrave, the British adviser to the Ruler; and Cairo Radio continued to thunder against British power everywhere, even broadcasting in Swahili.

The visit to Egypt a week after Lloyd of Pineau, the French Foreign Minister, had been preceded by a resumption by France of the sale of arms to Israel – twelve Mystères, which the French asked the USA to approve under the Tripartite Agreement. Eisenhower had agreed, 'pleased . . . that the French had queried us; their doing so seemed to prove that such co-

17. He had seen, in the British magazine *Picture Post*, General Glubb described as the uncrowned King of Jordan. Hussein's action was the climax of a long-growing antipathy to Glubb, encouraged by Jordanian army officers.

18. Evidence of a Cabinet Minister.

ordination between us was desirable and necessary'.[19] These were Mystères Mark IV. By now, however, French elections (in January) had brought a new Government to power, that of the socialist Guy Mollet with Radical support. This Government, for ideological reasons, was determined from the start to help Israel and in early February Mollet had also clashed with the French settlers in Algiers; he thereafter decided to follow a policy of war *à l'outrance* against the Algerian rebels. France had refused to sell 300 mortars to Egypt in February, on the grounds that they might be sent to Algeria. Immediately after he became Prime Minister, Guy Mollet received Shimon Peres, the Director-General of the Israeli Ministry of Defence, and told him: 'Now you will see that I will not be a Bevin'. Peres had already established contact with the new Minister of Defence, Bourgès-Maunoury, and his staff, while he had been Minister of the Interior in the previous government. Now contacts became much closer and more regular.[20]

France and Egypt were however still prepared to collaborate over one thing: their hostility to the Bagdad Pact, which France disliked as an attempt to preserve British power indefinitely in a region where France had once been influential. As in the case of Lloyd's visit, it is unclear precisely what happened while Pineau was in Cairo. According to Pineau, Nasser promised to cease helping the Algerian rebels, providing that the French continued their criticism of the Bagdad Pact.[21] Nasser later denied having made any such undertaking, and maintained that he had merely said that there were no Algerians training in Egypt and no Egyptians in Algeria.[22] In the event neither side kept their promise and both felt aggrieved. But neither could have kept such a promise; in the mood of alarm in England which had followed the dismissal of Glubb, the French Prime Minister, Guy Mollet, had visited England and in fact undertaken not to criticize the Bagdad Pact, in return for

19. Eisenhower, p. 29.
20. Shimon Peres, *David's Sling*, pp. 60–61.
21. Azeau, *La Piège de Suez*, p. 104.
22. Nasser on BBC TV, 20 September 1966, and Third Programme, 7 July 1966.

general British support over Algeria.[23] A sudden and surprising
warmth sprang up between the English conservative and the
French socialist, and Eden's always latent francophilia thereafter never died. Eden from that time became converted to the
view that Nasser was the main enemy of Britain in the Middle
East.[24] Julian Amery, secretary still of the Suez group, found
himself suddenly *persona grata* with the Foreign Office; already
in contact with Israelis such as Peres, of the Defence Ministry
in Tel Aviv, Amery visited Pineau in the spring in Paris to urge
an end to his policy of conciliation; and perhaps this advice of a
British MP was a minor factor in changing Pineau's mind. In
the weeks that followed, France gave up all thought that Nasser
could be bought off or conciliated. Thus by May Colonel Louis
Mangin, an aide to the French Minister of Defence, Bourgès-
Maunoury, was telling an enthusiastic audience of *anciens com-
battants* at Lyons that Nasser was a new Hitler, to be resisted
just as surely as their old enemy of the Wolfschanze. This was
apparently the first time that this celebrated analogy was employed. At the same time, it would appear that the Iraqi
Government, with at least the tacit support of the British and
US Governments, began to give financial and other backing on
a regular basis to Syrian exiles seeking to overthrow the pro-
Nasser regime in Damascus.[25]

Certainly the new policies were not consistently followed.
Pineau always found Nasser less an agent of anti-Christ than a
'*grand marchand de tapis*', between East and West, and he
never succumbed to the historical analogy popular in the
Ministry of Defence.[26] The Quai d'Orsay was always reluctant,

23. *The Times*, 12 March 1956. Eden says in his memoirs that at this
meeting at Chequers he and Mollet did 'good work in aligning our
policies' and that Mollet loyally thereafter 'refrained from criticizing the
Bagdad Pact' (*Full Circle*, p. 436). Pineau and Lloyd were still away in
the Middle East. Rumours about this meeting persist. Thus the Egyptian
weekly *Akhbar al Yom* (29 October 1966) alleges that an invasion of
Egypt on 20 March 1956 was planned. The plan was supposed to have
been delayed to permit Israel to increase her forces.

24. Anthony Nutting, *No End of a Lesson*, pp. 28–9. Nutting dates this
event as the time when 'Eden completely lost his touch'.

25. The evidence is summarized in Seale, pp. 270 ff.

26. Comment of a French Minister.

even in 1956, to depart far from the policy of the Foreign Office in London on these matters, and in consequence was not much consulted. About the time of Mangin's speech, French arms were still being sold to Egypt; thirty to forty tanks, 9,000 shells, and some 155-mm cannons left for Alexandria about 14 May.[27] But the armament now made available to Israel far exceeded this. The twelve Mystères approved by the USA crept up (secretly) to thirty-six. The Gaullist politician and anthropologist Jacques Soustelle, until January Resident-General in Algeria and now President of the Franco-Israeli Parliamentary Association, referred in private conversation to the Israelites with approval as the 'new Aztecs'.[28] A more dispassionate observer, Raymond Aron, told the readers of *Le Figaro* that 'Israel today fears the same enemy as we.'[29] The old anti-semitism of the French bourgeoisie flagged.

Israel and France were thus allies before the nationalization of the Suez Canal Company by Nasser, their friendship founded on a common distrust of Islam.

Though Britain reached a similar disillusion about Nasser before the nationalization of the Suez Canal Company on 26 July, this did not lead her rulers to a similar conclusion: they remained pro-Arab, even when most opposed to Nasser. Anyone who knew the Middle East well (and there were so many in Whitehall) could easily make the most invidious distinction between the Egyptians and those whom they took to be the *real* Arabs of the desert. Still, in the spring of 1956 Britain did sell six Meteors to Israel.[30] After March 1956 Eden knew that his policy of appeasement had failed with Nasser. Possibly the idea occurred in early 1956 to British policymakers that a convenient counter-revolution against Nasser might be arranged, as had occurred in the case of Musaddiq in Persia – though that had depended for its success on US help.[31] The problem of

27. Bar-Zohar, *Suez; ultra-secret*, p. 117.
28. Evidence of an observer.
29. *Le Figaro*, 21 February 1956.   30. Eden, p. 331.
31. For the CIA's part in the overthrow of Musaddiq, and the role played by Kermit Roosevelt, see Wise and Ross, *The Invisible Government*, pp. 110–14.

what would happen to the Suez Canal after the final with-drawal of British troops, planned for June, was on the Government's mind; this was a matter which Eden spoke about, though perhaps in elliptical terms, when Bulganin and Khrushchev visited London in April: Eden says in his memoirs that he told the Russians that 'the uninterrupted supply of oil was literally vital to our economy. They showed an understanding of our interest and appeared to be willing to meet it. I said I thought I must be absolutely blunt about the oil, because we would fight for it'.[32] But it is not clear that Eden explicitly mentioned the Suez Canal while, even if he had done so, Russia was far from absolutely controlling Nasser – as Eden must have known: further, the Minister of State, Anthony Nutting, and the Secretary of State for War, Antony Head, had both spent some time negotiating with Nasser in 1954, and had reported him to be, as he seemed to be on paper, a firm anti-Communist. (Nasser himself later remarked that two things caused him to be hostile to Communism: its atheism – he was a practising Muslim – and the need to take orders from Moscow.[33])

The British worries about Egypt continued. Egyptian agents seemed to crop up everywhere in the Middle East and the Government found it easy to attribute all their difficulties with Arab nationalism to these ubiquitous and well-financed trouble-bearers. Syria seemed about to become a Soviet satellite. The conflict between Nuri and Nasser, waged by radio, became daily more bitter. The commitment to help finance the Aswan Dam thus seemed increasingly irksome, particularly since Nuri es-Said was complaining that Egypt seemed to be doing better out of the West by bullying than Iraq was by co-operating:[34] the Aswan Dam was indeed far the most expensive project for development that had been launched in the Middle East. Critics of the Aswan scheme in Britain meantime concentrated on the technical and hydrological parts of the plan, while the Voice of the Arabs continued to attack Britain, in defiance of the alleged promise given by Nasser to Selwyn Lloyd. Lloyd approached the State Department in late June,

32. Eden, p. 358.   33. *Sunday Times*, 17 June 1962.
34. Eden, p. 421.

and found that they shared British 'apprehension for the future of the [Aswan] scheme'.[35]

Eden had also become irritated by the US administration. He and Selwyn Lloyd had crossed to Washington in January in order to persuade the US to 'put teeth' into the Tripartite Declaration. They failed. Britain also failed to persuade the US to bring pressure on the great oil business, ARAMCO, who, they knew, paid large sums to King Saud, some of which he in turn spent on undermining the British position in the Persian Gulf, particularly in respect of the Buraimi Oasis, where the US had openly supported Saud. But the US administration was prepared to collaborate with Britain over the withdrawal of the loan for the Dam as indeed they also seem to have been ready to collaborate in helping and financing the overthrow of the Syrian Government in conjunction with Iraq.[36]

Dulles's earlier doubts about the political disadvantage of being a creditor of Egypt on so large a scale had now grown because of new political worries: in May Nasser recognized Communist China and in June the new Russian Foreign Minister, Shepilov, arrived, while Egypt was celebrating the British withdrawal from the Canal, amidst a large display of arms sent from Communist countries; he was rumoured to have offered an interest-free loan of £50 million. The Secretary of the US Treasury, George Humphrey, decided that Egypt was holding an option on the Western offer while 'shopping round for a better offer' from Russia.[37] Humphrey also doubted whether, with the expensive new arms purchases, Egypt would be able to pay the interest and repayment on the loan. On 20 June the President of the World Bank, Eugene Black, received from Nasser a series of counter-proposals about the loan which persuaded both Dulles and Eisenhower that Nasser was 'not really interested in serious negotiation on the project'.[38] Ten days later the US financial year came to an end, without any firm commitment of funds being made: so if the project were to go ahead Dulles would have to go back to the Senate to ask for money – an idea which he would have disliked at all

35. Eden, p. 421. 36. Seale, p. 273.
37. Eisenhower, p. 31. 38. Eisenhower, p. 32.

times and particularly in the middle of the summer of an election year.[39] Much later Dulles admitted at a press conference that he was also thinking of the effect such a withdrawal would have on any other state which 'played both sides'.[40]

It was not however the USA but the British who made their decision on this subject first: Eden explains in his memoirs that 'in mid-July ... the Government came to the conclusion that they could not go on with a project likely to be increasingly onerous in finance and unsatisfactory in practice'.[41] This decision was taken by Eden, Lloyd and Macmillan (the Chancellor of the Exchequer) but it would seem that the other Ministers were circulated with the right papers,[42] so that there is no reason for the complaint by the Lord Chancellor, Lord Kilmuir, that the Cabinet had not been properly consulted.[43] This decision was not announced publicly. Eden 'would have preferred to play this long'[44] and therefore presumably not to have told Egypt for a while. Something leaked out, however, for *The Times* announced on 14 July: 'The attempt to stabilize the Middle East in co-operation with Egypt is now over.'[45] Meantime, friendships between the French and Israeli Ministries of Defence were being brought closer than ever and, at the end of June, France promised that she would secretly supply Israel with 'all she needed for her defence'.[46] This meant an end for the Israelis of months of lobbying in New York, London

39. It was the judgement of a senior Adviser (intimately involved with these matters) that this was the main reason for the rejection of the loan on 19 July.

40. *New York Times*, 3 April 1957.

41. Eden, p. 421.

42. Evidence of a junior Minister.

43. In his memoirs, he writes 'I ... have no recollection of this crucial aspect of the situation [the political consequences] being brought home to Ministers' (*Political Adventure*, p. 267).

44. Eden, p. 422.

45. It is still uncertain what the British Government really told the US on this issue at this time.

46. Jacob Tsur, *Prélude à Suez* (1968), p. 376. Tsur was Israeli ambassador in Paris at the time, but was himself only informed after the agreement had been concluded.

and Paris, and radically altered the military balance in the Middle East, such as it was. But this was a secret, jealously kept, so much so that the Quai d'Orsay knew nothing of it and Israeli diplomats in the other Western capitals continued to press for the sale of arms to their country, in order further to divert suspicion.

Dulles on 13 July told Egypt that the USA 'were not now in a position to deal with this matter, because we could not predict what action our Congress might take and our views on the merits of the matter had now altered'. He told the Egyptians that 'we would consult with them the next week'. Two days later, the Senate Appropriations Committee announced that funds previously earmarked for the Aswan Dam could not be used for that project unless they were again consulted.[47] This provision was, however, unconstitutional and Eisenhower did not accept it.

By this time Nasser must have realized that the West were no longer interested in going ahead with their plan. He seems already in fact to have decided to nationalize the Suez Canal Company, chiefly to get money to finance the Dam but partly to snub the West (and, through them, Nuri) in an obvious fashion. Naturally the idea of such an act had appeared in many previous Egyptian nationalist manifestoes. This decision, however, meant a reversal of Nasser's policy on the Canal: to try and get as many Egyptians into the Company's service as possible – to 'Egyptianize' it peacefully, that is, rather than take it over by an act of force though some idea of devising a pretext for nationalization may have been discussed earlier in the year. He had already set up 'a study group to submit plans for the future of the Canal'. Anyway Nasser was persuaded by his ambassador in the USA, Ahmed Hussein, a friend of collaboration with the West, to make a final bid for Western aid, and though no doubt he was still somewhat in two minds whether he really wanted the money from the West (on the same grounds as his original doubts),[48] Nasser agreed. Before leaving Egypt for Washington, Hussein therefore announced that he was returning to sign the Aswan Loan agreement; on his

47. Eisenhower, p. 32n.   48. *Sunday Times*, 24 June 1962.

arrival in Washington he arranged to go quickly to Dulles with his demands, which included an appeal for a Western commitment for the whole ten years of building.[49]

On 18 July Dulles decided to tell Hussein when he called on him the next day that he would cancel the loan. Sir Roger Makins, the British Ambassador, was told that day (giving him time to report to London and to receive a comment before the meeting), and Eisenhower was consulted about the same time.[50] At the meeting, the Assistant Secretary of State, Murphy, later recalled:

The Egyptian ambassador informed the Secretary of State that if the US would not guarantee to foot practically all of the Aswan bill, the Soviet Union would do so. Dulles told him in precise terms that the US did not submit to blackmail and that our offer of aid was withdrawn. Dulles added politely that he hoped relations between the two countries would improve so that the matter could be re-examined at some future time. Hussein pleaded the Egyptian case skilfully, saying that reports exaggerated the quantity of arms which had been purchased from the Soviet bloc, and declaring that Nasser was anxious for an agreement with the US, but Dulles reiterated that the American decision was firm.[51]

Two days later, the British announced that their offer was also withdrawn,[52] and the World Bank's offer, which had depended on the two Governments' loans, lapsed too, to the distress of the President of the World Bank, Black. Dulles's decision was accompanied by a press release which constituted the first news that the Egyptian Government had of it. The following week *Time* magazine commemorated this 'victory for the West' by showing a picture of the old chessmaster Dulles saying 'checkmate' to a spluttering Nasser. In fact it was the first time that

49. This paragraph owes much to the advice of a prominent diplomat.

50. Murphy, *Diplomat among Warriors*, pp. 459–60; evidence of a senior Adviser.

51. Murphy, p. 459; see Eisenhower, p. 33, for Dulles's letter to him of 15 September 1956 denying he had been abrupt.

52. Samuel Brittan (*The Treasury under the Tories*, p. 184) says that Thorneycroft was in favour of going ahead without the US, but with some European participation.

aid to underdeveloped countries had been openly used by the West as an instrument of policy.

Nasser was then in Brioni, Yugoslavia, in company with Nehru and Tito. Possibly the manner in which Dulles had acted irritated him, though perhaps not so much as to wound his pride, as Eden puts it in his memoirs,[53] and certainly not so much as to justify the comment that it was a 'stinging personal rebuff', as Lord Kilmuir puts it in his.[54] Actually Dulles had played into Nasser's hands and it is hard to believe that he really felt insulted.[55] He returned to Cairo accompanied by Nehru (whom he doubtless consulted),[56] and on the 24th made a violent attack on the USA. His anger was comprehensible because on the 22nd the Russian Foreign Minister, Shepilov, denied that he had made any firm offers to build the Dam, and indeed Russia did delay two years before she agreed to pay. Had it not been for this remark by Shepilov, it is just possible that Nasser would not have nationalized the Canal Company there and then though he has since firmly stated 'in the end we would have taken some similar action in any case'.[57] On the 26th he proclaimed the nationalization, in a three-hour harangue at Alexandria, ostensibly as a means of financing the Dam. He assumed control of the Company's offices in Egypt, imposed martial law in the Canal Zone, and forbade all employees of the Company, including foreigners, to leave their jobs. But shareholders were to be compensated (at 26 July prices). Imperialism, alliances in general, the Bagdad Pact, were all denounced and British and American policies were confounded; Britain was spoken of as being a mere satellite of the USA.

No one seems to have anticipated this move, except, presumably, *The Times* which on 27 July smugly remarked that it was 'not entirely unexpected'. Between 19 July and 26 July Suez Canal Company shares had actually gone up. In the traditional

53. Eden, p 422: 'the news was wounding to his pride'.
54. Kilmuir, p. 267.
55. His comment on BBC TV on 20 September 1966 however was that it was 'insultive' and a humiliation.
56. See Robertson, *Crisis*, p. 69.
57. *Sunday Times*, 24 June 1962.

end-of-session debate on foreign affairs in the House of Commons on 24 and 25 July, only Mrs Castle had mentioned the Aswan Dam.

The international quarrel which now began and preoccupied much of the world for three months was nominally about the Canal, but Nasser cared more about the Dam than the Canal. Egypt, though large, is mostly desert. Only the delta and the plain of the Nile are suitable for agriculture. On these six million acres (the size of Yorkshire and Lancashire together) most of Egypt's population of about 24 million made their living. This region has the highest density for a rural population in the world: 3,000 per square mile. The population was increasing fast so that by 1988 there would probably be 60 million Egyptians. Most people in Egypt were starving. The expectation of life was thirty-five years, per capita income £25 a year.

The Aswan Dam, the latest of many schemes through the ages for improving Egyptian agriculture, had become the main aspiration of the new Egyptian regime, an achievement 'seventeen times greater than the Great Pyramid'. Nasser, now thirty-eight, was, as well as having an almost Irish guile and charm, a puritan and an astute nationalist. The Dam was a symbol for the practical regeneration, even preservation, of the country. Nasser was resolved to build the Dam wherever the money for it came from. Its creation, he rightly believed, would help to resolve his countrymen's long-standing sense of inferiority; and the capture of the Canal Company too would help towards the same end. Since her first association with Egypt in the 1870s, Britain had always made mistakes with regard to her; as a result, Egyptian nationalism had been for a long time defined in terms of hostility to Britain, just as Cuban nationalism had always been anti-American. For Nasser, the decisive occasion indeed in the formation of revolutionary views was the occasion in 1942 when as a young lieutenant he heard that Sir Miles Lampson, the British ambassador, had ringed the royal palace with tanks in order to impose on King Farouk an Egyptian Government of Britain's choice, under Nahas Pasha.

In his speech on 26 July 1956, Nasser linked the Dam with the

Canal, by saying that the dues from the one would be used to pay for the other. But his promise of compensation at current prices brought him a new debt of £70 million. Dues, now £35 million a year, would no doubt have to be raised to compensate shareholders. The Dam would cost at least £100 million in foreign exchange. The question was: would the Canal be milked or run down to pay for the Dam?

One further point should be made: in politics, international or national, the manner in which actions are carried out is often as critical as the action itself – and there can be no doubt whatever that Nasser did his cause no good by his abrupt style. Aneurin Bevan put it quite clearly nearly a year later: 'if the sending of one's police and soldiers into the darkness of the night to seize somebody else's property is nationalization, Ali Baba used the wrong terminology.' [58]

58. *Hansard*, vol. 570, col. 680.

2

THE RHINELAND

The British Cabinet, seeking the line of least resistance, felt that the easiest way out was to press France into another appeal to the League of Nations.

Churchill on the German reoccupation of the Rhineland, March 1936

(The Gathering Storm)

It would be preferable for Great Britain and France to enter betimes into negotiations with the German government for the surrender on conditions of our rights in the zone while such surrender still has a bargaining value.

Eden (Facing the Dictators)

EDEN heard the news of nationalization of the Suez Canal Company on 26 July appropriately, in the middle of a formal dinner, all men, knee breeches and white ties, with Britain's chief Middle East friends, King Feisal and Nuri es-Said from Iraq.[1] Nuri gave encouragement to the British to act toughly, even if it is improbable that, loquacious and long-winded as he was, he was so laconic as to say (as he was afterwards reported by Eden himself): 'Hit him, hit him hard and hit him now.'[2] Getting rid of other guests such as Gaitskell and Shawcross, the Prime Minister summoned a meeting of Ministers, to which the Chiefs of Staff (the Chief of Air Staff was at dinner), the French Ambassador, Chauvel, and the US Counsellor of Embassy, Andrew Foster, were also invited. Eden said: 'The Egyptian has his thumb on our wind-pipe.' M. Georges-Picot, Director-General of the Canal Company, was summoned from the Ritz. In the passage, Eden gave him a silent handshake of sympathy.[3] Eden seemed furious and Nuri, lunching privately the next day with some members of the Suez group, remarked to Julian

1. Kilmuir memoirs, p. 268, for the scene; cf. *The Times*, 27 July 1956.
2. Evidence of an Adviser.　　　3. Azeau, p. 122.

Amery: 'I think Eden's woken up.' [4] It doubtless seemed to him high time: his own plans for a revolution in Syria seem to have been maturing only slowly.

Britain was the country most affected by Nasser's action since the Government owned a controlling interest (45 per cent) of the shares in the Company. Disraeli's purchase of the shares in 1875 was a legendary victory in imperial folklore; even so moderate a Tory as R. A. Butler felt Disraeli (seven Conservative leaders ago) behind his emotions in 1956.[5] Slightly less than a quarter of British imports came through the Canal.[6] A third of the ships passing through the Canal were British (4,358 out of 14,666 in 1955).[7] Eden believed that Britain had in July about six weeks' reserves of oil, at most, though in this matter the Prime Minister (like Attlee at the time of Abadan in 1951) was misinformed.[8] Ever since Churchill converted the Navy to the use of oil in 1911, British politicians have seemed indeed to have had a phobia about oil supplies being cut off, comparable to the fear of castration.

Britain had now withdrawn the last of her 80,000 men from Egypt under the treaty of 1954. But the huge base at Tel-el-Kebir was still there with its British technicians and its £40–£50 million worth of stores. About 60,000 British troops went through the Canal annually bound for the Far East. Further, a snub on this scale from Egypt 'of all countries' could not pass unchallenged. Britain's general position in the Arab world, which rested so much on prestige, was threatened even more than it had seemed to have been over the Glubb affair.

The morning after the nationalization, in a somewhat empty House of Commons, Hugh Gaitskell (Leader of the Opposition since December), affected by the strong pro-Israeli sentiments which then dominated much of the British Left (and his wife was Jewish), said: 'We deeply deplore this high-handed and

4. Evidence of Julian Amery. The lunch was given at the Café Royal by Kenneth Pickthorn.

5. Evidence of a senior Cabinet Minister.

6. President of Board of Trade on first nine months of 1956 (*Hansard*, vol. 560, col. 1112).

7. *The Times*, 27, 28 July 1956.

8. Eden, p. 429, with an Adviser's comment.

totally unjustifiable step by the Egyptian Government.' He asked (to cheers) if Eden would block Egyptian balances. Alfred Robens, Labour's foreign affairs spokesman, questioned whether there would be any further supply of arms to Egypt.[9] No member of the Labour Left, such as Crossman, was called, but even Bevan came up to Amery at this time and said encouragingly: 'This proves you were right.'[10]

Thus Eden initially had the impression that the Labour Party would be with him in any strong response. But he took no steps to associate the Opposition in his policy. The reason was partly personal: he 'had not met anyone with [Gaitskell's] ... cast of mind and approach to problems. We never seemed able to get on terms.'[11] Eden apparently had rarely met social democrats of professional background such as Gaitskell, who seemed schoolmasterly and who had fought in neither World War – an important point where Eden was concerned. (Gaitskell however liked Eden.[12]) Meantime, with the exception of the *Guardian*, the national daily press argued for a strong course: 'This reckless defiance of international decencies. . . . The British Government will be fully justified in taking retaliatory action.' Thus the *News Chronicle*. The *Herald* said: 'No more Hitlers.'[13] The *Mirror* suggested that Nasser should study the fate of Mussolini.[14] *The Times* leaders in the next few days were very strong for action, being headed TIME FOR DECISION, WHAT IS AT STAKE, A HINGE OF HISTORY, and RESISTING THE AGGRESSOR.[15]

After these exchanges in the Commons, on 27 July, there was a Cabinet, with the Chiefs of Staff present. Butler was absent, ill. Everyone else was there. The mood was kept at high tempo by the news that the Suez Canal Company's bank in Cairo had been ordered to hand over its balance of £2 million to Egypt.[16] Sterling had fallen to its lowest since the autumn.[17] Eden and

9. *Hansard*, vol. 557, col. 777, 27 July 1956.

10. Private information.

11. Eden, p. 320. This may have been a somewhat retrospective judgement.

12. Comment of Lady Gaitskell.

13. 28 July.

14. *Daily Mirror*, 30 July.

15. 27, 28, 30 July, 2 August.

16. Eden, p. 425.

17. *The Times*, 28 July.

his Ministers decided formally that, as he put it immediately in a telegram to Eisenhower: 'we are all agreed that we cannot afford to allow Nasser to seize control of the Canal in this way. ... If we take a firm stand over this now, we shall have the support of all the maritime Powers. If we do not, our influence and yours throughout the Middle East will, we are convinced, be finally destroyed.'

Therefore, the telegram continued, 'we ought in the first instance to bring the maximum political pressure to bear on Egypt ... [but] my colleagues and I are convinced that we must be ready, in the last resort, to use force to bring Nasser to his senses. For our part we are prepared to do so. I have this morning instructed our Chiefs of Staff to prepare a military plan accordingly'.[18]

The British Cabinet which took the decision to prepare this plan had now been led by Eden for fifteen months. It was a more orthodox Government than any of Churchill's. Apart from Walter Monckton, an eminent lawyer, none of the Cabinet had much position outside politics. Tough old outsiders like Lords Woolton, Waverley, Chandos, or Cherwell played no part in Eden's Cabinets, unlike Churchill's. Including Eden himself, eleven out of the eighteen Cabinet Ministers had been in the House of Commons before 1939, nine were Etonians, six (Eden, Macmillan, Gwilym Lloyd George, Monckton, Salisbury, James Stuart) had served in the First World War (three were MCs, including Eden); another four had fought in the Second World War.[19] All save two had been at Oxford or Cambridge. Four had been opponents of appeasement before the Second World War (Eden, Salisbury, Macmillan, Sandys), and five (Butler, Lennox-Boyd, Kilmuir, James Stuart and Home) supporters of it. The youngest Minister was Macleod (forty-three), the eldest Monckton (sixty-two); four Ministers (Monckton, Salisbury, Major Lloyd George and Macmillan) wore over sixty.

The Foreign Secretary was Selwyn Lloyd, aged fifty-two, a lawyer and wartime Brigadier, who had made a name as Minister of State and as Eden's deputy between 1951 and 1954,

18. Eden, p. 428.   19. Lloyd, Sandys, Macleod, Buchan-Hepburn.

but, promoted quickly, he was in a weak position to argue with Eden. Also he had been 'charmed'[20] by Eden whom he admired and whose experience in comparison with his own was infinitely greater. Lloyd was in fact a junior Cabinet Minister holding a senior post. He also believed himself to have been personally deceived by Nasser when the latter had promised to abandon propaganda against Britain during his own visit to Cairo.

There was no deputy Prime Minister. Butler, Leader of the House of Commons, was heir presumptive, though Macmillan, Chancellor of the Exchequer, was a strong contender for this role, being backed by the powerful anti-appeasement group, who remembered with hatred Butler's role as Under-Secretary at the Foreign Office in 1938 and 1939. Macmillan's advice seems to have been what finally decided Churchill to retire the year before.[21] Some of Butler's verve had left him since his first wife had died of cancer eighteen months before, and Butler had himself been ill in July. Since Eden had only recently taken over Churchill's mantle, the question of the succession should have been academic, though it never quite seemed so. 'It was not a happy Cabinet,' a junior Minister commented.

On the other hand, Eden 'dominated and dictated to the Cabinet more than Churchill had ever done'.[22] In foreign affairs his word was law. Thus in the unfolding crisis of Suez each decision taken by Britain was peculiarly Eden's.

After fifteen months of supreme power, Eden's health was still doubtful.[23] He had had a duodenal ulcer in 1945. In 1953 he had to have a stone in his bile duct removed. The operation was bungled. A second operation also failed. A third, successful, operation was done in the US. Though normally he might have recovered completely, the three operations weakened Eden, since he was left with a plastic join in the duct which

20. His own words to a friend in late 1956.

21. cf. Moran's chapter *'Et tu, Brute'* (*Churchill, the Struggle for Survival*, pp. 625–31).

22. The words to the author of a senior Cabinet Minister.

23. The following passage was submitted to and approved by a well-informed doctor.

left him liable to mysterious fevers and the normal consequences of a bad liver : a strong temper and impatience. These,
with hatred of criticism and obstinacy, were his weaknesses,
partly hereditary.[24] His virtues were honesty, courage and
negotiating brilliance. He was an accomplished parliamentary
orator and not an intriguer; in the House of Commons he never
lost his temper and rarely seemed even temperamental. His
real nature was thus hidden from the public by well-bred
though successful diplomatic platitudes.

There were however already doubts as to whether Eden lived
too much on his nerves for supreme power. His own Lord
Chancellor refers in his memoirs to the 'chronic restlessness
which . . . affected all his colleagues' and to his habit of interference in departmental affairs.[25] His skin seemed thin.[26] He
worried too much. He rang people up in the middle of the
night.[27] He could not relax. When he went away for the week-
end to his Wiltshire cottage, he was in persistent touch with his
secretaries. His eyes never rested on the green downs of Wessex
without seeing in them the shape of international struggles as
yet unborn.[28] The Creevey of the age, Lord Moran, had noted
in his diary on 21 July : 'The political world is full of Eden's
moods at No. 10. . . . Winston . . . sees that things cannot go on
like this for long.'[29] Churchill indeed had already begun to
wonder whether his successor was 'turning out a dud' and the
news of these magisterial doubts perhaps trickled to Eden,
causing further disturbance.[30]

Already in July 1956, Eden was taking many pills.[31] When
the crisis came he told an adviser that he was practically living

24. See for instance Eden's brother's volume (*The Tribulations of a
Baronet*, 1933), about their father Sir William Eden, the 'butterfly
baronet' of the Whistler controversy.

25. Kilmuir, p. 308.

26. Lord Kilmuir to the author.

27. Comment of a Minister.

28. See the study of Eden by one of his Foreign Office private secretaries, Valentine Lawford, *Bound for Diplomacy*.

29. Moran, pp. 702, 706.

30. Private information.

31. Evidence of a senior Cabinet Minister.

on benzedrine.[32] Yet to the world he was impeccable. Even to those Foreign Office officials who disliked him, he was the old master of diplomacy, the Foreign Secretary more commanding than any other, whose 'antennae' (a favourite word)[33] had led him to negotiating triumphs such as that at Geneva in 1954 to end the French war in Vietnam. Often later accused of acting in a nineteenth-century manner, he was a representative Prime Minister for England in the mid-fifties: for England too was in Churchill's dangerous shadow, affecting a superiority to Europe, with a vague feeling for the East (Eden liked to quote Persian poetry), acutely conscious and resentful of decline in relation to the USA, and unwilling to appreciate economic priorities. Eden was representative, though not typical; for no one else in English politics had quite so many gestures and no one else had such a reputation for good looks. In the thirties, this appeal, rivalling that of matinée idols, had helped him to advance in politics among a group of older Conservative leaders who looked on him as the survivor of the lost generation, the young men of the First World War; in the fifties Eden's looks also affected the female vote.

The unfolding tragedy of Eden was England's too, for precisely what England required in 1956 was a man such as Eden had been till then – a respected negotiator with the prestige and ability to pursue a foreign policy on occasion at least distinct from that of Foster Dulles. Younger son of an old family, far from rich, Eden seems in retrospect to have played the part in 1956 of an authentically tragic hero, caught up in the retreat from Empire, and, despite his aristocratic bearing, a man of his time, when Englishmen, like the nation, irritably lived beyond their means.

Eden had had a bad time as Prime Minister since he succeeded Churchill. To Conservatives, the Government seemed weak. His popularity during the 1955 election had slumped and, at a by-election at Tonbridge, the Conservative majority had fallen from 10,000 to about 1,000. On the Right, Eden was regarded as the man responsible for the 'scuttle' from Egypt in the first

32. Evidence of a senior official.
33. Comment to the author of Mr Anthony Nutting.

place. In January he had been violently attacked by the press (led by the *Telegraph*), 'waiting for the smack of firm Government',[34] and had taken the oddly defensive step of officially denying that he was thinking of resignation. Cyprus was proving not to be the promised safe haven for Britain in the Middle East after the retreat from Egypt: a guerrilla war had begun, Archbishop Makarios had been hastily banished against the advice of the Colonial Secretary,[35] military law imposed. For the first time, Eden had been cheered by the Right. In this new crisis on Suez, the Right feared another scuttle. 'No negotiation until the nationalization decree is revoked', ran a letter from Julian Amery in *The Times* on 30 July.

The pressures on Eden to take a tough attitude were strong. It was not only the Right of the Conservative Party. The Party as a whole had come out of its fifteen-year domination by Churchill specially prizing the bulldog reputation. Further, the nationalization of the Company seemed to have proved that the Suez group led by Amery and Waterhouse had been right and that Eden and the moderates had been wrong (the nationalization perhaps in truth proved that the Canal could only be held from Cairo, and that once Britain had left the capital of Egypt the 'Egyptianization' of the Canal was really only a matter of time).[36] Then the French Prime Minister Mollet had, as has been seen, abandoned all desire to be on good terms with any Arab and was to be far the strongest and most persistent influence on Eden for the use of force. Nuri was another important influence for force. Churchill too saw Eden on 30 July. He was 'very angry', thought 'we can't have this malicious swine sitting across our communications', and doubtless said to Eden (as he told Moran later): 'I want our people to take up a strong point on the Canal with a few troops and to say to Nasser: "We'll get out when you are sensible about

34. *Daily Telegraph*, 3 January 1956; written by Donald McLachlan (*Spectator*, 16 September 1966).

35. Evidence of Mr Anthony Nutting.

36. It is only fair to remember that the Suez group were not necessarily 'right-wing' on matters other than foreign affairs. Thus, Amery, Hinchingbrooke and Biggs-Davison favoured the end of capital punishment.

the Canal".'[37] In addition, Eden's new wife, a niece of Churchill, was, though non-political, interested in foreign affairs (she once wrote a Berlin diary for *Horizon*) and eager that Eden should assert himself against the calumnies in Conservative newspapers and drawing-rooms that he was a man of straw.

As important, however, for Eden was the pressure of memory: of being an infantry officer in the First World War (in which two of his brothers were killed) and of appeasement before the Second (in which his elder son was killed). These experiences marked Eden for life. In the thirties Eden as Foreign Secretary had tried unsuccessfully with Baldwin, his first benefactor, and Chamberlain to avoid war by means of negotiation, and had failed to take a strong stand over the Rhineland, the occasion when it had come to be thought that Nazism could have been nipped in bud.[38] He had resigned in February 1938 over whether there should be talks with Mussolini before Italian volunteers had been withdrawn from Spain. He was in many respects less an opponent of appeasement in the thirties than a practitioner of it who saw earlier than most that it could not work. Now Eden would become against Nasser the strong figure 'standing up against long dismal drawling tides of drift and surrender' that Churchill had praised in 1938, but which in fact he had never quite been in reality. One young Conservative MP put it less kindly: 'Eden had to prove he had a real moustache.' Eden had, too, an obsession with dictators at least ever since his personal clash with Mussolini in 1935; in his memoirs of the 1950s, *Full Circle*, Hitler or Mussolini were mentioned for purposes of comparison about fifty times. Possibly Eden subconsciously welcomed the nationalization of the Canal Company as an occasion to show that he could meet a challenge. Maps would be produced, chiefs of staff summoned, and Eden would prove once and for all that the cartoon which had appeared the previous year in *Punch* depicting him as a new Chamberlain had been misleading. Eden was indeed a brave man but, like Hemingway, whom he did not otherwise much resemble, perhaps was

37. Moran, p. 702.
38. See Eden, *Facing the Dictators*, pp. 330–42.

anxious to prove himself just a little braver. He was too a real internationalist, and hence was specially outraged by Nasser's act of nationalization.

The Foreign Office, unlike the Cabinet, were mostly hostile to any policy which risked difficulties with the Arab world, and were also instinctively critical of any policy which threatened to fall out of line with the 'special relationship' with the US and with the UN. (It was for the same reason that Churchill's desire for a meeting with the successors of Stalin had been unpopular in the Foreign Office.) But the head of the Foreign Office, Sir Ivone Kirkpatrick, an Irishman 'who never minded a fight' (as a colleague said of him),[39] had little interest in the Middle East and seems to have confined his observations to doubts whether Britain should have any arrangements with France.[40] He, too, an infantry officer in 1914–18, had unhappy memories of the thirties, when he had served as Counsellor in Sir Nevile Henderson's ill-fated Embassy at Berlin; he had been at Munich itself; he shared to the full Eden's and Mollet's historical analogizing about the lessons of the recent past.[41]

Any thought of going first to the UN or the International Court over Suez was rejected by the British Government partly on the ground that such a course would be too slow and partly because the British legal position was uncertain. Nasser had nationalized the Company (which had an unresolved nationality), not the Canal (as he himself pointed out on 1 September to the Editor of the *Times of India*).[42] The Company's concession anyway ran out in 1968, when ownership of all facilities would pass to Egypt. The Company, though its headquarters were in Paris, and its shareholders mostly British or French, with only five of the directors Egyptians, was Egyptian. Its rights in Egypt were legally decided by a series of 'concessions',

39. Comment of a senior Adviser.
40. Comment of a critically placed Minister.
41. cf. Robertson, *Crisis*, pp. 88–92.
42. The delicate legal character of the Canal Company has a large literature. cf. discussion in e.g. *The International Status of the Suez Canal* by Fr Joseph Obieta (the Hague, 1960, pp. 90–93). It is best to think of it as being both Egyptian and having 'an international character'.

recently reaffirmed by Nasser, but the Egyptian Government, a sovereign state, could abrogate them. The Canal itself was guaranteed as an international waterway by the ancient Treaty of Constantinople (1888). If it should indeed prove that Nasser was incapable of running the Canal – 'an international waterway of this kind cannot be worked by a nation without technical and managerial skills such as the Egyptians', *The Times* pointed out with antique contempt on 28 July – or of developing it to meet increased traffic, Egypt would be regarded no doubt as in breach of that treaty. But this had not yet happened, and Nasser desired the Canal Company staff to continue at their posts (indeed his first, rash, move was to order them to do so). Of course he wanted the dues too. Egypt had in addition been in breach of the Treaty of Constantinople since 1951 when she refused to allow Israeli ships through the Canal. Men as various as Truman, Stalin and Bevan had all suggested the internationalization of the Canal (i.e. some form of UN control) and other such waterways, but nothing had come of these plans.

The British Government believed that whatever law or international practice, the UN or any other experimental body might say, it was intolerable to have the Canal in potentially enemy hands. The Lord Chancellor was also convinced that Britain had a legal case: the Canal Company had been 'treated as an international entity'; to destroy this constituted aggression which could be answered by force under Article 51 of the UN Charter.[43] This doubtful legal argument (Lord Kilmuir remarked later in his memoirs that he could not get any international lawyer to support him except for Professor Goodhart) was in fact never tested.

The alternatives were thus these: either Nasser would be overthrown and replaced by a friendly government, the Canal Company being restored or, more likely (now that its vulnerable nature was shown), its powers being handed over to an international agency; or Nasser himself would be 'brought to his senses' by negotiation to accept such an international agency. Either way, the British Government were committing

43. Kilmuir, p. 268.

themselves to some form of international control of the Canal
– that is, altering the basis upon which the Canal had been
run, as an Egyptian entity under European control, since its
opening. The old idea of cutting off the Nile at source, in
Uganda, by some complicated act of hydraulic piracy, is incidentally believed to have flitted across the mind of one senior
official; it did not recur.

This crisis, nominally caused by international economic
demands, was, however, dictated by political calculations; for
the City and the world commercial community regarded the
act of nationalization as something to be accepted without
panic. Many in those quarters thought the Government was
reacting somewhat emotionally and looked on Eden as a
romantic and out-of-date man of postures more than policies.
Many too were scathing about the Government's reliance on
arguments provided by the Suez Canal Company.

In London on 27 July a Cabinet committee ('The Suez Committee') was nevertheless set up to control the situation (Lloyd,
the Foreign Secretary; Macmillan, the Chancellor; Lennox-
Boyd, Colonial Secretary; Salisbury, Lord President; Kilmuir;
and Thorneycroft, President of the Board of Trade). Watkinson, Minister of Transport, Monckton, Minister of Defence,
and Home, Secretary of State for the Commonwealth, often
attended as of course did Eden also.[44] The member of this
inner Cabinet who had most reservations about the use of
force was Lloyd, oddly enough, because of his Foreign Office
advice, his own inclinations, and his recollection of the difficulties which the Foreign Office had had in getting out of
Egypt before. These recollections also naturally occupied Eden
and the Secretary of State for War, Antony Head, who had
negotiated the treaty of 1954 with Nasser. The membership of
the Suez Committee did not, interestingly, include Butler. He
arrived at the group's first meeting and of course was allowed
to stay. But in the minutes he was listed as 'Minister in attend-
ance'; in the narrow world of political scheming, this was re-

44. Evidence of a Cabinet Minister. cf. Eden, *Full Circle*, p. 432.
Membership was shifting, but Eden's remark that there were only six
Ministers is probably misleading.

garded as a victory for Macmillan.[45] This special committee
of the Cabinet on foreign affairs was, though Eden did not
seem to remark the parallel, the first of its sort since the little
group of Ministers set up by Neville Chamberlain to run foreign
affairs in 1938.

The British Chiefs of Staff, meeting on 27 July, were meantime faced immediately by two problems, both of which dominated the following Suez crisis: first, the absence of a base
near enough to Egypt which would take big ships and landing
craft; and second, the fact that Britain's defence arrangements
were geared either to all-out nuclear war against Russia or to
counter-insurgency in colonies; almost no provision existed for
limited or conventional war of the old sort. Constant changes
at the Ministry of Defence since the Conservatives returned to
power in 1951 had indeed failed to bring about a consistent
policy on defence: Lord Alexander (1952–4) had been followed
by Harold Macmillan (1954–5), Selwyn Lloyd (April–December
1955), and now Walter Monckton (since December 1955). The
recent establishment of a Chairman for the Chiefs of Staff
Committee had not yet borne any fruit.

First the Chiefs of Staff discussed the possible dispatch to
the Canal Zone of such forces as the British then had in the
Middle East.[46] The aircraft carrier at Malta, the two cruisers
at Port Said and in the Red Sea, could not act by themselves.
The 10th Armoured Division in Libya and the 10th Hussars in
Jordan probably could not be used against another Arab
country. The Royal Horseguards, eight infantry battalions, the
3rd Commando Brigade, and three battalions of the Parachute
Regiment were all in Cyprus.[47] But the infantry were occupied
with EOKA, while the parachutists had done no recent training; there were no amphibious specialists, and the transport
aircraft in Cyprus were only enough for a battalion; above all,
there were no pilots trained – an indispensable requirement for

45. Evidence of an Adviser, confirmed by a senior Cabinet Minister.

46. An authoritative article in *Air Pictorial*, August 1965, argued that
'several months before 26 July Britain and France had been considering
the use of force in Egypt if necessary and the basis of a plan existed at
the date of announcement'. (No authorities were given, however.)

47. *The Times*, 3 August 1956.

an airborne attack.[48] The use of airborne troops without cer-
tainty of support within twenty-four hours was also militarily
taboo since Arnhem. Though the Egyptians' capacity to use
their weapons was exaggerated, the weight of their material
was impressive – at least 100 MiGs, 100 medium tanks, 30
Ilyushin bombers. The Egyptians even had better rifles than
Britain – a good Czech semi-automatic rifle, where Britain had
old Second World War breech-loading rifles.[49] More important
and perhaps even critical, Britain had no airborne battalion
anti-tank gun. No one knew whether the Soviet technicians
who were training the Egyptians would be manipulating their
material.[50] The Egyptians had anti-aircraft guns which were
expected to bring down slow troop-carrier aircraft, for they
were manned by British-trained men.[51] Egypt under Nasser
thus seemed a different proposition from what it had been
under Arabi Pasha in 1882.

Possibly if the Parachute Brigade had immediately landed at
the Canal they might have seized the old British base with its
stores and equipment for 80,000 men and met only spasmodic
resistance. Just possibly they would have also triumphed if dispatched to Cairo, as proposed by a future Conservative Secretary of State for Air, Hugh Fraser, in the *Sunday Express* on
29 July.[52] But such audacious moves could have led to a terrible
disaster. They could not have been supported for ten days. The
Chiefs of Staff, Sir Gerald Templer, Lord Mountbatten, Sir
Dermot Boyle and Sir William Dickson (the Chairman),
hinted that they would resign if the Cabinet insisted on the
immediate use of airborne troops.[53] Eden did not overrule the

48. Evidence of a commander.

49. Evidence of a commander, and of General Beaufre.

50. This point was stressed by General Beaufre.

51. *The Times*, 3 August, speaks of this. cf. too the speech by Lord
Head in the House of Commons on 16 December 1958 (*Hansard*, vol.
597, col. 1070–76).

52. He stood by this view in conversation with the author in 1966, and
several later critics of the Suez policy have explained that they thought
that the only thing to do would have been to send airborne troops
immediately.

53. Evidence of a Minister. This was half admitted by Head in the
House of Commons in December 1958 (*Hansard*, vol. 597, col. 1071).

Chiefs of Staff. No doubt all his predecessors would have done the same. There would be no immediate riposte by Britain. This fact was known to the Cabinet by lunchtime on Saturday, 28 July.[54]

Nasser later claimed to have made a similar appreciation of the likely British speed of reaction from 'Egyptian liaison officers working secretly in Cyprus, Malta and Aden': 'It was clear to us that Britain would not be able to have a military movement before three or four months.'[55]

54. Evidence of a Cabinet Minister.

55. BBC TV, 20 September 1966, and Third Programme, 7 July 1966. See also Muhammed Heykal's article in *Al Ahram*, 7 October 1966 (quoted in *The Times*, 8 October 1966), and *Sunday Times*, 24 June 1962.

3

THE GRAND ALLIANCE

England has always had the armament which she needed. She always fought with those weapons which were necessary for success.

Adolf Hitler, Mein Kampf

GUY MOLLET had been Prime Minister of France since January, with a Cabinet comprising Socialists, Gaullists and Radicals. Mayor of Arras, a Resistance hero, and Secretary-General of the French Socialist Party since 1946, he was an anglophile ex-schoolmaster who had written text-books on the English language. Relations between him and English Conservative politicians dated from their concurrent period out of power in the late forties; thus Kilmuir had met Mollet at Strasbourg in 1949. Before the Suez crisis Eden and Mollet had not known each other well, but they were never as far apart as Eden and Gaitskell.[1] Mollet's Government seemed the last natural combination of parties in the French political spectrum. If it failed, what would happen to the Fourth Republic? In the event, less than two years separated his administration from the collapse of the regime.

Many Frenchmen regarded the nationalization of the Suez Canal Company less as a disaster than as an unexpectedly good chance of justifying the use of force against Nasser. For Mollet, the supreme objective was to win the war in Algeria. The critics within the Socialist Party of a forward policy in Algeria (such as André Philip or Daniel Mayer) had been defeated at the Socialist Congress at Lille in June. Mollet, like his predecessors, Mendès-France and Edgar Faure, still believed that the money, arms and *élan* behind the Algerian rebels came from Cairo (a false assumption; many of the arms for the rebels were stolen or even bought from the French Army itself). The US Ambassador, Dillon, reported to Washington on 31 July that the

1. Evidence of a critically placed Minister.

French Government believed Nasser to be working with Russia in order to gain peace in Algeria and secure a neutral France – a tall tale which the French doubtless hoped would influence the US to help them.[2]

French public opinion on the other hand was quickly stirred by the Suez crisis because of France's role in building the Canal, the number of French shareholders in the Company (Canal shares were freely quoted on the Bourse though not on the Stock Exchange), the fact of the Company's headquarters in Paris and, too, because Nasser was already popularly regarded as the elemental enemy – the Algerian rebels seemed to have no leaders whom the French could recognize and, therefore, hate. Quite independently of Britain, Mollet also began to talk of Nasser as an apprentice dictator, a new Hitler. Nasser's *The Philosophy of the Revolution* seemed a new *Mein Kampf*. In Mollet, as in most people of his Government, the 'anti-Munich reflex' was at least as strong as in the British Cabinet. From the first, therefore, Mollet and Eden reinforced in each other these powerful considerations, though the Foreign Minister, Pineau, continued to disagree with Mollet's identification of Nasser with Hitler, despite reports to Eisenhower by US Ambassador Dillon to the contrary.[3]

When on the night of the nationalization Eden began to speak on the telephone about a conference, Pineau agreed to go over to London two days later (29 July). Dulles might then also be over from the US so that his anger, as the French hoped it would be, might be harnessed to the cause. Meantime, the Defence Minister, Bourgès-Maunoury, like the British Chiefs of Staff, said that he needed time for military action.[4] The French had even fewer forces immediately available than the British. The Mediterranean fleet was in *tenue d'été*: the *De Grasse* not ready, the *Georges Leygues* in careenage, the *Arromanches* in repair, while the battleship *Jean Bart* had only one turret. But France began to prepare. All the main French

2. Dillon to Dulles, 31 July.

3. Dillon to Dulles, quoted in Eisenhower, p. 36. Eisenhower's comment has been corrected after discussion with a French Minister.

4. Robertson, *Crisis*, p. 75.

ministers involved (Mollet, Bourgès-Maunoury, Pineau, Lacoste, the Minister Resident in Algeria) were from the beginning partisans of military intervention.[5] All French women and children were thus ordered to leave Egypt – a tougher policy than the British mere recommendation to the same effect. It may be that the French toughness was partly explained by the fact that at the end of July their representatives were secretly seeing Algerian representatives in Yugoslavia; to break Nasser now might induce compromise by the Algerians.[6]

One fact dominated US reaction to Suez: it was election year. Eisenhower, who at sixty-six had recovered from his bad heart attack in 1955 and an intestinal operation that June,[7] was standing for re-election in November, and as the Prince of Peace. Only 15 per cent of US oil imports came through the Suez Canal. While the route to Europe from the Persian Gulf via the Cape was two thirds longer than via the Canal, to the USA it was only two fifths. US investments in the Canal Company itself were negligible. The recent decision on the Aswan Dam had satisfied senators who feared that the ensuing development of the Nile waters would make for increased competition from Egyptian cotton.

When news came of the nationalization, Dulles was in Peru watching the installation of a new president. He returned to Washington four days later, reflecting bizarrely that if there were going to be war, Latin American support would be essential.[8] In his absence, the State Department quickly decided that they would not regard the act of nationalization as an occasion for the use of force – indeed the idea never occurred as a remote possibility – and told the British and French Ambassadors so. Eisenhower also sent to London a very experienced official, Robert Murphy, an old colleague of Harold Macmillan's at Algiers in 1943, to 'discourage impulsive armed action'[9] and to 'hold the fort ... see what it's all about'.[10]

5. General Ely, *Mémoires*, vol. II, p. 86.
6. *Le Monde*, 26 June 1960, p. 2.
7. Emmet Hughes, *Ordeal of Power*, p. 176.
8. Finer, *Dulles over Suez*, p. 58.   9. Eisenhower, p. 37.
10. Murphy, p. 464.

Murphy arrived late on 28 July (a Saturday: Eden was making a speech in Wiltshire). On Sunday afternoon he saw Selwyn Lloyd and Pineau, who had come from Paris; Murphy's impression was that his allies were not going to use force immediately and that they wanted not the restoration of the old Company but a Western consortium to operate the Canal, to be established if need be by force.[11] They, on the other hand, understood that Murphy was an observer, not a maker of policy, and did not say much of importance to him.

That night Murphy dined at No. 11 Downing Street with Harold Macmillan. In the course of the dinner Macmillan remarked that if England did not accept 'Egypt's challenge', she 'would become another Netherlands'. 'Suez was a test which could be met only by the use of force.' Field-Marshal Lord Alexander was at the dinner, and to Murphy appeared (though he was retired)

obviously ... in close touch with the campaign plans and approved them ... military moves might start in August and 'would not take much' – perhaps a division or at the most two.... It would all be over in ten days, with the Suez Canal returned to international control.... The British did not like the risk and expense ... [they] had set aside £500 million ... but 'Nasser has to be chased out of Egypt'.... Macmillan and Alexander conveyed the impression of men who have made a great decision and are serene in the belief that they have decided wisely.[12]

Next day Murphy reported, 'on a most secret basis', the Anglo-French decision 'to employ force without delay or attempting any intermediate or less drastic steps'.[13] But Macmillan was in truth exaggerating somewhat, perhaps in order to show the USA how seriously the British were taking the situation, and thereby try and persuade Eisenhower and Dulles to bring pressure on Nasser in conjunction with Britain and France.[14] Murphy, therefore, misunderstood his old friend, just as Macmillan's scheme to bring along the Americans failed. A

11. Murphy to Eisenhower; cf. Eisenhower, p. 38, and Murphy, p. 462.

12. Murphy, pp. 462–3. The figure of £500 million there appears as £5 million but this was a printer's error, as was made clear to the author by Robert Murphy in a letter dated 17 August 1967.

13. Eisenhower, p. 664.   14. Evidence of a Cabinet Minister.

particular irony is afforded by the fact that over the brandy, Murphy, who was quite in favour of strong measures, thought that what Macmillan told him made 'good sense'.[15]

Actually, as has been shown, the British Cabinet knew at least by the Saturday at lunchtime that they could not use force immediately.

Harold Macmillan at this time was the most skilful politician in the Cabinet and the most decisive. He had reached political success quite late in life, having been almost fifty before he got his first major appointment, in Churchill's Cabinet in the war, as Minister Resident in Algiers. He was three years older than Eden, for whom he had always had an aversion : Macmillan the clubman, who enjoyed good conversation and shooting, found Eden too feminine in his reactions and too yielding to be a good leader of his country. Macmillan, though ambitious, knew that if Eden's prime ministership ran its natural span he, Macmillan, would be too old to be a possible successor. Butler was ten years younger. Yet no doubts seemed to have troubled Macmillan. Eden had made him Foreign Secretary in April 1955, an arrangement which did not work well, since Eden naturally wished to undertake much foreign policy himself and Macmillan was the last person to enjoy interference in his department. When Macmillan moved to the Treasury in December, he had agreed reluctantly on the condition that Butler should not be appointed Deputy Prime Minister and that he, Macmillan, should be undisputed 'head of the Home Front'.[16]

Macmillan had been influenced by Churchill in many ways more than Eden had. He hated with all his soul the decline of Britain as a great power. He, as his own prime ministership later showed, was prepared to be realistic about winds of change, but realism is easier for men charged with power. In the summer of 1956 he became quite quickly the obvious second-in-command of the Cabinet, the experienced older man to whom Eden could turn for encouragement He relished the atmosphere of crisis, realized that he could keep his nerve in it more easily perhaps than any other Minister, and enjoyed some of the

15. Murphy, p. 463.
16. Harold Macmillan, *Tides of Fortune, 1945–55* (1969), pp. 692–3.

cloak-and-dagger side of preparations now set on foot. If his reason (and his Economic Secretary, Sir Edward Boyle) told him as Chancellor that force might be risky and expensive, his emotions drove him to try and prove that there was life in the old lion still and that Churchill's successors were worthy of their immortal predecessor. Was not Egypt, after all, easily conquerable and therefore likely to afford a triumph even to a Britain with diminished power? [17] As with most Conservatives, and as with Churchill, there was no insincerity in Macmillan's belief that the nationalization of the Canal Company was a challenge to Britain which could only be met by Nasser's humiliation, either by force or not.

Macmillan, on the other hand, did not have the resentful view of the USA which marked and ultimately dominated Eden. He still believed that Britain should play the part of the Greeks in a new Roman Empire directed by the USA;[18] he did not hanker for a separate foreign policy. He believed that the USA would always back Britain in the long run whatever they did.

Meantime, Nasser was beginning to assume in the British public mind, as in the French, the proportions of a familiar enemy. It was a Labour MP, curiously enough, R. T. Paget, who first compared Nasser's act with Hitler's 'week-end technique' (he later withdrew the comparison).[19] Many people, particularly the old, the war-weary, the veterans of the Somme as much as (if not more than) those of the Western desert, began like Eden and Mollet to see in the nationalization of the Canal Company another occupation of the Rhineland, foreshadowing that Empire from Agadir to Karachi, of which Nasser had already dreamily talked, just as the Rhineland had foreshadowed the armed expansion of the Third Reich.

The most curious side of this identification of a present threat with a past bogey was that it followed a long period of un-

17. See the article by Hugh Massingham, *Sunday Telegraph*, 28 August 1966; also Anthony Sampson, *Macmillan*, especially Chapter 7.

18. Richard Crossman, *Sunday Telegraph*, 8 February 1964, gives a piece of Macmillan's table-talk in Algiers. But he often said the same to others (e.g. Murphy, p. 206).

19. *Hansard*, vol. 557, col. 779, 28 July; vol. 557, col. 1894–5, 3 November.

successful appeasement by both Britain and France as well as by the USA. A complication was, however, that Nasser's writings, such as *The Philosophy of the Revolution*, did sound threatening; and many read that work, for it was short. *Mein Kampf* had been long, verbose and might mean anything. No one had read it.

It was clear by Monday, 30 July, that the US would not prepare for force, at the very least before a conference of maritime powers. On that day therefore and the next the British joint planners had to discuss what military means they had if they were to act without the US. On the 30th, the French chief of naval staff, Admiral Nomy, accompanied by the French naval attaché in London, and by General Martin, of the French General Staff, were present at a meeting of the Chiefs of Staff committee in London. The British were, it seems, surprised at the determination of the French and at the size of the forces which they wished to make ready for an attack on Egypt.[20] On 31 July Colonel Prieur arrived in London from Paris to tell the planners that France could contribute the 10th Parachute Division under General Massu and the 7th Light Mechanized Division. This might have been enough for the Canal Zone, but not for Cairo; and Cairo might have to be the aim. But this question of the ultimate aim of force does not seem to have been immediately decided.

Britain and France still however hoped that the US would play a role: Eden remarked to Murphy on 31 July (Tuesday) at lunch that, if Britain and France settled scores with Egypt, he hoped 'you will take care of the Bear': that is, presumably, to provide a nuclear umbrella if need be. The French Foreign Minister, Pineau, in the intervals of disputing about who was to blame for leaks to the press, had insisted to Murphy that since the US was 'responsible for the Aswan decision it should not disinterest itself from the consequences'.[21] Both countries also continued throughout the crisis not only to hope but to assume that they would be able to rely on the USA for oil if the worst came to the worst; so there was always a certain unreality about plans to 'go it alone'.

20. Ely, p. 91.   21. Murphy, pp. 465–6.

But the US was actually hardening against the Anglo-French ideas. Eisenhower for instance thought the British had no legal case for force. He had once been personally occupied with the daily operation of the more complicated Panama Canal and he did not believe in the argument that only European technicians could operate the Suez Canal. Admiral Burke, Chief of the US Naval Staff, normally no sluggard when the call for action was heard, said the same. Others in the US administration wondered what would happen if the Canal Zone were reoccupied; would troops be kept there indefinitely? Wouldn't that simply mean a return to the bloodshed that had attended the last years of the last British occupation of the zone, which, after all, had only ended the previous month? [22]

These arguments were put by Eisenhower to Eden in a letter of 31 July; he told of his 'personal conviction, as well as that of my associates as to the unwisdom even of contemplating the use of ... force at this moment. ... I realize that the messages from both you and Harold stressed that the decision ... was firm and irrevocable. But ... I hope you will consent to reviewing this matter once more in its broadest aspects. ... [So] I have asked Foster [Dulles] to leave this afternoon to meet with your people ... in London.' At the same time Eisenhower publicly said: 'We must make certain that the rights of the world are not abused.' [23]

Dulles arrived in London on 1 August with instructions to prevent military intervention. Over the next weeks he gave himself over to this difficult task. Aged sixty-eight and ten years older than Eden and Mollet, probably already, without knowing it, suffering from cancer, Dulles was with the President's approval the unfettered chief of US foreign policy. He assumed that 'the danger of bellicose action would disappear if negotiations were prolonged'.[24] Here he erred.

To achieve his aim, Dulles gave the impression to Eden that he really believed that 'a way had to be found to make Nasser disgorge what he is attempting to swallow'.[25] Eden found this remark comforting. Murphy later explained that it 'was to be

22. Eisenhower, pp. 39–40.   23. Eisenhower, pp. 664–5.
24. Murphy, p. 468.   25. Eden, p. 437.

taken with a warehouse full of salt'.[26] Pineau, however, never thought that Dulles purposely sought to deceive: 'His policy was always clear enough.'[27]

If Eden and Dulles had been friends, mutual incomprehension, which often settled down over them like a dark cloud, would doubtless have been avoided. But behind them stretched years of animosity. Eden had even asked Eisenhower not to appoint Dulles Secretary of State.[28] Disputes over Vietnam, Quemoy and Matsu, and finally Eden's glittering success at Geneva in 1954 had fanned the flames. There were, further, psychological differences between the two of them: Dulles liked to seek the intellectual basis for his actions; Eden relied on intuition and became bored with Dulles's long analyses. Both men openly criticized each other behind their backs, but were scrupulously polite when they actually met. Dulles, like Eisenhower, hated the 'My dears' with which Eden laced his private conversation (in contrast to the 'My friends', his style of addressing the public). In 1956 the relations between these statesmen already resembled those of Lucan and Cardigan at Balaclava. There was now a reversal of roles: Eden, until now the intuitive negotiator, became morally insistent; Dulles, the intellectual moralist, became the diplomat of improvisation. Throughout the crisis there was to be misunderstanding; Dulles seemed to agree with British hatred of Nasser when he was with the British; in the USA he would publicly talk against old-fashioned colonialism. Dulles saw himself as the advocate of the West against Communism: a career at law suitably crowned by representing the free world in a permanent brief. He distrusted Eden's independence. Believing that the British influence in the Middle East was certain to disappear one day, Dulles wanted the USA to be on good terms with those he supposed to be the inevitable successor states. A man of formidable and in so many ways admirable qualities, his view of the world was Manichean: he represented the moral force of liberty, Russia the amoral one of tyranny; and the old corrupt Europe was not going to stand in his way, as it had in that of his

26. Murphy, p. 470.   27. Evidence of a French Minister.
28. Eisenhower, *Mandate for Change*, p. 142.

old chief President Wilson, with whom he had gone, thirty-seven years before, to the Paris Peace Conference.

On 1 and 2 August the French seemed anxious to use force as soon as possible. Dulles was as determined to oppose it, though he had not shown his hand and his allies thought that he believed with them that if Nasser 'got away with it', similar disasters would follow throughout Africa: a foretaste of the domino theory so beloved by Americans in respect of Asia in the sixties. Eden, at the mercy of conflicting pressures, stood somewhere between the French and Dulles, though inclined towards a conference. The British Chiefs of Staff then made all the politicians' decisions for them.[29] They reported that if there were no US help, an Anglo-French military force capable of restoring international control of the Canal Zone could not be mounted for at least six weeks. For instance, Nasser's new MiGs were too powerful even for jets on the only aircraft carrier available. Further, in any situation of limited war, reservists would have to be recalled. The occupation of the Canal Zone (as had been discovered in 1952–4) would solve nothing with a hostile Cairo; the Allies would have to be prepared to occupy much of Egypt even though at this stage the Joint Planners expected allied forces to land at Port Said.[30] This advice made it easy for Eden and, with greater reluctance, Mollet, to agree to a conference. At all these delays both British and French public opinion were critical. Michel Debré spoke in the Chamber of 'criminal impotence', Paul Reynaud of 'these men who have been talking for six days, not acting'.

The British Cabinet on 2 August then seems to have taken, with all members present, the main decision in the whole Suez crisis: that while a negotiated settlement should be sought, force would be used if negotiations failed within a measurable time. The decision thus taken covered all subsequent actions by the British Government. To it faint-hearted or sceptical Ministers could be referred and told that they were proposing to go back on a decision already taken by the supreme execu-

29. Evidence of a Minister.
30. *The Times*, 4 August 1956; General Stockwell, *Sunday Telegraph*, 30 October 1966.

tive of the country. But at the moment, with the possible exception of Monckton, no one was critical. The actual decision was apparently taken very much 'on the nod', without much discussion, about one o'clock, 'with some members slipping out to lunch'.[31] To some it seemed that in the heady mood of the time major decisions of peace and war were thus taken in a rather hasty way;[32] but a similar charge might be levied against the Liberal Cabinet of 1914 and of course against the Cabinet which agreed with Palmerston to go to war against Russia in 1854: then several members were actually asleep.

On 2 and 3 August there followed debates in the House of Commons and the National Assembly respectively. The tone in both was similar, with significant minor differences. Pineau delighted the French Right (who had previously regarded him almost as Nasser's agent), by saying that the Government 'would continue on the path upon which it has begun without abandoning either sang-froid or resolution'. The French Government won its vote by a crushing majority of 422 to 150, the Opposition being all Communists. In the words of one later French writer, 'the French bourgeoisie thus freed itself from the American tutelage to which it had been subject ... since 1946'.[33] (A little later, ironically, Vice President Nixon would make a similar claim that Dulles's foreign policy towards Europe constituted 'a new declaration of independence'.[34])

In the House of Commons, Eden was quieter. Reserves, he said, would be called up, as part of 'certain precautionary measures of a military kind', because 'no arrangements for the future of this great international waterway could be acceptable to Her Majesty's Government, which would leave it to the unfettered control of a single Power which could ... exploit it purely for purposes of national policy'.

Gaitskell still seemed closer to Eden than to Eisenhower. His case against Nasser was based on Egypt's prevention of Israeli

---

31. Evidence of an Adviser. A senior member of the Cabinet disputes the importance of this meeting: 'Things were changing so much all the time'.

32. Evidence of an Adviser.   33. Azeau, *La Piège de Suez*, p. 147.

34. Emmet Hughes, *Ordeal of Power*, p. 184.

shipping from passing through the Canal. He also pointed out that Nasser could not at the same time keep up and develop the Canal, compensate the shareholders, and finance the Dam out of Canal dues unless these were raised (though later Denis Healey argued that even if the tolls were raised five times, the price of petrol would only go up 1d. a gallon in England). Further, alluding to Nasser's pan-Arab ambitions, Gaitskell said: 'It is all very familiar. It is exactly the same as that we encountered from Mussolini and Hitler in those years before the war.' [35] This sentence cheered up Churchill, who said he must have gravely misjudged Gaitskell in the past.[36] It was a dangerous remark, one which identified Gaitskell with Mollet, as with the rising tide of xenophobia in Britain, and one which was not forgotten.

Nevertheless, in a long conclusion to his speech (drafted by Kenneth Younger), Gaitskell did support a conference and hoped that a UN agency might eventually take over the Canal. (In the Shadow Cabinet only Younger and Philip Noel-Baker seemed at this moment interested in the UN aspect of the crisis.[37]) Agreeing with Eden's preliminary recall of reserves, and admitting that 'there are circumstances in which we might be compelled to use force', Gaitskell added: 'it would be difficult to find . . . in anything he has done any legal justification for the use of force.' Any force used ought to be consistent with the UN Charter. The Conservatives, however, only remembered those parts of this speech which they had cheered; and in fairness to them, even in print, the first part of Gaitskell's speech makes a stronger impression than the second.

In the same debate, Herbert Morrison, Foreign Minister at the time of Abadan, went much further than Gaitskell and said: 'If the US will not stand with us, we may have to stand without them. . . . I ask the Government not to be too nervous.' A large number of other speakers recalled Hitler and the thirties, and it is hard, reading Hansard without knowing the identities of speakers, to decide upon which side of the House many stood. Perhaps only Julian Amery saw the situation as a

35. *Hansard*, 3 August 1956. See Appendix 3.
36. Kilmuir, p. 269.   37. Evidence of Kenneth Younger.

'gleaming opportunity' to redeem what Britain had lost in the Middle East. But Conservatives over-estimated the extent to which they were supported by Labour. In fact once again no left-wing Socialists were called (except William Warbey) and Morrison was somewhat discredited by then.

With such apparent general support, Eden must have felt that he had 'recovered his poise', as *The Times* put it on 4 August, and was in command of his party for the first time for months. The next morning, 3 August, there was another short (hour-long) Cabinet meeting. But the Cabinet were apparently not told that, after the debate on the 2nd, Gaitskell had written to Eden explaining that the Prime Minister might have mis-understood him: he could not back the use of force without UN approval, a policy which William Clark, Eden's press officer, had, in agreement with Eden, told the press would be inevitable if the conference failed. Clark (previously a journal-ist on the *Observer*, and whose appointment had testified to Eden's past political moderation) never made any secret that the Government intended to use force 'if need be'. Some jour-nalists (such as Cecil and Michael King of the *Mirror*) believed him, some (such as his old *Observer* colleagues) did not. Some thought that Clark was exceeding his instructions, and Richard Crossman (who then wrote a column for the *Daily Mirror*) talked about 'Clark's War'.[38]

Gaitskell also personally twice at this time saw Eden and said that the Opposition would not back force except through the UN.[39] Eden appears to have regarded these acts as a simple disassociation by the Opposition from his policy, which en-titled him henceforward to ignore them.[40]

The three-power discussion had ended at 8 p.m. on 2 August. It had called for a conference of twenty-four maritime powers to begin in London on 16 August. Britain and France had agreed to delay orders by the Canal Company to withdraw their employees from working in Egypt, since the consequent disruption would in Dulles's view destroy support in the US

---

38. Evidence of a journalist.

39. Gaitskell in September in the House of Commons, *Hansard*, vol. 558, col. 177.   40. Evidence of a Cabinet Minister.

for sacrifices to make up for oil shortages in Europe.[41] Although Britain and France with the USA represented a majority of ships using the Suez Canal, their action in calling for this conference was somewhat high-handed; the other signatories of the Statute of 1888 were not consulted. Nor did invitations go to *all* interested powers, only to a selected few. Thus Israel received no invitation. Dulles nevertheless returned to Washington after thirty-six hours in London to tell Congressional leaders that he alone had prevented Britain and France from going to war immediately.[42] He said that he had been told by the British and French that 'to let Nasser, "a wild man brandishing an axe", get away with it would risk a world war and cause Britain to sink to the level of a third-rate power'.[43] Macmillan had told Dulles: 'This is Munich all over again'.[44] But of course the big differences between the Allies remained: Britain and France saw the proposed conference as something to fill in time till the military preparations were ready. Dulles saw it as the end of the road.

No doubt, with the election campaign opening, both Eisenhower and Dulles had decided, at least in their own minds, that force should never be used over Suez unless the Canal became unworkable;[45] if so, this decision was not communicated to Eden, who always remembered Dulles's remark about making Nasser 'disgorge'.[46]

41. Dulles to Eisenhower.

42. Sherman Adams, *First Hand Report*, p. 200.

43. Robertson (*Crisis*, p. 81) puts this otherwise: he makes Dulles say to Menzies that Eden and Lloyd both said that they would risk a world war rather than sink to the level of a third-rate power.

44. Murphy, pp. 469–70.

45. This is the clear implication of Eisenhower's memoirs, though Eisenhower apparently used different language sometimes, e.g. to Menzies, to whom he had used words such as 'tyranny of weakness' and 'how long are we going to stand for it?' (evidence of a senior officer to whom Menzies spoke). In his memoirs Eisenhower says: 'If Nasser was wholly arrogant the US would have to support . . . counter-measures [including] . . . the use of force under *extreme* circumstances' *and*, implicitly, if this led to a failure (a) of operation of the canal and (b) to keep the 1888 convention.   46. Eden, p. 437.

4

EUROPE IN DECAY

> Was the hope drunk
> Wherein you dress'd yourself? hath it slept since
> And wakes it now, to look so green and pale
> At what it did so freely? . . . Art thou afeard
> To be the same in thine own act and valour
> As thou art in desire?
>
> *Macbeth*, I.7.35

IN London, Parliament went into recess. Eden gave the impression, in a speech on 8 August on TV and wireless, that he regarded the struggle as a personal one between Nasser and himself ('Our quarrel is not with Egypt – it is with Nasser') – a speech which made it more difficult for Nasser to attend the conference in London as, against the advice of his colleagues, he apparently had wished.[1] His imagination excited by the resolution of the French, Eden had, according to one opinion, already decided that 'the world was too small for both himself and Nasser'.[2] Eden certainly thought that Nasser, in showing himself as untrustworthy as Hitler in matters of contracts, threatened to be as dangerous; as one who believed in the value of conventional rectitude in public and international affairs, he interpreted Nasser's action as an affront to his whole policy as Foreign Secretary towards Egypt. To those critics whom Eden could not avoid seeing (such as Anthony Nutting, Minister of State at the Foreign Office) he would exclaim: 'You don't understand politics.'[3] Butler, a possible critic, was away, still recovering from the illness from which he had suffered in July. He listened at his country house to Eden's speech of 8 August with some alarm.

The situation in the country was changing. The Labour Shadow Cabinet took up a position critical of the use of force

1. *Sunday Times*, 24 June 1962; *The Times*, 9 August 1956.
2. Nutting on BBC TV in 1966.
3. Evidence of Anthony Nutting.

without UN approval and secured that Parliament should resume for two days in September. The Shadow Cabinet were united on this position, Bevan taking as strong a line as Gaitskell,[4] and Eden could have been left, after further discussion with them, in no doubt at all as to the Opposition's attitude. Eden and his wife began to hear boos outside Downing Street.[5] The *Daily Mirror* followed (or led) the Labour Party into outright hostility. *The Times* on the other hand kept to a tough line. It celebrated the opening of the conference with a famous leader entitled ESCAPERS' CLUB, which alluded with some contempt to those who, preoccupied with the charms of Diana Dors and of Test matches, failed to remember that Venice declined when the Turks blocked the caravan routes to the East.[6] After this, the editor, Sir William Haley, left the country for some weeks and his newspaper slowly modified these angry sentiments.

Public opinion in France needed no such exhortation. Even the Communists gave only token opposition. The further movement of sentiment away from the USA was unmistakable. *Combat* wrote: *'Depuis dix ans, la France a démontré sa solidarité totale avec l'Amérique. Elle lui a sacrifié souvent ses intérêts. . . . Aujourd'hui c'est la France qui est en cause.'* [7] Here was to be seen the first articulate expression of a long felt if long disguised anti-Americanism among the French bourgeoisie which later would find its full flowering in Gaullism.

Nasser did his best to lower pressure during these days, perhaps under the influence of Nehru and of the US.[8] Thus he answered the invitation to the conference with a conciliatory letter. Ships continued to go through the Canal, the British and French continuing to pay their dues to the old Company in Paris. Two ships under charter to Israel even passed through. The US and others paid dues to Nasser's nationalized company (the US Government had in fact no power to compel US ships

4. Evidence of Kenneth Younger.
5. Eden, p. 448.
6. *The Times*, 27 August 1956. See Appendix 2.
7. *Combat*, August 1956, quoted in Azeau, p. 138.
8. Evidence of a prominent diplomat. cf. also Robertson.

to act otherwise). By mid-August Nasser was receiving 35 per cent of the dues. The Company was furious.

This further weakened the 'special relationship', as did the scarcely tactful remark of Charles Wilson, the US Secretary of Defence, that 'the Suez Canal thing was a ripple'.[9] On 12 August Nasser abandoned any idea of devoting the income of the Canal to the Aswan Dam. World opinion, so far from being 'mobilized' against Nasser, was decidedly now in support of Dulles: 'The crisis was fundamentally a business dispute over the control of an international public utility in a monopolistic position.'[10] The USA did at this point instruct their Ambassador in Moscow, Bohlen, to make an appeal to Russia to keep out of the Middle East and away from the Suez crisis, but it appears that he had been merely instructed to 'emphasize the seriousness of the situation if a peaceful solution were rebuffed by Egypt'.[11] This was however not quite what Britain and France wanted.

At the conference, eighteen of the twenty-two countries, under a strong lead from Dulles, supported a scheme for a board of user nations, together with Egypt, to run the Canal. The overwhelming desire of all the minor countries was a peaceful settlement. India, who could have exercised an influence for compromise, was unfortunately represented by Krishna Menon, who always maddened British Conservative politicians and who acted as Egypt's advocate. Russia, led by her Foreign Minister, Shepilov, kept to assertions of Egypt's right to nationalize the Company and argued that they ought only to be discussing freedom of navigation. Menzies, the Australian Premier and the only Commonwealth leader wholly with Britain on these matters, set off to present the eighteen-nation plan to Nasser, though knowing 'his chances were ninety-nine to one'.[12] Dulles refused an invitation to go, not wishing to commit his prestige.[13] He had actually begun the conference with a long private talk

9. Eisenhower, p 49.

10. D. C. Watt, *Documents on the Suez Crisis*, p. 5.

11. Bohlen to Dulles, 17 August 1956.   12. Kilmuir, p. 269.

13. Finer has this interpretation, which seems to be accurate (*Dulles over Suez*, p. 174).

to Shepilov in which he had said that the USA agreed completely with Britain and France that they should not be forced to rely on Egyptian promises.[14] But before the end of the conference Shepilov had denounced the Western plan as designed to reimpose colonial control of Egypt.

By this time, Anglo-French military preparations had gone far. Some was overt 'sabre-rattling' to persuade Nasser to compromise on Anglo-French terms. Thus it was made known in early August that three aircraft carriers (*Bulwark*, *Theseus*, *Ocean*), a squadron of Canberras, some tank landing craft, the Life Guards, not to speak of the French Fleet, were either on their way to the East Mediterranean or had arrived there.[15] The British public knew too that independent airlines were transporting reinforcements to Cyprus in requisitioned aircraft.[16] Nasser realized that secret radio stations were broadcasting on wavelengths close to the 'Voice of the Arabs' – close to it too in virulence – calling for revolution in Egypt. Could Nasser be overthrown by a *coup d'état*? This possibility was the background to the arrest, trial and imprisonment of the Maltese merchant Zarb with James Swinburn and Charles Pittuck, English 'businessmen', in late August, and the expulsion from Egypt of two 'passport officers', Mr J. B. Flux and Mr J. G. Gore, of the British Embassy, Cairo. Eden from this time on is believed to have relied on information about Egypt from a number of secret sources and to have discounted telegrams from Sir Humphrey Trevelyan who did not believe there was any alternative to Nasser.[17]

On 5 August a joint team of Anglo-French military planners had gone to work.[18] Bourgès-Maunoury and his chef du Cabinet, Abel Thomas, crossed the Channel several times.[19]

14. Dulles to Eisenhower, 16 August 1956.

15. *The Times*, 3 August 1956.   16. *The Times*, 3 August 1956.

17. Evidence of an Adviser. The *Daily Express* on 24 October 1966 alleged that Zarb and Swinburn were betrayed to Russia by George Blake and that Russia passed on the information to Egypt. One useful British source at this time was ex-King Zog of Albania who had until recently been living in Alexandria.

18. Stockwell in the *Sunday Telegraph*, 30 October 1966.

19. Tournoux, p. 112.

It was agreed that in any invasion of Egypt, Britain would provide the Supreme Commander (General Sir Charles Keightley, a cavalryman who was already British Commander-in-Chief Middle East land forces) with a French deputy (Vice-Admiral Barjot) who would also command all French forces. The Staffs would follow the same scheme: General Sir Hugh Stockwell, of the 1st Corps in Germany, would be the commander on land; the able General André Beaufre, who had until August commanded the Algerian-Tunisian frontier, would be his deputy. The naval task force commander would be Admiral Maxwell Richmond, with Contre Amiral Lancelot his deputy; the air task force commander was Air Marshal Denis Barnett, and General Brohon beneath him. The planning team, working under the Thames in old Second World War secret apartments, was instructed to 'be prepared to mount joint operations against Egypt to restore the Suez Canal to international control', a somewhat complicated order which had also to envisage the destruction of the Egyptian forces.

The integration of command was never popular with the French and was later explicitly criticized by de Gaulle.[20] Still, the British would contribute most – a Medium and Light Bomber force, the fighter and ground attack force, and 50,000 men (half reservists), the French only 30,000; there would be over a hundred British warships, thirty French,[21] hundreds of landing craft and nearly eighty merchant ships carrying stores and baggage.[22] Seven aircraft carriers, five British, were gathered, as well as 20,000 vehicles. Some airborne troops would be used but, since Britain had only old and inadequate transport aircraft, the bulk of the forces would reach Egypt by sea. Airborne troops would not be dropped till after a naval bombardment.

20. Tournoux, p. 176. Beaufre, *L'Expédition de Suez*, criticizes the plan explicitly (p. 40).

21. Keightley, Despatch, p. 5327 of the *London Gazette*, 10 September 1957. The French would provide 10 warships, 13 auxiliary vessels, 10 amphibious craft, 2 submarines, 14 minesweepers, the rearmed *Pasteur*, 5 packetboats, 1 hospital ship, 45 cargo vessels, 7 tankers, 2 sweet-water tankers; 25,000 men were on board, and 9,500 vehicles (Tournoux, p. 150).   22. cf. Harold Watkinson, *Hansard*, vol. 561, col. 1226.

The problem was, where should this armada be assembled? Cyprus, specifically taken by Disraeli in 1878 as a *place d'armes*, had no harbours adequate for so splendid a gathering. The Chiefs of Staff indeed had been demanding a real port on Cyprus for months, but without success. Libya and Greece were out of the question, though it was hoped that the former would not oppose an advance by the British 10th Armoured Division established there. Malta was the only alternative, nearly 1,000 miles away from Port Said and five to six days' steaming for heavy transport ships (such as tank landing craft) from Egypt. But the British fleet and Commandos assembled at Malta, the 3rd Division trained at home, while the French assembled at Algiers.[23]

Difficulties loomed. It was desirable because of the absence of tides in the Mediterranean to land at a big port capable of receiving tank landing craft.[24] But should this be Port Said or Alexandria? A new armoured brigade for the 3rd Division had to be formed. There was a persistent shortage of landing craft and air transport. The necessity to base the fleet at Malta and Algiers, with some ships not leaving England before the start of operations, gave any large-scale plan a straitjacket as regards time from which it could never escape. Then British and French equipment was not interchangeable, not to speak of rations (wine or tea? centigrade or fahrenheit thermometers?). Few British signallers knew French. The operation was first known as 'Hamilcar', after that successful North African, but the British had painted large Hs across cars as aircraft recognition signs before they discovered that the French spelt it 'Amilcar'. The plan was then christened 'Musketeer'. Only a small number of commercial ships could be requisitioned. Reservists needed training, while 1940 Army lorries and 1944 landing craft had to be refurbished.[25]

23. For the military preparations see Beaufre, pp. 37 ff.; A. J. Barker, *Suez: The Six Day War*, Chapter 2; B. Fergusson, *The Watery Maze* (history of combined operations), Chapter 16; and General Stockwell in the *Sunday Telegraph*, 30 October 1966.

24. Evidence of a task force commander. But some beaches near Alexandria were possible.

25. See Stockwell on his difficulties (*Sunday Telegraph*, 30 October 1966).

Hundreds of little comedies therefore occurred daily on the winding roads of Dorset and East Anglia. Shortage of lorries meant that civilian vehicles had to be used, but civilians took much longer, especially when working by union rules. One officer wrote: 'Gilbertian situations arose in the loading of guns and equipment when the Port authorities, Board of Trade and Ministry of Transport continued to follow peacetime regulations'.[26] Food, fuel and lodgings had to be found at Malta and Cyprus. EOKA terrorists were therefore afforded opportunity to steal stores and arms.

The plan prepared in London in the second week of August assumed that operations would be preceded by an ultimatum presented to Egypt, who would reject it. The fleet would already have started for Egypt, and then thirty-six hours' bombing by aircraft operating from Cyprus and carriers would destroy the Egyptian air force. Cyprus would be the headquarters. When the fleet arrived, British and French airborne troops would drop to the south of Alexandria (not Port Said, as at first envisaged by the planners), which would have previously been bombarded from the sea. Marines would land on the waterfront. Alexandria captured, the Allies would, after a few days' 'build-up' and after the arrival of the 3rd Division from Southampton, march on the main Egyptian army and on Cairo down the desert road.[27] General disembarkment would be on 15 and 16 September; and the fleet would leave Malta on the 9th and 10th.

The problems of organization of this great assembly were gloomily described by the Chiefs of Staff as being harder than planning 'Overlord' in Normandy in 1944, though 'Overlord' was the model.[28] Given its size and the short time available, the

26. Letter of a colonel, 19 September 1966.

27. Evidence of a Minister, a task force commander, a French commander, and a commander, cf. Beaufre, p. 42, and Azeau, pp. 188, 207–8. General Stockwell, however, says that one of his eight assumptions in planning was 'we would not enter Cairo' (scc *Sunday Telegraph,* 30 October 1966). It was perhaps assumed that the allied forces would have made for the Canal across the Delta to the north of Cairo but Beaufre assumed a 'new battle of the pyramids' (p. 50).

28. Evidence of an Adviser.

achievement of the co-ordinated amphibious force was remarkable. A curious aspect of the plan however remained – it never
specified exactly its political aims, and some officers spent
fruitless hours attempting to get this clear.[29] Would Egypt be
reoccupied or not, would a new Government be found for
Cairo? The truth seems to have been that the fall of Nasser
was assumed by the politicians, probably before the armies
reached Cairo. So there would be no need to enter the capital
which would by then be the seat of a friendly Government.
This was evident to French officers such as General Beaufre
but it never became so to the English.[30]

The plan was ready on 8 August, accepted on the 10th by
Eden and later confirmed by Mollet.[31] It does not seem that
either questioned the size of the operation planned and indeed,
given Malta as a starting point, a cut in the size of the force
would not have had any effect on the time needed to get to
Egypt. But the British planners seemed to their French colleagues to be unenthusiastic about the whole enterprise. Probably, a certain malaise was communicated by the doubts of the
Minister of Defence, Walter Monckton,[32] evidently shared
by the First Sea Lord, Mountbatten,[33] presumably on political
grounds – for no force of this size had ever been assembled by
any British Government without the support, much less the
knowledge, of the leaders of the Opposition. Keightley thus
had more men under his command than Wellington at Water-
loo and the total expedition was about the size of that at Anzio.
Gaitskell, with Parliament away, heard by chance of the scale
of the undertaking from the Maltese Prime Minister, Dominic
Mintoff, who chanced to be in London. He did not believe him,
though Bevan did.[34] It was perhaps unfortunate for the leaders
of the Opposition that they had recently accepted the resignation of Colonel Wigg, who was always fully informed, from

29. Evidence of a British commander.
30. Beaufre, p. 45.
31. Azeau (p. 188) has the 18th for Mollet's approval.
32. Evidence of Lord Kilmuir, a Minister and an Adviser.
33. For the doubts of Mountbatten, see Ely, pp. 164, 170.
34. Evidence of an adviser to the Labour Party.

the post of Opposition spokesman of the Army: Gaitskell refused to listen to Wigg.[35] Eden's neglect to inform Gaitskell of
the magnitude of the proposed operations helps perhaps to
explain the violence with which Gaitskell later attacked him.
Nor was Gaitskell informed that the Anglo-French leaders
already had various ideas for a new puppet government, perhaps led by Neguib, more likely by Nahas Pasha, the old
Egyptian politician with whom Eden had negotiated the Treaty
of 1936, who had been foisted on Farouk in 1942 and with
whom some Conservative friends of a strong policy, such as
Julian Amery, remained in contact.[36]

Eden did not trust Gaitskell, whose position in the Labour
Party, because of the Bevanite controversy, was not strong.[37]
Eden perhaps thought that Gaitskell would be bound to tell
anything that he was told to the Labour Shadow Cabinet, some
of whom were so opposed to force as a matter of principle that
they would stop it by fair means or foul. Had Attlee, major in
the First World War and Deputy Premier in the Second, still
been Labour leader, it might have been different, since Eden
respected him and no doubt would have felt he had to consult
him. In these respects the French Government were more cir-
cumspect. But for them it was easier. All the Government
parties knew what was planned and the Government's opponents to the Right were critical only on the grounds of slowness. De Gaulle was throughout kept informed by the Minister
without Portfolio, Chaban Delmas.[38] As it was, Gaitskell
seems to have been only persuaded that Eden was serious in
talking of force after discussion with Cecil King, the pro-
prietor of the *Daily Mirror*, who with other newspaper
chieftains was regularly and privately briefed by the Prime
Minister.[39]

News filtered through to the US. Indeed, US forces in
France gave material to the Allies, such as new anti-tank guns

35. Evidence of a Labour MP.
36. Evidence of an Adviser and private information.
37. Evidence of a Cabinet Minister.
38. Pineau, *Le Monde*, 4 November 1966.
39. Edelman, *Daily Mirror*, p. 159.

and liquid oxygen apparatus; the recently developed U2 reconnaissance aircraft took photographs of the Canal, which were shown to the British.[40] Italy, no doubt with US approval, allowed French aircraft bound for Israel to refuel at Brindisi.[41] Perhaps the President was not informed of this. Anyway, at the end of August he was wondering 'whether the British and French Governments were really concerned over the success or failure of the Menzies mission. . . . The French and British had given orders to begin evacuation of their nationals from Egypt, Jordan, Syria, and even Lebanon. . . . Such . . . hardly showed an intent to work for a peaceful solution'.[42]

The news that the French Foreign Legion (accompanied by numerous 'nurses') had been given permission to land in Cyprus to 'protect' French nationals in Egypt 'if the occasion arose', was menacing.[43] The day that Menzies arrived in Cairo, 2 September, Eisenhower wrote to Eden; after some preliminary politeness, he said: 'I am afraid, Anthony, that from this point onward our views on this situation diverge. . . . I must tell you frankly that American public opinion flatly rejects the thought of using force, particularly when it does not seem that every possible peaceful means of protecting our vital interests has been exhausted without result.' [44] Eden found this letter 'disquieting'.

Eden replied to the President on the 6th and in detail compared the threat of Nasser to that of Hitler. The nationalization of the Canal Company was but one step in a long-prepared programme to destroy the Western position in Africa and the Middle East. His letter ended: 'I can assure you that we are conscious of the burdens and perils attending military intervention. But . . . it would be an ignoble end to our long history if we accepted to perish by degrees.' [45] About the same time he is said to have told another US diplomat, the Arabophil Loy Henderson (the US representative on the Menzies mission): 'I

40. Private information.   41. Tournoux, p. 155.
42. Eisenhower, pp. 48–9.   43. Eisenhower, p. 48.
44. Letter in Eisenhower, pp. 666–8.
45. Eden, pp. 46–7. The existence of this letter became known to the press later.

would rather have the British Empire fall in one crash than have it nibbled away.' [46]

Eisenhower replied to Eden immediately with a clever letter of moderation:

Dear Anthony, Whenever, on any international question, I find myself differing even slightly from you, I feel a deep compulsion to re-examine my position instantly and carefully. But permit me to suggest that when you use phrases in connection with the Suez affair, like 'ignoble end to our long history' ... you are making of Nasser a much more important figure than he is. We have a grave problem confronting us in Nasser's reckless adventure with the Canal, and I do *not* differ from you in your estimate of his intentions and purposes. The place where we apparently do not agree is on the probable effects in the Arab world of the various possible reactions by the Western world. You seem to believe that any long, drawn-out controversy ... will inevitably make Nasser an Arab hero.... This, I think, is a picture too dark ... I believe ... we can expect the Arabs to rally firmly to Nasser's support [if] ... there should be a resort to force without thoroughly exploring and exhausting every possible peaceful means of settling the issue ... Nasser thrives on drama. If we let some of the drama go out of the situation and concentrate upon ... deflating him through slower but sure processes [such as economic pressures, Arab rivalries, a new pipe-line to Turkey, more oil for Europe from Venezuela] ... I assure you we are not blind to the fact that eventually there may be no escape from the use of force.... But to resort to military action when the world believes there are other means available ... would set in motion forces that could lead ... to the most distressing results.... With warmest regard. As ever your friend. ...[47]

This letter was not widely circulated, though the Prime Minister of course was entitled to keep such communications to himself.[48] Anyway, he thought that it was written by Dulles (thereby making the common English error of supposing that Dulles and Eisenhower could be considered apart). He said: 'the only thing that's true to Ike in that is his signature and that's

46. Finer, p. 192.   47. Eisenhower, pp. 669-71.
48. A senior Cabinet Minister, a Cabinet Minister and a senior Adviser all said they did not remember it.

illegible.' [49] In fact Dulles and Eisenhower wrote the letter together; one unwise sentence by Eisenhower had been cut by Dulles. It had run: 'It took your nation some eighteen years to put the original Napoleon in his proper place but you did it. You have dealt more rapidly with his modern imitators.' Dulles pointed out that Napoleon had been overthrown by force.[50]

Menzies meanwhile had had no luck in Egypt. Nasser's morale was probably strengthened by a remark by Eisenhower at a press conference while Menzies was in Cairo that the US would go to every length to secure a peaceful settlement.[51] This perhaps cancelled out in Nasser's mind Menzies's arguments that Britain and France were ready for force. (On his way back to Australia afterwards, Menzies went out of his way to see Eisenhower in Washington and told him brutally that 'he had pulled the rug clean out from under his feet'. Eisenhower somewhat weakly replied: 'What can I do, this is a democratic country!' Menzies replied that the task of a President was to be a leader.[52] But Menzies had really no chance of success, for he did not go to negotiate – only to present a point of view, demanding what was in effect not the mere return to the *status quo* before 26 July but the formal internationalization of the Canal. Nasser himself greeted the failure of Menzies's mission by proposing a conference of *all* Canal users to deal with freedom of navigation, dues and Canal maintenance (that is, all matters save management and control), under an agreement which would give rights to all and be lodged with the UN, who would act as arbiter. Such a new plan was, of course, unacceptable to Eden and Mollet who anyway had gone to some trouble to keep out Soviet satellites from the first conference.[53]

Britain and France had now proposed to go to the UN, feeling that 'if we successfully passed a mandatory resolution, Nasser would have to give way. If as was almost certain there was a Soviet veto, then force would be justified'.[54] Keightley's

49. Evidence of an Adviser.   50. Eisenhower, p. 50.

51. Menzies always thought so. (Evidence of a senior Adviser and a senior official.)

52. Evidence of a senior officer.

53. *The Times*, 12 September 1956.

54. Comment of a Cabinet Minister.

armada could set off as planned though already D-Day had been put back (on the 4th) to the 19th and then (on the 6th) to the 26th.[55] Everything suggested that by then the Canal would really be closed – a final justification. For the Canal Company in Paris planned to announce that all their non-Egyptian personnel would be withdrawn from service of the Canal. M. Georges-Picot, director of the Company, had repeatedly told the two Governments that if the pilots left the Canal, Egypt would not be able to operate it.[56] The Company had had great success with this line of argument with both British and French newspapers and so far as the latter were concerned had even started to reward them for presenting their point of view, as became clear when a cheque for 100,000 francs (£100) rashly made out to a left-wing opposition paper, *Libération*, was published in facsimile. This forced other papers to return their cheques. *Le Figaro* wrote: 'We shall not be too harsh on you for a gesture whose friendliness and lack of judgement are equally evident. *Le Figaro* will continue to publish whatever it thinks expedient and our relations with you will not be the less cordial because they cost you nothing.' Company officials, embarrassed, attributed these mistakes to their 'ignorance of the ways of the press': they said they had confused 'reports of board meetings which rank as advertisements with statements at press conferences which rank as news'.[57]

There were at that time 205 pilots on the Canal Company's books: sixty-one British, fifty-three French, forty Egyptian and fifty-one others. Despite salaries of between £200 and £500 a month, all 165 non-Egyptian pilots said that they would not stay on with Nasser; fifty-eight of these, who were on leave, said they would not even go back to Egypt. Britain and France, through Georges-Picot, had urged the others to stay at their

55. General Stockwell's timing (*Sunday Telegraph*, 30 October 1966). There is a discrepancy between this and that in Azeau (pp. 208–9) and Beaufre who says that on 2 September the disembarkation was put back to the 25th (p. 69).

56. See Pineau in *Le Monde* 4 November 1966.

57. *The Times*, 1 September 1956.

posts till after Menzies returned from Cairo, and this instruction had been issued on 31 August.[58]

Dulles saw that the Anglo-French scheme of going to the UN could easily lead to the use of force being more generally accepted, and prevaricated: he would not support it. He accused Britain (to Sir Roger Makins in Washington) of 'trying to enlist the aid of the Security Council to force a new treaty on Egypt'.[59] Lester Pearson, the Canadian Foreign Minister, told Selwyn Lloyd firmly on 7 September 'that neither Canada nor the USA would stand for the UN being employed as a cover for war'. Lloyd replied: 'If things drag on like this, you know, Israel might take advantage of the situation to move against Egypt. Frankly, I wouldn't blame them if they did. They'd probably win, Nasser would go and most of our troubles would be solved.' Pearson implored Lloyd 'not to do any urging in that direction', since such action would clearly unite all the Arabs against us.[60] This was the first suggestion of an intoxicating idea which was later to grow on Britain, on French insistence, in the coming weeks.

Deprived of an extra legal justification, the question was now nevertheless posed clearly to Eden and Mollet: to order the armada to set off on 15–16 September (to arrive on the 26th) or not. For the situation envisaged throughout August had now arrived: Nasser had rejected the West's proposals. The fleet was ready. The Allied Commander-in-Chief, General Keightley, was in London.[61] Seven troopships lay along the quay at Southampton. Parliament had been called back to meet on the 12th and approve the action. (This decision had been taken at a Cabinet meeting on 6 September – the Service Ministers Antony Head, Lord Hailsham and Nigel Birch also attend-

58. *The Times*, 1 September 1956.

59. Eden, p. 475 (on 7 September).

60. This conversation is reported in Robertson, *Crisis*, p. 101; he is usually reliable where Pearson is concerned. On the other hand, he makes Lloyd say not 'I wouldn't blame them if they did' but 'I wouldn't mind if it happened.' I have ascertained that my version is correct.

61. Keightley was in London 2–13 September (Minister of Defence in House of Commons, *Hansard*, vol. 561, col. 1242); he had also been in London 22–30 August.

ing.) [62] On the weekend of 8–9 September Eden and his wife flew to Balmoral; the Queen was doubtless apprised of the possible imminence of battle. The French Minister of Defence Bourgès-Maunoury later recalled: 'From 1 September the French forces were ready.' [63]

Mollet (back from a two-day visit to Algiers) was all for action. Once again a Frenchman would bring back battle honours from Egypt. Algeria and the Republic would be saved. In his Cabinet only René Billères and one or two other Radicals apparently were critical. But the decision was Eden's and Eden wavered. On the one hand were forces for action: the vociferous Conservative Right; leading Cabinet Ministers such as Macmillan, Salisbury and Lennox-Boyd; the Tory papers who had accused him of weakness; even *The Times*; ghostly voices from dead comrades on the Somme; Churchill's voice in the Rhineland crisis; perhaps the memory of Mussolini's strident voice in Rome.

But other voices, duller, perhaps thinner but no less persistent, were also in Eden's mind, urging caution or at least delay: his past record as a negotiator, the memory of the League of Nations and the UN, of the Anglo-Egyptian Treaties of 1936 and 1954,[64] the Atlantic partnership, all the solid though doubtless drab fabric of international order. Lord Hailsham the new First Lord of the Admiralty, was critical of the plan to bombard Alexandria.[65] Lloyd and the Foreign Office tugged towards the UN, at the very least as 'an essential preliminary to the use of force'.[66] Monckton and Butler (who now often attended the meetings of the Suez Committee) were sceptical,[67] though it is said that neither spoke out strongly in Cabinet.[68]

62. *The Times*, 7 September 1956.

63. He added that 'only the political conversations at London as much as in Paris and New York delayed their departure' (*Journal Officiel, Débats Parlementaires*, 7 December 1956).

64. Eden negotiated both these treaties.

65. Evidence of an Adviser. Lord Cilcennin had resigned as First Lord on 28 August.

66. Evidence of a Cabinet Minister.

67. Evidence of a senior Cabinet Minister.

68. Evidence of a Cabinet Minister.

Other Cabinet Ministers were dubious – though most of these
were junior (Macleod, Buchan-Hepburn, Eccles, Amory). The
Treasury had prepared a paper in August suggesting that the
effect of blocking the Canal would not be so serious after all.[69]
The TUC had also unanimously opposed the use of force
without UN consent.[70] A junior Minister openly expressed the
view that 'we shouldn't use force to safeguard oil supplies'.[71]

Mollet and Pineau came over on Monday, 10 September, in
the evening to resolve these doubts and Menzies returned from
Cairo to consult with the four of them after dinner.[72] Ironically,
never since Munich had French ministers flown backwards and
forwards to London so frequently.

First the two Prime Ministers decided that in any event the
point of assault would be changed from Alexandria to Port
Said: a return, that is, to the first plan of the Joint Planners.
The Canal Zone would first be occupied and then, unless
Nasser had in the meantime fallen, there was a tacit political
understanding that 'we would turn right to Cairo'.[73]

The reasons for this decision were various; partly Eden had
become aware of the changed political climate, so that it
seemed that public opinion would not stand for an assault on
Alexandria; Mollet and his military advisers also hankered for
a plan which would make greater use of paratroops and bring
the Canal to Western hands in, as they thought, a shorter
time.[74] Detailed implications of this changed plan were not
clear and the decision to use force at all was still in the balance,
when news of Dulles's most masterly scheme of evasion,

69. Evidence of a junior Minister. This Memorandum was written by
Robert Neild.

70. *The Times*, 7 September 1956.

71. Evidence of a junior Minister.

72. *The Times*, 11 September. Also present were Butler, Salisbury,
Macmillan and officials.

73. Azeau, p. 215; Robertson, pp. 108–9. Evidence of a French
commander. See General Stockwell's views also.

74. Beaufre, pp. 63, 73. As Ely points out (p. 105) there may have
been other reasons for this seemingly simple decision, at least in the
minds of some officials in the French Ministry of Defence, namely, that
an operation in the Port Fuad-Port Said area could be more easily combined with an Israeli offensive.

SCUA (Suez Canal Users' Association), began to arrive in several long telegrams. Worked out by Dulles during the Labor Day week-end at Duck Island, Ontario (where he often repaired for fishing), SCUA was planned as an international organization, with ships at each end of the Canal, to deal with all problems of Canal passage, including such measures as alternative methods of getting oil. Dulles and Eisenhower had begun to plan the Canal Users' Association about 4 September for use if Nasser should reject Menzies's proposals: and Eden had already heard of it vaguely in Eisenhower's letter of the 8th.

Over the next twenty-four hours, on 11 September, there were several discussions between Eden and Dulles on the telephone. Dulles was ever willing to talk. Eden thought Dulles told him that if Egypt refused to accept SCUA, the three Allies would jointly carry the flag of decency down the Canal, gunboats on all sides. But it is likely that Eden read more into SCUA than Dulles meant.[75] Personally he thought it 'a cock-eyed idea, but if it brings the Americans in, I can go along' (a remark by Eden to Gwilym Lloyd George, then Home Secretary).[76]

Two other factors played a part: first, there was the knowledge that not all the tank landing craft put aside for the operation had yet reached Malta; some officers at least thought this the main reason for postponement.[77] Secondly, there was still no adequate airfield at Cyprus: Akrotiri would be ready only in late September.[78]

On 11 September, Eden persuaded first the French and then his own government to accept SCUA. Some were dubious: one Minister thought it 'too good to be true'.[79] Macmillan appeared the leader of the war party.[80] Lloyd thought it better to take the issue straight to the UN.[81] But in the Cabinet of the after-

75. cf. *Survey of International Affairs* for 1956–8, pp. 33–4.
76. Evidence of Gwilym Lloyd George (Lord Tenby), July 1966.
77. Evidence of a task force commander.
78. Evidence of a British commander.
79. Evidence of a Minister.   80. Evidence of a junior Minister.
81. Evidence of a Cabinet Minister.

noon of 11 September, Eden triumphed. Most of the Cabinet were relieved.[82]

Pineau was scornful about SCUA: 'I think this is just another Dulles bluff. . . . Trying to unravel this latest scheme will get us all so involved that by the time we find the whole affair is impracticable, everyone will be bored to death by our threats.'[83] But the French Cabinet, to the anger of their military advisers, also agreed. Operation Musketeer was further postponed, though, contrary to what was generally supposed, it was merely put back to a new date during which the further political possibilities could be explored.[84]

The next morning, the 12th, Selwyn Lloyd called on Eden and said he had had a night of 'indifferent sleep, during which he had turned over and over again in his mind this question' of SCUA. On reflection, he had decided 'we had better not' (i.e. better not accept SCUA). Eden and he talked and Eden, persistently anxious to preserve the 'special relationship', persuaded him to hold on to the course proposed, 'with a full consciousness of the risks'.[85]

82. Evidence of a junior Minister.   83. Robertson, p. 111.
84. Beaufre, p. 76. The plan of 12 September was that disembarkment (at Port Said) would be on 1 October, while the first ships would leave England on 21 September.
85. Eden, p. 481.

FRIENDS APART

Did Marianne take John Bull to a secret rendezvous? Did
Marianne say to John Bull there was a forest fire going to
start and did John Bull then say 'we ought to put it out' but
Marianne then said 'No let us warm our hands by it, it is a
nice fire.' Did Marianne deceive John Bull or seduce him?
Aneurin Bevan in the House of Commons,
5 December 1956

THUS conflict was delayed. Yet on 12 September *The Times*
published a leading article which clearly assumed that war was
imminent: Egypt had 'neither the experience nor the money'
to keep the Canal 'going efficiently'; 'reference to the UN may
prove wholly abortive. What then? . . . There is no formula by
which the Government could undertake not to use force except
in certain hypothetical circumstances.' On this day too a rather
ill-timed letter from Marshal Bulganin reached both Mollet
and Eden telling them that he knew that Britain and France
had stationed troops on Cyprus (hardly a secret) and that
Russia could not stand aside if there were an invasion of
Egypt: there was a danger 'that small wars can turn into big
wars'.[1]

Parliament returned temporarily from the holidays on the
afternoon of the 12th. The tone of the debate was extreme:
'Weakness or faint-heartedness now can mean carnage for our
children within years,' remarked Sir Victor Raikes; Patrick

1. *Izvestia* (23 April 1957) and *Soviet News* (29 April 1957) published
the letter; it is reprinted here as Appendix 4. The Government thought
that they had accurately assessed Soviet intentions. They believed that
Russia was out to make mischief. On the other hand, the Soviet leadership was cautious, they were inferior in nuclear weapons to the US and
they were reluctant to intervene militarily. It would appear that Eden
did not send this letter to Dulles till the end of September. But it is clear
from a report by the Paris correspondent of *The Times* on 14 September
that the existence of these letters was well known in Paris then.

Wall proposed that Britain should nationalize the head waters of the Nile in Uganda. Eden spoke glowingly of the virtues of Dulles's Canal Users' Association (SCUA); indeed he launched it to the public gaze for the first time, and implied clearly that it would, if need be, be backed by force. The Labour Party had a much calmer attitude than six weeks before on 2 August, demanding that force should only be used, if at all, with the backing of the UN. Some Conservatives, for instance the ex-Attorney General, Sir Lionel Heald (in a speech which clearly shook the Government), spoke critically on that theme too. A special irony is afforded by the fact that the Opposition were pressing the Government to the one thing – to go to the UN – which they actually wished to do for other reasons, but had been prevented from doing by Dulles. The Chief Whip, Edward Heath, told Eden that the Opposition would not press a division if the Government could say that they were taking the issue to the UN; but that they could not do.[2] These days of debate were conducted on a basis of utter ignorance of the facts on both sides of the House; on the first day Gaitskell denounced SCUA as an aggressive conspiracy which, on Eden's definition, over-reached the UN; Conservatives praised it, as an organization which would cause the USA to bristle with daggers at last.

The critical point occurred on the second day of debate, when the news came that Dulles at a press conference, apparently after a visit from the Egyptian Ambassador calling for the denunciation of force, had said that he had never envisaged SCUA would shoot its way through the Canal: 'It may be that we have the right to do it, but we don't intend to do it. . . . If we are met by force, which we can only overcome by shooting, we don't intend to go into that shooting. Then we intend to send our boats round the Cape.'[3]

Eden was convinced that Dulles, that 'terrible man'[4] as he frequently described him, had consciously deceived him. It is improbable. Much of the negotiation of this scheme had been on the telephone, so that misunderstanding was only too likely.

2. Eden, pp. 481–2.   3. *The Times*, 14 September 1956.
4. Evidence of an Adviser.

Dulles told Emmet Hughes that he 'did not know anything to do except keep improvising'.[5] But Dulles's manner was inexcusable: to slap in the face an allied statesman whom he knew to be thin-skinned, and to do it at a press conference, was to invite a riposte. Dulles and Eden, who disliked each other before, were henceforth scarcely on speaking terms. Tragedy was now probably inevitable, though in Dulles's defence it must be said that he always treated the US press to intemperate remarks which were not intended to define US policy to foreign governments. 'How we longed,' Eden later however recalled, 'for the brisk "no comment".'[6] Whatever judgement one may make of Dulles, it is evident that he did not make himself clear before he persuaded Eden to accept SCUA.

Meantime at Suez itself, the old company pilots left (to the music of 'God save the Queen' and 'The Marseillaise', played by the Egyptian Government), but Nasser, with his Egyptian pilots (supplemented soon by fifteen Russians and later nearly 200 others from other nations), triumphantly let pass forty ships on 16 September – more than the average number – and 254 within a week. There was some congestion, some delay, but shipowners had helped by rerouting some vessels round the Cape. Lloyds soon dropped the emergency premiums on ships passing through the Canal. The Egyptians had shown that they could cope. The proposal for SCUA which had assumed that the Egyptians were incapable of managing the Canal was thus further undermined.[7]

Nevertheless, SCUA had its conference. Russia did not attend, calling it, predictably, 'an imperialist plot', another example of splendid misunderstanding. Few of the delegates were happy. Dulles still tried to prevent Britain and France from going to the UN. The conference ended indecisively, calling for a third London conference to draw up precise rules, to open on 1 October. The meeting had been memorable only for a *mot* from the French delegation: *il faut coloniser le canal*

5. Hughes, *Ordeal of Power*, p. 178.
6. Evidence of an Adviser.
7. cf. *Survey of International Affairs* for 1956–8, p. 35.

ou canaliser le colonel.[8] Eden observed bitterly that the US conception of SCUA 'was now evolving so fast that it would end as an agency for collecting dues for Nasser'.[9] Dulles's senior adviser, Murphy, later wrote: 'If J. F. Dulles ever was actually convinced of the possibility of organizing a Canal Users' Association to operate the Suez Canal, I was not aware of it.' [10] In the circumstances, Dulles could hardly complain if he was henceforth not fully informed. On 22 September, Eden and Mollet announced, without Dulles's backing (and without specifically telling him that they were going ahead now), that they would put their case to the Security Council, which decided on the 26th that they would discuss the matter on 5 October. Dulles, who was flying back from London when this appeal to the UN was announced, now in his turn believed that he had been misled.[11]

Both Labour and dubious Conservative MPs however now put aside their private war books.[12] Nasser also believed that the crisis was over.[13] In the last days of September rumours of war seemed to be abating. Newspapers began to demand the release of reservists. In Cyprus and Malta themselves both reservists and others chafed. Commandos went back to chase Cypriots. Even the French Chief of Staff, General Ely, confided to his diary that he thought there was no possibility of military intervention any more. Peace seemed to have broken out.

It was an illusion, for the Supreme Command still anticipated 1 October as D-Day.[14] Nor were Ministers wavering: Harold Macmillan had told Dulles at the US Embassy during the SCUA conference that he would rather pawn the pictures in the National Gallery than accept humiliation at Nasser's hands.[15] Behind Macmillan was still much of British public opinion, for whom the 'gypos' remained a convenient target for their frustrations. Durham miners, for instance, in the Chester-le-Street by-election were quite surprised to find the

8. As recalled by a member of the Spanish delegation.
9. Eden, p. 490.   10. Murphy, p. 470.
11. Finer, p. 261.   12. Evidence of a junior Minister.
13. *Sunday Times*, 24 June 1962.   14. Beaufre, p. 76.
15. Eden, p. 520, describes the incident without naming the Minister.

subject even a matter for controversy.[16] Churchill had been depressed in mid-September and left for the South of France on 17 September with the thought: 'I am afraid that we are going downhill.'[17] The Prime Minister was aware of these gloomy predictions. An opinion poll at the end of September suggested that slightly less than half the population were behind Eden, though of course his critics might have thought him either too weak or too tough: a decided weakness in the poll concerned.

The shadow of Munich in fact hung over both the British and French Governments and now the French, who in the thirties had been so often the prisoners of the British, became the decisive partners during what were, as has since become evident, the last weeks of the Entente Cordiale.

The strong man of the French Government was now Maurice Bourgès-Maunoury. De Gaulle's delegate to the Resistance in 1944, grand-nephew of Marshal Maunoury, he had, unlike Mollet, been almost permanently in power since 1945. He had an admirable war record both for bravery and for organization in difficult circumstances. He was Minister of Defence; under Edgar Faure he had been Minister of the Interior and responsible for Algeria. His devoted aide, Colonel Mangin, one of the sons of the great General Mangin, had actually been his predecessor as de Gaulle's representative in the Resistance. Bourgès and his staff, a resolute group of patriotic men, but living still somewhat in the world of the Resistance, became the driving force of the administration. On 18 September the Minister of Defence told General Ely that the Government was still determined on military intervention and that Eden had recently written to Mollet in the same sense.[18]

France in September 1956 had another ally as well as Britain: namely, Israel. Ben Gurion had been desirous for nearly a year to wage a preventive war against Egypt. His aim remained to destroy the bases in Gaza for the *fedayun* (self-

16. Evidence of William Rees-Mogg, Conservative candidate.
17. Moran, *Churchill, The Struggle for Survival*, p. 706.
18. Ely, p. 112.

sacrifice) commando raids on Israel, free the Gulf of Akaba for Israeli shipping as an alternative to the Suez Canal (the Gulf was dominated by two Egyptian-held islands) and tarnish Egyptian military prestige before the creation of a united Arab command dedicated to the extinction of Israel.

These plans implied the commitment of regular troops to the Sinai Desert, which affords no cover to infantry. The campaign demanded therefore effective command of the air, which could be secured only by the destruction of the now potentially powerful Egyptian Air Force before the attack began. Bombers would have naturally to be bought as well as fighters, or an alliance would have to be reached with a country who had both the bombers and the bases near enough to use them.[19] The importance of air power had been shown by a clash on 29 August when two Israeli Meteor F8s had met four Egyptian Vampire FB 52s over Gaza, and on 31 August when a similar clash took place over Israel. Three Vampires altogether had been destroyed. But Meteors would be no match for well-handled MiGs.[20]

Israel had also to square or to confuse the Governments of Britain, France and the USA, who, as has been seen, in the Tripartite Agreement had agreed in 1950 both to prevent the crossing of the Arab-Israeli armistice lines and to keep sales of arms to both the Arabs and Israel so that the balance remained roughly equal. After the nationalization of the Canal Company, Israel's plight seemed likely to be worse than before, since Egypt could now hold up any ship which had merely anchored in an Israeli harbour.

In his first telephone call to Eden on 27 July, Mollet is believed to have suggested collaboration with Israel – a proposition Eden energetically rejected.[21] There was apparently an important meeting between Israelis (headed by Shimon Peres, the Director-General at the Defence Ministry) and

19. Evidence of General Dayan. He said the same to Calvocoressi on the BBC Third Programme: 'We should have ... taken care to gain air superiority on [?over] the Egyptians before we could have committed our infantry forces going in the naked desert.' (Transcript of programme on 18 July 1966, p. 25.)

20. *Air Pictorial*, August 1965.   21. Azeau, p. 124.

French officers and politicians on 28 July in the Bois de Boulogne.[22] Prophetically on 29 July 1956 the Spanish Falange paper *Arriba* said that if Britain wanted a war with Egypt 'London will be busy looking for some sepoys; she might fall back on the Israelis'.[23]

From early August the Israelis received more or less whatever arms they asked for from France. French sources make much of another Franco-Israeli meeting in Paris on 7 August.[24] The French kept Israel in touch with the military plans made in conjunction with Britain; thus it is evident from his published diaries that General Dayan, the Israeli Chief of Staff, knew details of Operation Musketeer (and presumably its probable date of execution) as early as 1 September.[25] He knew too that the Anglo-French threat had caused Nasser to withdraw half his army from Sinai (including his armoured brigade).

In August the French had suggested that the justification for the start of Operation Musketeer might be afforded by the dispatch of an Israeli ship to the Suez Canal. Again, the British turned down the idea; it would align them publicly with Israel against Egypt and so offend friendly Arabs.[26]

There is some discrepancy as to the attitude of Nuri es-Said: at one moment he is supposed to have said: 'Act quickly but keep away from the Jews and the French.'[27] But according to two reliable sources, he suggested 'you should get the Jews to do the job for you'.[28] Nuri anyway was still preoccupied with his plots with Syrian exiles and his long-term plans for establishing Iraqi unity with Syria.

Maddened by Dulles, and by the indecision of Eden only to a slightly lesser extent, Bourgès-Maunoury and his staff began to co-ordinate military plans with the Israeli military attaché in Paris, Colonel Nishri, from the moment that it was clear that they had been, as they put it, *'menés en bateaux'* by

22. Azeau, pp. 128–9.   23. *Arriba*, 28 July 1956.

24. Dar Zohar, *Suez: ultra-secret*, p. 141.

25. Dayan, *Diary of the Sinai Campaign*, p. 20.

26. This idea eventually got into the papers. cf. *The Times*, 17 October 1956.

27. Evidence of Anthony Nutting. See also *No End of a Lesson*, p. 48.

28. Evidence of a Cabinet Minister.

Dulles.[29] Neither Foreign Ministry was concerned or even knew anything was planned. Even the Director-General of the French Ministry of Defence, Geoffroy de Courcel, was kept in blissful ignorance since his Minister knew him to be critical of these new ideas.[30] According to one account, France had told Ben Gurion that if he wanted support from France, Israel would have to attack Egypt at some date carefully fixed close to the US elections (on 6 November), so that (as was hoped) Eisenhower would not be able to react. Indeed, Ben Gurion seems to have been told that the date must be that which the French wanted or never. 'Is this an ultimatum?' Ben Gurion had asked. '*Si vous voulez*', the French representative, Colonel Mangin, had replied.[31]

This conversation apparently occurred some time during the first fortnight of September. It lends colour to the idea that behind the agreement to shift the Anglo-French point of assault from Alexandria to Port Said, lay some expectation that the allied expedition to Egypt might be co-ordinated with an Israeli attack. Antony Head, the Secretary of State for War, thus told the Conservative Defence Committee in November that 'the original plan was to land at Alexandria; but as the ostensible reason was to separate the Jews from the Arabs it was thought better to land at Port Said'.[32] The serious attacks by Israel on Jordan, a strategic diversion from their plans for a war against Egypt, date precisely from 10 September, the day that the point of assault was changed to Port Said.[33]

It is against this timing that one must judge the instruction by General Dayan, the Israeli Chief of Staff, on 7 September at his Air Force Headquarters that 'our political circumstances

29. Remark of an officer in the French Ministry of Defence.

30. Evidence of a French official.

31. Ben Gurion so told a French Minister, whose letter of 17 November 1958, describing the conversation, I have seen.

32. From the diary of a Conservative MP present. As earlier suggested, this view was held by some in the French Ministry of Defence. See Ely, p. 106. Shimon Peres (p. 185) reports that Bourgès-Maunoury had asked him how long it would take Israel to cross the Sinai peninsula as early as May. Peres replied 'five to seven days'.

33. This point is made by Azeau, p. 231.

obliged us to be capable of going into action and operating all our aircraft ... and not to be caught in a position in which we would have to pass up favourable political opportunities to strike at Egypt'.[34] Ten days later, on 17 September, Dayan was ordering his staff to examine among other things plans for the capture of Sinai itself – an Israeli war aim which had never appeared before (except among dreamers who coveted the return of the seat of Moses to Israel) and could only have point if co-ordinated with an Anglo-French attack on the Canal Zone. 'Military action', Dayan recorded (on that date), 'may be taken by us at our own initiative, *either in association with the forces operating against Egypt* [my italics] or without ... them.'[35]

During the next week there was much secret coming and going between Tel Aviv and Paris: Abel Thomas (chef du Cabinet to Bourgès-Maunoury) and Mangin flew to Tel Aviv on 20 September[36]; both these able men were passionate supporters of the idea of military intervention.[37] Shimon Peres flew to Paris on 24 September.[38] Relations were evidently close enough for Ben Gurion on the 23rd to be able to burst out at a party meeting: 'soon we shall have a true ally'.[39] But Mollet would not act without Britain; indeed, despite the arguments of Admiral Barjot to the contrary, it would be almost impossible to act independently of Britain because of the integration of commands in the forces. Israel also knew that only Britain had the bombers necessary to destroy the Egyptian Air Force. Dayan made the point strongly in his diary: 'if it were not for the Anglo-French operation, it is doubtful whether Israel would have launched her campaign; and if she had, its character, both military and political, would have been different'[40]; that is, without Britain and

34. Dayan, p. 21.

35. Dayan, p. 22. Dayan's diary was substantially reworked by him before publication in 1966 but doubtless the dates are genuine.

36. Randolph Churchill, *The Rise and Fall of Sir Anthony Eden* (p. 264), contains this information. Azeau identifies them (p. 216). See Bar-Zohar, p. 146.

37. Ely, pp. 86, 124.   38. Dayan, p. 24.

39. Evidence of Bar-Zohar on Ben Gurion's testimony; see also André Fontaine, *Le Monde*, 30 October 1966.

40. Dayan, p. 3.

France, Israel would not dream of crossing Sinai; she might even not try to free the Gulf of Akaba. Israel might of course have taken a risk and attacked Egypt without any arrangement with France, much less Britain (whom Ben Gurion distrusted), chancing that the Suez crisis would enable her to carry through a preventive war against a doubly-beset Egypt. But without bombers Israel would not have committed infantry.[41]

The British position was meantime in some confusion. The Foreign Office remained on the whole anti-Israeli and pro-Arab. The Government had made no change whatever in their general policy over the supply of arms to Israel. At the end of August the Chiefs of Staff had been disturbed at the thought that the Middle East might be further complicated by an Israeli attack against Jordan, with whom Britain still had a Defence Treaty. But the Minister of Defence, Walter Monckton, as well as being sceptical of the desirability of force against Egypt, was the leader of those within the Government who were anxious to help Israel by selling her Centurion tanks to the same number that had been sold to Egypt.[42] Head's remark to the Conservative Defence Committee suggests that even if a new policy towards Israel was not the only reason why the Allies planned to land at Port Said, rather than at Alexandria, the two matters were connected. Britain knew of Israel's desire for a preventive war and as early as 7 September (as has been seen) Lloyd told Pearson that if Britain did not act against Nasser, the Israelis might do so. Two days before, on the 5th, Colonel Robert Henriques, a writer, ex-Regular officer and a member of a leading Anglo-Jewish family, seems to have been a witness of a change in the British official attitude. It is a curious little tale. A non-Zionist and about to visit Israel for the first time, he first consulted Sir Hartley Shawcross and then Walter Monckton about his legal position if war should come in the Middle East. Shawcross told him to keep out of Israeli uniform. Monckton sent him on to General Oliver (Vice Chief of the Imperial General Staff) and General Charles

41. Evidence of an Israeli commander. See also Beaufre, pp. 104–5.
42. Evidence of Colonel Henriques who consulted Monckton in early September (see below).

Haydon, chief of military intelligence in the Middle East, both of whom, as the luck of the old boy network would have it, had worked in Combined Operations with Henriques in the war; and from them he went to see yet another old comrade from the war, by now a Minister of the Crown.

On 5 September (when D-Day for Musketeer was still fixed for the 19th), over lunch at the Savile Club, this Minister first sought to dissuade Henriques from going to Israel at all and then agreed that, if he did go, he might unofficially tell Ben Gurion: 'Israel must at all costs avoid war with Jordan. But if, when Britain went into Egypt, Israel attacked Egypt too, it would be a bisque.[43] Britain would doubtless denounce Israel's aggression but at the peace conference afterwards Britain would probably help Israel to get the best possible treaty.' The British Chiefs of Staff seem to have been in fact so worried at the possibility of receiving a rebuff at Egypt's hands that they thought that the extra insurance of a simultaneous Israeli attack would be helpful. However, when Henriques did see Ben Gurion about 20 September, Ben Gurion made as if to say: 'We have heard such promises before.'[44]

News of Franco-Israeli plans was meantime passed on rather gloomily during these weeks to Lord Montgomery (in Paris, as deputy supreme commander of NATO) by the French Chief of Staff, General Paul Ely.[45] Ely, a politically experienced general of great intelligence, was critical of the military enterprise, though he appears not to have voiced his criticisms on the grounds that if it never happened, the French Army would be blamed by the politicians for preventing it.[46] Through Montgomery at least the British Government must have been fairly well informed of the details of planning by France and Israel; and on 20 September Montgomery saw Eden at No.

43. An extra stroke in golf or croquet to be taken when desired.

44. This story first appeared in an article by Henriques in the *Spectator*, 5 December 1959, and in subsequent correspondence. It has been developed as a result of further conversations with Colonel Henriques and others.

45. Evidence of an officer.

46. Beaufre, p. 110. This view is not apparent in Ely's memoirs, however.

10[47]: presumably this was the occasion of which the Field
Marshal spoke in the House of Lords in 1962:

When the Suez operation was being teed up I was in Paris and in
close touch with the French Chiefs of Staff. The Prime Minister ...
asked me if I would come over here and see him, which I did; we
had some conversation, and after that I said to him 'Will you tell
me what is your object? What are you trying to do?' And he replied:
'To knock Nasser off his perch'. I said that if I were his military
adviser – and I made it very clear that I was not – that object would
not do. I should need to know what was the political object when
Nasser had been knocked off his perch ... because it was that which
would determine how the operation was best carried out, what was
the best disposition for our forces and so on. In my judgement, it
was the uncertainty about the political object of our leaders which
bedevilled the Suez operation from the beginning.[48]

*The precise moment when the British Government, or, at
least, some members of the British Government were first
apprised of the hopes and plans of the Israelis remains a matter
for controversy. In the first edition of this book, it was suggested that the idea of a joint operation with Israel was propounded at least in vague terms by the French Foreign Minister
to the English Prime Minister at the end of September. I have
now accepted the timing of this put forward by Mr Anthony
Nutting in his book* No End of a Lesson,[49] *since Mr Nutting
was present when the scheme for joint action was, as he believes, first propounded on 14 October. Mr Nutting, as will be
seen,[50] suggests that on this occasion the English Prime Minister
was both pleased and surprised. On the other hand it is possible
that Mr Nutting has mistaken the true timing of these things and
that there was previous contact with France or Israel on the
matter to which Mr Nutting, despite his eminent position, was,
like many other prominent persons, not privy. Thus Christian*

47. *The Times*, 21 September 1956.
48. *Hansard*, Lords, vol. 238, col. 1002–3. Montgomery evidently
changed his mind about the Suez operation. Early on, he was clearly an
outright opponent of all military action. By November, he was in favour
of the operation as it was launched and hoped it could be hurried up. See
Ely, pp. 170–71.
49. Nutting, Chapter 10.   50. See below, p. 111.

Pineau, the French Foreign Minister, told a British BBC audience in 1966 that 'Israel said to the French first: "We have the firm intention to invade the Sinai. What will you do?" ... And personally at this period I went to London and said to Eden: "That is [now] the question [i.e. position] of Israel, what will you do?" And Eden said: "We have to discuss this question together ...".'[51] This could not have been the occasion described by Mr Nutting since on that day the French Government were represented in London by General Challe and Monsieur Albert Gazier then acting as deputy to Monsieur Pineau who was in New York. Further, Monsieur Pineau is also believed to have told the Canadian journalist Terence Robertson that he had two meetings with Eden on the matter on 23 September and 3 October respectively.[52] A French Minister also spoke to me specifically of a date 'early in October' as being the occasion for the broaching of the project and a date late in September also seems more probable from a careful reading of the diaries of General Dayan. General Beaufre speaks of a collusion 'more or less secret' with Israel being discussed by Eden in late August.[53] Monckton, the Minister of Defence, is now known to have sent his letter of resignation to the Prime Minister on 24 September, and it is possible to derive the impression from a slightly ambiguous memorandum written by him later that one of the reasons for his resignation was that he 'did not like the idea of allying ourselves with the French and the Jews in an attack upon Egypt'.[54] Two English Cabinet Ministers read through the relevant paragraphs of an earlier draft of this work when it appeared in the form of articles and, though raising other matters of correction, did not venture to criticize the dates. Nevertheless, politicians often have bad memories and

51. Third Programme, 18 July 1966; see also Christian Pineau, *Le Monde*, 4 November 1966, and an article by André Fontaine, *Le Monde*, 30–31 October 1966.

52. Robertson, pp. 124, 134–5.

53. Beaufre, p. 94. The English edition of this book unforgivably translates this as '*early* August'.

54. Lord Birkenhead, *Walter Monckton*, p. 307. This comment, written later, is incidentally the only public admission by a Cabinet Minister of the time that there was an Anglo-French alliance with Israel.

Mr Nutting's evidence is clearly impossible at the moment to set aside. Monsieur Pineau in an article in the Daily Telegraph[55] also spoke of 'mid-October' as the deciding time. The following narrative should however be read with the above considerations in mind. The memoirs of the Earls of Avon and Kilmuir, it should be said, are silent on all these matters.

On Sunday 23 September, anyway, Bourgès told Shimon Peres, the Director-General of the Israeli Ministry of Defence, that though Eden wanted military action, he had met strong opposition in the Conservative Party. But Bourgès and his staff were determined on action even if France were to act alone: 'If she does, they believe that Britain, in the end, will join in.' Peres had earlier brought to Paris new reports of Soviet armaments in Egypt.[56] Peres returned to Israel in order to propose, on Bourgès's behalf, a top-level Franco-Israeli discussion to begin very soon.

The next day, Eden and Lloyd flew to Paris to fulfil a long-standing engagement to discuss the Common Market, then an economic idea of doubtful future. There was also discussion about the Queen's visit to Paris in 1957. Publicly, the Entente Cordiale seemed at its height. Eden had even asked Nutting before this meeting to re-examine Churchill's proposal of 1940 for common citizenship between Britain and France, since the idea of European union was not attractive to him.[57]

The Times, noticing that Eden, Lloyd, Mollet and Pineau met for several hours in Paris alone, on 27 September, welcomed 'a return to secret diplomacy'.[58]

Eden was still placing some hope in the Security Council; the French only agreed to go to it at all on the clear understanding that force would be used if nothing came of it. Eden 'wanted to reassure our allies that we would not abandon our main objective, to remove the Canal from the control of a single Government or man.... The French were sceptical about the UN and more sceptical still about SCUA ... [and]

55. *Daily Telegraph*, 6 June 1967.
56. Peres, pp. 189–90; Dayan, p. 25.
57. Nutting, pp. 68–9.   58. *The Times*, 28 September 1956.

favoured action at an early date'.[59] There was apparently some discussion about Jordan, where there were to be elections in three weeks: perhaps the defeat of the Nasserite forces there might be so severe a blow to Nasser that he himself might fall? Vain hope! Was there also perhaps some anxiety about Nuri's plans against Syria? It seems possible that Mollet raised in a vague form the question of an Israeli attack on Egypt but that on this matter 'nothing much happened'.[60] At all events, Mollet the next day assured the Israeli ambassador in Paris, Tsur, that the fate of Nasser was certainly sealed, and that the 'attitude of Great Britain had in no way weakened'.[61]

The questions raised by the Franco-Israeli collaboration were left undecided for the rest of the week after Eden and Lloyd got back from Paris. On one of these days, Robens and James Griffiths went to see Eden on behalf of the Labour Party and assured him once again that under no circumstances would the Labour Party accept force against Egypt without UN approval.[62] But the mood was still high in France. Mollet made on 30 September what *The Times* referred to as 'possibly one of the strongest speeches' he had ever made on Suez.[63] In the succeeding days his Government's desire to finish with Nasser was further stimulated by more murders in Algiers – eleven killed on 30 September alone.[64] It was about this time apparently that influential members of the French administration began to wonder whether they should not act alone, independently of Britain though together with Israel.[65]

Golda Meir (then Israeli Foreign Minister), Moshe Carmel (transport minister), Dayan and Peres flew to Paris from Tel Aviv on 29 September to make a final demand for 'urgent and essential' arms, without, however, saddling 'our army with the complication of having to absorb at the last moment more new equipment than is absolutely necessary. Nor do we wish to

59. Eden, p. 496.
60. Bar Zohar, pp. 156–7; comment of a Cabinet Minister.
61. Tsur, p. 61.   62. Evidence of Lord Robens.
63. *The Times*, 1 October 1956.
64. *The Times*, 1 October 1956.
65. Thus Beaufre (p. 99) records General Ely asking him to think out the implications of this idea.

clutter up the comparatively few roads which will be serving the fronts.'[66] On 30 September Dayan and Peres met with Pineau, Bourgès-Maunoury and his staff. It 'became clear that France would support Israel if Israel acted alone', by strengthening the Israeli army, and on 1 October, General Ely, the French Chief of Staff, promised these emissaries from Israel, at a secret meeting in Colonel Mangin's flat in the Rue de Babylone, a large number of tanks and trucks. The Israeli army, if they were really going across Sinai, needed a great many vehicles which they had not had before, quite apart from the still unsolved matter of control of the air. Probably Ely disliked these secret arrangements but he fitted well into them, for he had been predecessor of both Mangin and Bourgès as de Gaulle's military representative with the Resistance in 1943. Ely agreed to send Generals Challe and Martin, with Colonel Simon, of the General Staff, to Israel the next day to decide finally what Israel needed.[67]

On his return to Israel, Dayan on the 2nd told his staff cautiously that 'as a consequence of British and French reactions to the nationalization of the Suez Canal, a situation might emerge in which Israel could take military action against the Egyptian blockade of the Gulf of Akaba.... My news ... electrified the meeting'. The campaign would begin on 20 October and would probably last three weeks.[68] Challe and his colleagues had meantime set off for Israel.

These days appear to have been critical in Britain. On 1 October Eden lunched with Lloyd, and afterwards, with SCUA holding its forlorn opening meeting in London, Lloyd flew to New York, while in London there was a meeting of Ministers – Butler, Home, Lennox-Boyd, Monckton, Watkinson (Minister of Transport), with Head and Nigel Birch, Ministers of War and Air respectively, and the Chiefs of Staff. This was, of course, the Cabinet Suez Committee as at first formed at the end of July though with its membership now altered. That day the Allied Commander-in-Chief General

66. Dayan, p. 29.   67. Ely, pp. 124–6; Peres, pp. 196–7.
68. Dayan, p. 32. Dayan bought 100 super-Sherman tanks, 300 half-track vehicles, 1,000 bazookas.

Keightley came back (and remained in London for the next three weeks)[69] and Eden telegraphed to Eisenhower on a somewhat new tack, perhaps hoping to rouse the President to anti-Communist apoplexy, on the basis of the reports about the Soviet arms piles in Sinai which must have derived from Shimon Peres: 'Nasser ... is now effectively in Russian hands, just as Mussolini was in Hitler's. It would be as ineffective to show weakness to Nasser now in order to placate him as it was to show weakness to Mussolini. ... I feel sure that anything which you can say or do to show firmness to Nasser at this time will help the peace by giving the Russians pause.'[70] Eden hoped, of course, for some kind of message from Eisenhower to cheer up the SCUA conference. He had also just received another heavily threatening letter from Bulganin.[71]

The next day, 2 October, Dulles gave what must be regarded as his reply to Eden. He brutally dissociated himself from Britain and France in their whole handling of the Suez crisis, refused to identify himself with the 'colonial powers', and added the gratuitous comment on SCUA: 'There is talk of teeth being pulled out of the plan, but I know of no teeth; there were no teeth in it.'[72] Whatever may be the truth behind Dulles's earlier confusing remarks in September, it is hard to believe that on this occasion he did not know what he was doing. Under considerable Congressional pressure to avoid anything which threatened war in this last month before the election, Dulles perhaps thought that it was now his duty to prick the bubble of British pretensions in the Middle East. But this further insult to Eden was made when the British Cabinet, weary after two months of persistent crisis, needed only a little to push them over the brink. Nutting, in his book, suggests that Dulles had heard through the CIA of the French dealings with Israel.[73] But this scarcely acquits him of the charge of tactlessness. On this day incidentally the British Government had

69. Statement by the Minister of Defence, 5 December 1956 (*Hansard*, vol. 561, col. 1242).

70. Eden, p. 498.

71. Dated 28 September 1956, published in *Izvestia*, 23 April 1957, and mentioned by Eden in his memoirs.

72. *The Times*, 3 October 1956.   73. Nutting, pp. 68–9.

given their planners orders to work out a 'winter plan' of action which would bury the idea of a military action in the near future.[74]

That same morning, Macmillan had returned from two weeks in the US talking to the annual conference of the IMF but breathing fire nevertheless. He had made no secret in the US that Britain still intended force over Suez: 'Britain would go down against Egypt with flags flying rather than submit to the Suez despoliation' (a remark reported by General Bedell Smith).[75] After a brief courtesy call on Eisenhower,[76] he had apparently convinced himself that 'Ike will lie doggo until after the election'.[77]

But in fact Eisenhower was still wondering in late September 'what was the true purpose of the French and British in going to the UN? Was it, we wondered, a sincere desire to negotiate a satisfactory peaceful settlement … or was this merely a setting of the stage for the eventual use of force in Suez? We were apprehensive'.[78]

On his return to London Macmillan was immediately whirled back into a series of meetings: on the afternoon of 2 October a discussion with Eden, Butler, Lennox-Boyd, Home, Monckton and the three Service Ministers with Anthony Nutting (Lloyd was in New York).[79] Dulles's fatal remark about SCUA was at that time coming through on the tape and it is clear from Nutting's book that this played a great part in persuading several Ministers previously wavering in support of Eden's policy that they could expect nothing from the US. During the day Eden revealed something of his state of mind when he wrote privately to Sir Robert Boothby (in answer to a disturbed letter from him) that it would be disastrous if the result of negotiation was a settlement which strengthened

74. Beaufre, p. 99. The winter plan was approved by the Commanders-in-Chief on 12 October and was supposed to be enacted as from 21 October.

75. Finer, *Dulles over Suez*, p. 278.

76. A senior Adviser confirms it as 'a brief courtesy call'. Suez was not mentioned in the talk.

77. Evidence of a senior Adviser.   78. Eisenhower, p. 52.

79. *The Times*, 3 October 1956; Nutting, p. 69.

Nasser's position. Britain would then be finished in Asia and
Africa. The essential point was that Nasser should not be
judged by the world to have got away with it. Britain stood a
chance of achieving the objective by negotiation only if she
showed the greatest firmness and resolution. But it was not
more than a chance. Eden knew that Boothby agreed with this
and expressed himself as especially grateful for what he had
written, 'if the last resort of force was all that was left to us'.[80]
There was a meeting of the full Cabinet on 3 October.[81]

About the role of Macmillan at this time there has been
controversy. He was anxious for action. He may have noticed
on his return from the US a certain weakening of Eden's resolve, a new predisposition for negotiation. Eden probably had
missed his strong personality during the weeks when he had
been away. It was now, apparently, that Macmillan took the
French line very strongly and threatened to resign unless, if the
UN failed to accept British demands, force were used.[82] He
had, he said almost menacingly, 'taken soundings' in the Conservative Party – the Party Conference was a week off – which
caused him to think that at least his own friends (such as his
son-in-law, Amery, who had written to *The Times* in July: 'If
our American allies cannot or will not join us, then Britain and
France must go ahead without them . . . not for the first time')
would not stand for a negotiated settlement.[83]

Eden's health had held up quite well during these discussions,
though he had seemed under strain throughout. The Israeli
Ambassador, lunching with him in September, noticed that he
talked without ceasing throughout the meal. Now, however,
there was a serious suggestion that all was not well. On Friday
5 October, after yet another meeting of Ministers (Salisbury,
Kilmuir, Butler, Macmillan),[84] he visited his wife in University

80. Eden to Boothby, reported by Boothby in *My Yesterday, Your
Tomorrow*, pp. 64–5. Boothby produced his letter to Eden, advising
against force, to his constituency in November.

81. *The Times*, 4 October 1956.

82. Evidence of an Adviser. This is apparently written down in the
Cabinet minutes.

83. cf. also Amery's speech on 2 August.

84. *The Times*, 6 October 1956.

College Hospital where she was understood to be recovering from a dental inspection.[85] While there he went down with a shivering fever. His temperature reached to between 105 and 106 degrees.[86] This fever was of course connected with his old bile trouble.[87] It would be interesting to know what drugs were prescribed. Nevertheless he went back to Downing Street on the Monday, though that day and the next Butler took the chair at Cabinet meetings.[88] Those who worked with him noticed a curious change: throughout the crisis he never again lost his temper. According to one who worked closely with him at this time, he was henceforth in 'a state of acute intoxication in the technical sense of the word'.[89] In retrospect the reason is perhaps clear: the critical decision had already been taken. Britain would act – if necessary without the Americans. But nevertheless he managed a short personal letter to Eisenhower in his own hand in honour of the President's birthday on the 14th: 'Our friendship remains one of my greatest rewards. Public life makes one value such a relationship more than ever in these anxious times.'[90] Eden also on the 6th sent off a fairly sharply worded letter to Bulganin in reply to the Marshal's previous missive of 28 September; and on that day the task force commanders had received from Keightley the new instruction earlier decided upon: to prepare the 'winter plan' for 'Musketeer' to be held indefinitely in a state of readiness, ten days being the expected notice of action.[91]

At this moment the Minister of Defence, Monckton, decided that the time had come to hand over; he had wanted to leave in August. To the Cabinet he said that health was the reason; a perfectly good excuse at a time when the Minister of Defence was obviously about to be faced with great burdens and when in fact he had been ill in August. But to the American Ambassador he said that he was going because he thought the use of

85. *The Times*, 8 October 1956.
86. Eden, p. 568. An Adviser says that it was only 105 degrees.
87. This passage was read by an informed doctor.
88. *The Times*, 9 and 10 October 1956.
89. Evidence of an Adviser.
90. Eisenhower, p. 53.
91. Stockwell, *Sunday Telegraph*, 30 October 1966.

force a great blunder.[92] To the Canadian High Commissioner
he had complained that 'nobody in Government seems to feel
it his duty to bring forward bad news'.[93] Nevertheless, he remained in the Cabinet, as Paymaster-General. He had apparently told Eden that he desired to resign on 24 September[94]
and his actual letter of resignation was dated 11 October,
but was held up till the 18th so that 'he could tell his con-
stituents'.[95] One critically placed Minister commented: 'Poor
Walter had all the right ideas but never quite summoned up
the courage to fight for them.'[96] Monckton was appropriately
succeeded by Antony Head, Secretary of State for War,
who had been promised the reversion to the Ministry of
Defence as long ago as 1954 (by Churchill, in succession to
Alexander) and who had done most of the work for the past
few weeks.

Head was one of the most gifted of the Conservatives who
had entered Parliament in 1945. Before the war a regular officer
in the Life Guards, he had been a planner at the Cabinet office
in the War. Having negotiated with Nasser in 1954 he knew
very well the nature of Egyptian nationalism. Since he had seen
how difficult it had been for the Government to withdraw from
Suez in 1954 it is hard to believe that his instinct in 1956 was to
advocate a policy which might lead to the reoccupation of
Egypt. But with Eden (to whom he was personally loyal)
occupying himself with so much, Head approached the problems ahead as a technician.

Pineau and Lloyd were now in New York, and the former
told Dulles, according to Eisenhower, on 5 October that 'in
effect they did not believe that any peaceful way existed. They
urged ... that only through capitulation by Nasser could the
Western standing in Africa and the Middle East be restored.

92. Eisenhower, p. 64.

93. Robertson, p. 124.

94. Lord Birkenhead, *Walter Monckton*, p. 308. Monckton explicitly
told Eden in a letter of 24 September that he would not have thought of
resigning there and then had it not been for 'fundamental differences
with my colleagues over the size of the forces and over Suez'.

95. Evidence of a Minister.

96. cf. also *Observer* profile, 23 October 1960.

Foster disagreed vehemently.'[97] But Pineau at least regarded this as adequate prior warning to the US as to what would happen.[98]

Within a few days, however, the situation seemed to have been improved. Lloyd and Hammarskjöld persuaded Pineau to negotiate privately with Fawzi, the Egyptian Foreign Minister, in his office.[99] Possibly inspired by Nehru, Fawzi was extremely forthcoming. By 12 October, Hammarskjöld could make a list of six principles worked out by Selwyn Lloyd where agreement could, it seemed, be reached. The principles were: (1) free and open passage through the Canal; (2) respect for Egyptian sovereignty; (3) insulation of the operation of the Canal from the politics of a single country; (4) SCUA and Egypt to fix tolls; (5) allocation of a fair percentage of tolls to development; and (6) arbitration to be agreed between Egypt and the old Company.[1] On 14 October the Security Council unanimously approved the principles, though Russia vetoed the second part of the resolution which stated these points to be embodied in SCUA and the London Conference. Still the assumption was that Pineau, Lloyd and Fawzi would meet again later in the month, maybe in Geneva, to begin detailed negotiations. The responsibility for resuming discussions (and making detailed proposals) was however left with the Egyptians.

Would Egypt have stuck to these principles? 'Insulation from Egyptian politics' was surely one thing over which Nasser could never really give way, despite Fawzi's forthcoming attitude on the subject.

The British Government, it seems, also had been advised by the Secret Service to discount anything agreed by Fawzi on the

97. Eisenhower, p. 52. It would seem that Pineau said this to Dulles in Lloyd's presence. Dulles's telegram to Eisenhower (saying that Lloyd said the same) is therefore misleading.

98. Evidence of a French Minister.

99. This had nothing to do with Dulles, despite what Eisenhower says in his memoirs (p. 53).

1. *The Times*, 13 October 1956. See Nutting, pp. 72 ff., for a description of Eden's reactions.

grounds that he was too close a friend of Hammarskjöld.[2] As Eden says, Egypt might have procrastinated.[3] Still, the settlement boded well. Selwyn Lloyd set off back to England 'quite pleased',[4] though conscious that Dulles had no thought of trying to influence Nasser to make him accept a settlement on British terms.[5] Eden himself in his book pooh-poohed the agreement: 'Six principles, when it had taken us three months of negotiation to carry practical working proposals for the future of the Canal to the UN, only to have them smothered. . . . Plunder had paid off.'[6] But Eisenhower (maybe for electoral reasons) said on the other hand 'it looks as if a very great crisis is behind us'.[7]

If he really thought that, he was seriously misinformed. For on 5 October Challe and his mission had returned from Israel, after being much impressed by the state of preparedness in the Israeli armed forces. He brought back not only a detailed list of military requirements but also a message from Ben Gurion to Mollet that he would definitely not engage the Israeli army unless he was certain not only of French assistance but at the very least of British neutrality. On 8 October, Admiral Barjot had been instructed to study the possibility of a French military action against Egypt without British assistance, except perhaps for facilities on Cyprus, and, on 11 October, the very day that President Eisenhower was feeling so sure that peace had come, General Challe was in New York telling Pineau in person of the state of negotiations with Israel: Pineau expressed himself much encouraged and determined as much as ever on the use of force.[8]

The Conservative Party Conference meantime had begun at Llandudno on 11 October. It was an occasion for heady enthusiasm. Many resolutions demanded firmness. Gaitskell's reservations on the use of force were described as treacherous. Julian Amery said that if the Security Council failed 'to bring Nasser to his senses' the Government should use force with or

2. Evidence of a political Adviser.   3. Eden, p. 505.
4. An Adviser's comment.   5. Evidence of a Cabinet Minister.
6. Eden, pp. 505–6.   7. *The Times*, 13 October 1956.
8. Ely, p. 136; Challe, *Notre Révolte*, pp. 25–6.

without US backing. The Government's policy, of course, was to keep everyone's spirits up. Salisbury had been allocated the task of the major foreign policy speech, a real ginger-up, but unfortunately became ill with heart trouble. Eden therefore instructed Nutting to do this and, despite the fact that he was critical of the use of force at all, to make use of Salisbury's angry notes: 'The country would not flinch from the hard test.'[9] Nutting actually made what seemed a speech of great power and apparent passion, doubtless compensating in this way for the scepticism that he really felt about the policy. Butler also appealed to Conservatives not to 'knuckle under to predatory nationalism' and to follow Eden in his 'valiant resolve ... for liberty, progress and the rule of the law'.[10] Eden, speaking on the 13th in the final rally, made one of the most successful speeches of his life. Nevertheless, Waterhouse and Julian Amery could regard the conference as a triumph for them since they successfully added an amendment to the Government's resolution (which merely approved Government policy) to ensure that the Conservatives backed full international control of the Canal.

Meantime, Israel had been for a month deliberately fomenting acute tension on the Israeli-Jordanian frontier, as a diversion from their plans against Egypt. It was *primarily* a diversion but became a real crisis. On 10 October, with immense speed, Israel launched a punitive counter-raid at the Jordanian police fortress of Kalkillah, using artillery and airborne units. This action caused a greater stir than any other had done on the Jordanian front. Would Nasser act and so give the French an excuse to draw the British in to intervene on the Canal?[11] But King Hussein asked Keightley in Cyprus to put into effect the Anglo-Jordanian Treaty, and send the RAF to help Jordan. The next day, the 11th, Peter Westlake, the British Chargé d'Affaires in Tel Aviv (in the dark like everyone else outside the

9. Nutting, pp. 82–3. See also the review of Nutting's book, *No End of a Lesson*, by Lord Lambton, *Sunday Telegraph*, 2 July 1967; *The Times*, 12 October 1956.

10. *The Times*, 15 October 1956.

11. See the suggestive paragraphs by Azeau, pp. 232–6.

Cabinet about any proposed relationship),[12] told Ben Gurion that an Iraqi division was about to enter Jordan, to bolster Jordanian defence; if Israel took further military action, Britain would go to Jordan's aid.[13] Eden in his memoirs says: 'Our aircraft were on the point of going up.' [14] Dayan commented: 'I must confess to the feeling that, save for the Almighty, only the British are capable of complicating affairs to such a degree. At the very moment when they are preparing to topple Nasser ... they insist on getting the Iraqi army into Jordan, even if such action leads to war between Israel and Jordan in which they, the British, will take part against Israel.' [15] Through Eden (and through Nuri's complacency) the French secured that the Iraqi contingent in Jordan should be limited to only one regiment.[16] But this was not enough for Israel and Britain in mid-October 1956 remained in the curious position of considering military action against both Egypt and Israel.

12. Apparently.   13. Dayan, p. 52.
14. Eden, p. 512.   15. Dayan, p. 59.
          16. Nutting, p. 86.

THE DECLARATION OF INTENT

A Cabinet Minister: It was all a question of 'when' or 'if'.
The author: Aren't they the same words in German?
The Minister: I dare say they are in French and Hebrew
for all I know.

Conversation in London, August 1966

ON Sunday, 14 October (the day after the end of the successful
Conservative Conference), General Challe, major-general of the
French armed forces, and Albert Gazier, French Minister of
Labour (a close *confidant* of Mollet), crossed secretly to London
to see Eden.[1] Mollet had decided that the Iraqi complication
made it essential for him to take Eden fully into his confidence
about the possibility of collaboration with Israel.[2] Challe, who
had been to both Israel and New York in the last ten days, had
devised the strategic plan for Israel–Allied collaboration.[3] Since
the last contact between Eden and the French, Israel and France
had come close to an actual decision on their joint plans. General
Beaufre with his staff had been working not only on the British
'winter plan' but on the problems posed by '*l'hypothèse Israel*'.
About 9 or 10 October, Admiral Barjot had finished a general
direction on French collaboration with Israel which assumed
'a benevolent neutrality on Britain's part which permitted our
use of their Cypriot bases'.[4]

It is evident that the possibility of French action independent
of Britain was a serious possibility but the Israelis were sus-

1. Challe's visit was first revealed by the Brombergers (*Les Secrets de
Suez*, p. 13); it was confirmed to me by an officer in the French Ministry
of Defence. Azeau confirms too (p. 240). Gazier's visit was confirmed to
me by a senior (British) official. The visit is described in detail by
Nutting, pp. 74–8, and is naturally briefly mentioned by Challe in his
recent memoir (p. 27), and by Ely (p. 136).

2. Evidence of an officer in the French Ministry of Defence; and of
a critically placed Minister.   3. Beaufre, p. 108.

4. Beaufre, loc. cit. Barjot's plan was the limited one of France seizing
Port Said as a bargaining counter.

picious of any assumption of British neutrality and also desired British aerial support. Anyway, Gazier and Challe proposed a new plan to Eden at a meeting at Chequers. Challe stood before a map: 'The Israelis here, the Egyptians there. Where is our position? *On the Canal*.'[5] In Nutting's words, 'the plan was that Israel should be invited to attack Egypt across the Sinai peninsula and that France and Britain, having given the Israeli forces enough time to seize all or most of Sinai, should then order "both sides" to withdraw their forces from the Suez Canal, in order to permit an Anglo-French force to intervene and occupy the Canal'.[6] This was of course a good time to tempt Eden with such a plan. He had postponed and re-postponed all plans for attack on Egypt in the interest of keeping in step with the US. But he knew now that the US would never march. He believed that Nasser would never negotiate. He was 'thrilled at the idea' proposed by Challe,[7] much to that officer's surprise: 'If M. Gazier had not been with me and de-rived the same impression as I did, I should have said that Eden was making fun of me,' Challe confided the next day to General Ely.[8]

It would seem that on this day Eden received a letter (dated the 11th) from Eisenhower, in answer to his own sending Bulganin's communication of late September. Eisenhower, after agreeing that Bulganin wrote in a style 'hardly to be expected in communications of this sort', commented: 'It is clear that the Soviets are playing hard to gain a dominant position in the Near East area, and it is likely they have developed quite a hold on Nasser. This problem will probably remain with us whatever may be the results of the talks in New York. ... With warm re-gards.' What, however, did these *points de suspension* exclude? Is it possible that this letter added, as alleged by the French sources to whom Randolph Churchill spoke, some paragraphs

5. The Brombergers, *Les Secrets de Suez*, p. 13, and Challe (loc. cit.) describe the discussion in almost the same terms. Challe writes: 'Then I presented [to Eden] ... the pretext, or, better, the scenario which he was waiting for ... *Bonne idée, me dit Eden, j'irai demain à Paris en discuter avec Guy Mollet!'*

6. Nutting, p. 77.   7. Nutting in conversation, 12 May 1968.
8. Ely, pp. 137–8.

which Eden thought gave him *carte blanche* to act providing he did so *after* the presidential elections of 6 November?[9] If so, neither Eisenhower nor Eden mentions the fact in their memoirs. One can hardly doubt that whatever the letter contained, Eden read more into it than was intended; anyway he did not delay until after the elections. For, as has been seen, Macmillan, on what turned out to be unreliable evidence, had decided that action would be possible providing it came *before* the elections, an argument also pressed by France because of what they believed would be the nullifying consequences of the Jewish vote.

Of course, Eden and his close advisers were traditionally reluctant to enter into any arrangement, formal or informal, covert or overt, with Israel. The slightest contact with Israel was anathema to the Foreign Office. It would be absurd in an operation designed to avoid losing face in the Middle East for Britain to associate militarily with the one country at war with all the Arabs. Then above all there was Jordan. King Hussein of Jordan was already being accused by Cairo of connivance with Israel and tried to compensate for this slander by openly encouraging terrorist activity. Israel's continuing reprisal raids might be aimed at diverting attention from her Egyptian border, but they were causing a real crisis in Jordan, with whom, of course, Britain had a defence treaty and where elections were now only a week away. Any open arrangement with Israel would also evidently imperil the lives of all British subjects within the whole Middle East. Still, if Israel provided the only way ahead, an arrangement such as France suggested would have to be considered more seriously; and perhaps there were other advantages. Eden personally had always been closely identified with the Arab cause in the past. His speech at the Guildhall in November 1955 had caused the greatest misgivings in Israel. Yet already before General Challe's temptation he seems to have changed his mind. Nutting has described him as saying about 12 October in relation to the Iraqi–Jordan crisis that he would not allow him 'to plunge this country into war merely to satisfy the anti-Jewish spleen of you people in

9. Eisenhower, p. 54, and Randolph Churchill, p. 295.

the Foreign Office'.[10] Such a view would have been improbable in the extreme a year before.

The US now got wind of Israel's military preparations. High-flying reconnaissance showed that Israel now had sixty Mystère fighter-bombers (there may have been more), not, as they had been told, twelve[11] : a new miracle of loaves and fishes seemed to have occurred in Israel. But the US still thought that Israel, whom they realized to be mobilizing, was going to attack Jordan, not Egypt. Eisenhower recalls that 'from about this time on, we had the uneasy feeling that we were cut off from our allies'.[12]

On 16 October, Eden tells us in his memoirs that there was in the morning a meeting of Ministers[13]; these were in fact Macmillan, Monckton, Kilmuir and Lennox-Boyd, together with Nutting, representing Lloyd until he should return from New York; Head and the Chiefs of Staff were present too. The six principles were discussed and specifically dismissed as unlikely to lead to a swift solution. SCUA held no further promise. Macmillan and Kilmuir firmly backed the plan as presented by Challe and Gazier. Nutting and Monckton alone opposed it. Eventually Lloyd arrived from New York. The Foreign Secretary, still dubious on the use of force and initially disposed to agree with Nutting that Challe's ideas were mistaken, but unable to recommend to his colleagues that the UN discussions, either in New York or in Geneva, would really lead to anything, had become aware that Dulles would never back SCUA on the matter of dues.[14] Exhausted after his flight and weeks of incessant work, he was swept along by Eden,[15] and no more was heard of the 'six principles' nor indeed of the Tripartite Declaration, or of the UN Charter, or of the 1954 Agreement with Egypt. Eden tells us that though 'we could have found a pretext for going to Geneva . . . I could not return from Geneva with a piece of paper . . . when I knew it had no real value. This would have lulled people . . about a dictator whose intentions

10. Nutting, p. 73.   11. Eisenhower, p. 56.   12. Eisenhower, p. 56.
13. Eden, pp. 508–9; *The Times*, 17 October 1956.
14. Evidence of a Cabinet Minister.
15. Despite, apparently, initial hesitation expressed to Nutting.

were, I was sure, predatory'.[16] This comment should perhaps be placed against the view ten years later of Pineau: 'If the Egyptian Government had not maintained its boycott of Israeli ships a formula would without doubt have been achieved.'[17]

That same afternoon (not the 18th, as previously planned) Eden and Lloyd went over to Paris at a few hours' notice and saw Mollet and Pineau without any advisers being present. A disturbed British Ambassador (Sir Gladwyn Jebb) was informed by Eden that this was due to French insistence.[18] In his memoirs Eden says that, after some talk of Jordan, it was accepted at this meeting that *'if Israel were to break out ... it was better from our point of view that it should be against Egypt* [my italics] ... then there would be other worries, for example the safety of the Canal. In common prudence, we had to consider what our action should be, for our two countries were, as we knew, the only powers to have effective military forces at our command in the area'.[19] This comment reveals as much of the truth of what transpired as Eden desired anyone should ever know; and indeed it tells a lot.

Although Eden doubtless did his best on this occasion to avoid direct commitment, there is today no doubt that he did indeed now nail Britain's colours to the unfamiliar mast of Franco-Israeli collaboration. Lloyd is said to have been still critical of going ahead but Eden was apparently convinced by Mollet's urgent contention that this was in effect the last chance for action before winter. This was a naval point: to carry out an amphibious assault in the Mediterranean in November was anyway risky. By this time, of course, Mollet knew Eden well and how to persuade him best. Eden and Mollet decided to invite Ben Gurion to come soon to Paris in order to co-ordinate action, which would now be on the lines of the plan presented to Eden by General Challe.[20] Mollet saw Eden alone for about three quarters of an hour, and Lloyd came out of the meeting

16. Eden, p. 509. 17. *Le Monde*, 4 November 1966.
18. Evidence of a senior official. 19. Eden, p. 513.
20. General Ely is the only person to have given any detailed account of this discussion (op. cit., pp. 142–3).

to say cryptically to the British Ambassador that the balance of the meeting had been 'three against one'.[21] The Ambassador was still left in the dark. A debate in the National Assembly had just shown Mollet that if he 'acted' he could still count on French opinion. A right-wing deputy in the Chamber shouted: 'Are the Government going to wait till the Cossacks are watering their horses in the Tuileries fountains before making up their minds?'[22] Pineau could not contain himself and had assured the Assembly that the Government had a 'new trump'.[23]

Afterwards the few informed people in both Governments began now to work over the intricate problems of timing raised by their new decision. Brigadier Bernard Fergusson prepared to go to Cyprus to discuss 'news policy if the British radio services there had to be taken over in a crisis'.[24] In Tel Aviv the US Military Attaché ceased to receive information from his French and British colleagues [25] (the US Air Attaché seems to have concealed his knowledge of Franco-Israeli preparations out of sympathy for Israel[26]). There was now no British Ambassador in Washington: Makins had left on 11 October and Caccia conveniently did not arrive till 8 November, by sea.[27] Clark, Eden's press officer, who had been shown as sceptical on the use of force, went away on a week's holiday.[28] Until now relations between the Government and the press had been entirely frank and truthful; the Government had always said they would use force if need be though not all the press had believed them. But henceforth there was little communication.[29]

On 17 October, Ben Gurion, presumably informed from

21. Evidence of a Cabinet Minister.
22. *The Times*, 17 October 1956.
23. *The Times*, 17 October 1956. Mr Arthur Lewis later secured from the Government the useful information that this visit of Eden's to Paris cost £330 11s. 8d. (*Hansard*, vol. 561, col. *157*).
24. He arrived on 22 October (cf. *Hansard*, vol. 561, col. 1496).
25. Dulles to the Washington press, 31 October 1956 (off the record).
26. Bar-Zohar, pp. 180–81. On evidence of an '*officier supérieur français*'.
27. Evidence of a senior Adviser.
28. Evidence of a journalist.
29. Evidence of a journalist.

Paris that the British were now ready, made a big speech in the Knesset, ignored the question of Jordan, and announced unexpectedly that the 'gravest danger facing Israel was that of attack by the "Egyptian fascist dictator" '.[30] For the first time for some years, Ben Gurion said some agreeable words about Britain, thanking her for giving them economic aid. Israeli Ambassadors in London, Paris, Washington and Moscow were called back for consultations.[31] Eden, back in London on the 17th, opened the annual motor show with sang-froid and hastened away to jerk the machinery of 'force' into action, while the ever peripatetic General Challe flew off again to Israel to bring Ben Gurion back to Paris the next week.

On the 18th, Eden and Lloyd, at a meeting of some members of the Cabinet in London (according to Eden) 'went over the ground which we had covered in our discussions in Paris. . . . We described the . . . growing danger that Israel, under provocation from Egypt, would make some military move.'[32] 'Every senior member of the Government . . . remembered the mood in which we had taken our first decisions. The others were their consequence.' Thus Eden ends a chapter in his memoirs rightly entitled 'Prelude October 13–October 23'. It was an allusion to the decisions of 27 July–2 August to use force if necessary. It seems that now was the first time that Ministers other than those present on 16 October were let into the secret, in however guarded a fashion, about the Franco-Israeli plan. This was doubtless the occasion to which Butler made some reference in a TV interview in 1966:

I was informed by Eden [after returning from Scotland and Calder Hall, where he had been since the Conservative Conference] . . . that a series of meetings [i.e. diplomatic meetings with France, for Butler had been present at the Cabinet meetings and meetings of Ministers before the 11th] had been held at which it had been decided to go in to the Suez Canal to stop hostilities in the event of Israel invading Egypt. I agreed to this plan . . . and I supported Eden's courage in deciding upon such a move.[33]

30. *The Times*, 17 October 1956.	31. Tsur, p. 409.
32. Eden, p. 514. Nutting interestingly makes no allusion to this meeting.	33. BBC TV, 26 July 1966.

The action planned was now all but irreversible. Nevertheless a majority of the Cabinet Ministers consulted were apparently not made aware, perhaps did not wish to be made aware, of the precise military details of the manner by which the two attacks would be co-ordinated. Nor is it known whether they were apprised that later in the month an Iraqi *coup d'état* was planned for Syria – though Nuri's plots against Syria had been numerous and ineffective.

On 18 October, General Beaufre, deputy military commander and supreme French commander on land, encountered General Gazin, Chief of Staff to Admiral Barjot, in a train at the Gare de l'Est in Paris. Gazin told him: 'the decisions are taken. *Enfin les Anglais marchent. Mais avec* MUSKETEER RE-VISED B.' [34]

The full enormity of the news will only be realized if it is understood that this plan had been prepared between 10 and 14 September, after the decision to disembark at Port Said rather than at Alexandria. It laid special burdens of responsibility on the air task commander, Air Marshal Barnett, a New Zealander of wartime Bomber Command and, until earlier in 1956, commander of the RAF in Egypt. For the plan assumed that Egypt could be conquered by forty-eight hours of bombing to destroy the Egyptian Air Force, accompanied by eight to ten days of aero-psychological warfare – pamphlets and broadcasts 'to break the Egyptians' will to fight', accompanied by bombing of troop movements and defences. After this, the allied fleet would surely be able to land the armies at Port Said without fighting. Indeed they would probably not land until the commander-in-chief could report the magic phrase 'there is no opposition' or 'all opposition can be ignored'.

Eden had found this plan appealing on the grounds that it would cut all casualties to a minimum.[35] It seems to have been

34. Evidence of General Beaufre, See also his book (p. 116).

35. This description of the plan owes much to a French commander, General Beaufre in *Le Figaro*, 8 November 1966, says that to begin with there was to be an aero-psychological phase lasting 'at least ten days'. An earlier idea had placed an even greater reliance on aviation (see Stockwell's articles).

chiefly the work of the chairman of the Chiefs of Staff, Air Chief Marshal Sir William Dickson.[36] The French had accepted it just possibly because it answered the demands of a joint Anglo–French–Israeli offensive which some *officials* even then were already hoping for.[37] But the French *commanders* on the other hand had opposed this delay of eight to ten days. Beaufre had pointed out that contemporary world politics made it impossible to carry out so long an aerial propaganda and bombing attack.[38] The French were less preoccupied by fear of casualties; General Massu, the airborne commander, said grandly that he would have accepted thirty to forty per cent casualties.[39] The Navy, who anyway had preferred to land at Alexandria, pointed out that the plan enabled the Canal to be blocked by Egypt.[40] Beaufre asked what would happen if the Egyptians gave in after only two days. To whom could they surrender? This point went home. After some other arguments were brought forward, 'Musketeer Revised' was replaced by 'Musketeer Revised A'. Airborne troops would be kept in readiness at Cyprus for an immediate landing, along with some light landing craft and minesweepers.[41] (Somewhat confusingly these two plans were also together referred to, by the British, not the French, as 'Plan 2'.[42])

'Musketeer Revised A' was still not very satisfactory to the French. The main fleet would still take a long time to get to Egypt, 6 days $5\frac{3}{4}$ hours for tank landing craft. The journey naturally took longer from Algiers, where the main body of the French were gathered, and from Southampton, whence the 3rd Division would embark. Cyprus could accommodate only a few minesweepers and no tank landing craft. Delays prevented the

36. Beaufre, p. 85.

37. See above, p. 92. Antony Head's reported comment to the Conservative Defence Committee suggests some British connivance. It should also be said that on 10 September the French were disposed to accept almost any alteration of plan if only it made the British hurry up (evidence of a British commander).

38. Evidence of General Beaufre (cf. *Le Figaro*, 8 November 1966).

39. Evidence of a task force commander.

40. Evidence of a task force commander.   41. See Beaufre, pp. 85–6.

42. Stockwell, *Sunday Telegraph*, 30 October 1966.

accumulation on Cyprus of the necessary forces. No photo reconnaissance was allowed to be carried out. However, this plan was militarily an improvement on its predecessor. It is easy to imagine, therefore, the commanders' dismay when they were now instructed to go back to the old plan.[43] This new change seems to have been decided upon by 10 October, to limit casualties.[44] (Neither of these plans had anything to do with the British 'winter plan' which, as has been seen, was called for on 2 October, issued on 12 October and which according to Stockwell was 'dead' by 15 October.)

Beaufre flung himself once more into controversy. He managed in the next week to dispatch to Cyprus in requisitioned French civilian aircraft all the paratroops then in Algeria so as to make possible a variant of Plan 'A' 'on the day' if in fact it chanced that Nasser should fall quickly or if there really were no opposition. This idea later became known as 'Plan Omelette'.[45] Bourgès-Maunoury crossed to London to see Head.[46] The French deputy air commander, Brohon, though normally under Air Marshal Barnett, became the chief of French operations for Israeli collaboration – an activity he successfully disguised from his comrades: Brohon would ask leave to go to Paris; in fact he would fly off eastwards to Tel Aviv.[47] The number of days of aero-psychological warfare was also cut to six, to coincide with the shortest time for slow ships to come from Malta.[48] Instead of landing on 8 or 10 November, the disembarkation would be on the 6th, provided that the weather held. So ultimately what was put into effect was what Beaufre later described as 'Musketeer Revised B with elements of A'.[49] The aim of this operation was specifically to occupy the Canal Zone, though in the minds of some commanders and perhaps some of the politicians there remained an expectation

43. Evidence of a French commander.
44. Beaufre, *Le Figaro*, 8 November 1966.
45. Evidence of General Beaufre. See also his book, pp. 124–5.
46. On the 21st. Evidence of a Minister and J. S. Ambler, *The French Army in Politics*, p. 228.
47. Evidence of a British commander.
48. Evidence of a French commander.
49. Comment of General Beaufre, Tangiers, August 1966.

that 'we would turn right into Cairo at Ismailia' depending on whether the Egyptians gave battle before Ismailia or on the Cairo–Ismailia road. The political aim of the campaign remained somewhat obscure to the officers designated to carry it out.[50]

On 18 October, D-Day was only eleven days off. But the 'final operation order' was not given till 24 October. Although, as General Stockwell has now told us, 'things began to happen rapidly' by 20 October,[51] there was no clear picture in England as to when precisely action would begin. The French fleet in Algiers was being loaded from 20 October onwards, but since all French officers were deputies to British commanders this had no effect whatever on the likelihood of their reaching Egypt before the British acted. The probable sequence of events filtered through to, rather than was communicated to, the responsible English commanders: one commander came down about the 19th to the operational chiefs of staff after a talk with Keightley, and told them, 'unless I'm having hallucinations the hooknosed boys are going to be brought in'.[52] General Beaufre has since commented: 'The British, wishing to avoid all appearance of collusion with Israel, refused to begin loading the warships before the start of the Israeli attack, of which they, like us, knew the date. We therefore started off ten days late.'[53]

The British and French were now assisted by the coincidence of, first, the Polish, and then, on 22–23 October, the beginnings of the Hungarian revolution. These events swept aside public and international consideration of the Middle East, though Dulles speculated that the British and French might go to war after the elections, in the hope that the US would then join in.[54]

50. Evidence of a British commander. This uncertainty characterized even the Alexandria plan. A British commander has described how on one occasion Monckton was beguiled to attend a meeting in the planners' room and he confessed he did not know what was precisely the aim of the operation.

51. Stockwell, *Sunday Telegraph*, 30 October 1966.

52. Evidence of a British commander.

53. See Beaufre, *Le Figaro*, 8 November 1966.

54. Eisenhower, p. 56.

Dulles's papers make clear that their Ambassador in Paris (Dillon) reported France to be preparing for war on 19 October, but he did not know when hostilities would start.[55] On 21 October the long-awaited Jordanian elections gave, despite British efforts, a resounding victory for Nasser's friends and Jordan quickly cancelled her military arrangements with Iraq. The irony was not lost on General Dayan, particularly since at the very moment that the French military attaché was telling him that France had failed to persuade Britain to abandon her Iraqi project, the results of elections in Jordan were already known.[56] A little later Nasser announced that he would give King Hussein military aid whenever he needed it.

Despite the telegrams and instructions exchanged between 16 and 21 October, the general plan for the co-ordination of Operations Musketeer and Kadesh (as the Israeli plan was named) was not yet clear even to the protagonists. Israel was understandably still uncertain about Britain. So on 22 October, Ben Gurion, Dayan and Peres were flown to Paris by Challe and Mangin in the DC4 given to de Gaulle by Truman after the war. (This aircraft had been used by the Franco-Israeli planners for the past two or three weeks.) Landing at the military airport of Villacoublay, this party drove a mile or two to a villa at Sèvres, a suburb of Paris. They were later joined there by Pineau, Bourgès-Maunoury and Mollet. The meetings were secret.[57] Ben Gurion came for several things. He wanted to confirm first that the Egyptian Air Force would be destroyed before he started across Sinai; and he wanted an aerial watch over Egyptian airfields from the moment that Israel crossed the Egyptian frontier. Only the British had the aircraft for this. For Israel to move at all Ben Gurion wanted a written

---

55. Dillon to Dulles.   56. Dayan, p. 59.

57. The visit of Ben Gurion and the Israelis to Paris was confirmed to me by a French Minister present; Pineau also spoke of it on the BBC Third Programme on 18 July 1966 and in *Le Monde*, 4 November 1966. It is in effect now an open secret. General Ely (pp. 140–7) also mentions it, as does Peres in some detail (pp. 200–205). The meeting was described to me by an officer in the French Ministry of Defence. I have been assisted by an unpublished Israeli account of this meeting. Mollet has confirmed the meeting on several occasions (cf. Bar-Zohar, p. 162).

agreement, signed by all three countries, together with the presence at the final discussion of a responsible British Minister. Ben Gurion had doubts about Britain, both because of her traditional Arabism and because of Eden's known hesitations.[58]

The French Cabinet was now in a curious mood, of mingled anger and anxiety, due first to the capture of the yacht *Athos* loaded with Egyptian arms bound for Algeria, and secondly because of the odd affair of the capture on 22 October of the Algerian rebel leaders, Ben Bella and Ben Khider, in transit to Tunis, by orders of the Minister of War, Max Lejeune, contrary to the wishes of his Prime Minister, Mollet. The French Ambassador to Cairo was recalled, but Trevelyan stayed on.

Mollet and Ben Gurion confirmed at Sèvres the Franco-Israeli side of the plan, such as a *ceinture maritime* of French naval ships along the Israeli coast, an 'umbrella' of French fighters to protect Israeli cities, and French parachute drops of food, ammunition and trucks to the advancing Israelis by Cyprus-based aircraft.[59] That evening the 'responsible British Minister' and an official flew secretly to Paris. There is no reason now to doubt that this was Lloyd and the official Patrick Dean.[60]

Lloyd appeared, according to one who was present, like an 'old-fashioned family lawyer'.[61] Seeming to disapprove of the whole project, he keenly argued how it should be most effectively presented. Appearances had to be kept up. The Anglo-French should appear at all times to be defending the Canal against both sides.[62]

Britain had not wanted to begin bombing Egyptian airfields until seventy-two hours after the start of the Israeli offensive; France was ready to start bombing immediately – though of

58. From an Israeli account; Robertson (*Crisis*, p. 156) has the same; Azeau (p. 248) makes the point about the aerial cover. It is echoed by André Fontaine in *Le Monde*, 30–31 October 1966.

59. Azeau, p. 247; Bar-Zohar, p. 163; an Israeli account.

60. See Nutting, pp. 87–8, and Ely, p. 147. Christian Pineau in the *Daily Telegraph*, 6 June 1967, wrote: 'It is a fact, and it would be ridiculous to deny it, that three-sided conversations took place between Israel, Britain and France.'

61. An Israeli account.   62. An Israeli account.

course her bombers would not mainly be responsible. A compromise was proposed: thirty-six hours.[63] There would, however, be a British aerial watch over Egyptian airfields from the
start.[64] Britain argued also that the Israeli attack had to be made
to seem not simply a border raid, such as Ben Gurion had
mounted against Jordan. Anything less than a full war could
not be said to threaten the Canal and therefore justify the great
ruse.[65] But Ben Gurion remained all through most suspicious of
Britain and demanded very firm assurances that Eden would
commit himself.

The British attitude derived primarily from the hope that we
could keep friends with the Arab world as a whole even after
attacking Egypt. Many (maybe most) Arab leaders of different
political persuasions distrusted Nasser and Egypt. But the desire
of Britain to appear virtuous while being Machiavellian resulted in what was (as Pineau has explained publicly) one of
the main mistakes in the whole project. The plan tied the hands
of Britain and France and when it came to the point caused
them both to be more ineffective and seem more treacherous.[66]
Dayan questioned the delay between the start of British bombing and the landing of troops but the British pooh-poohed these
doubts: Malta was five to six days from Egypt and that was
that.[67] There appears to be no truth in the allegation put about
later by Dulles that Israel was promised a slice of Jordan in the
eventual share-out after the victory. But one day no doubt it
will become clear whether the plans for Nuri's *coup* in Syria –
according to one witness timed for 28 October – played any part
in Britain's behaviour.[68]

Lloyd stayed for as short a time at Sèvres as possible, perhaps
an hour and a half in all, between about 6.30 and 8.30 p.m.
and, though he left behind Dean to draw up a draft document,
there remained some doubt in Franco-Israeli minds about
British commitment. The Foreign Secretary seems to have

63. An Israeli account.   64. Azeau, p. 248.
65. An Israeli account.
66. See Pineau in *Le Monde*, 4 November 1966.
67. Evidence of an Israeli commander.
68. See the discussion in Seale, *The Struggle for Syria*, p. 280.

thought, in fact, that if anyone were going to sign a secret agreement with Israel and France it should be Eden and not he. So
the next night, with Ben Gurion and his party still in France,
Pineau flew to London and buoyed up Eden. Pineau's movements were carefully noted in London by *The Times*: dinner
with Lloyd at Carlton Gardens, visit of Eden at 10 p.m., his
stay for an hour and Pineau's return flight at midnight.[69]
According to Nutting, Lloyd told him the next day that Pineau
left London with assurances for Ben Gurion that he need have
no fear of being left in the lurch.[70] At all events, it is clear from
the account of Shimon Peres that it was on 24 October, still at
Sèvres, that Ben Gurion took the decision to go ahead.[71]
Dean meantime prepared a Three-Power document in three
copies, one for each participant. He signed for Britain, Ben
Gurion for Israel and Mollet for France. Ben Gurion, however, angrily refused to accept an official's signature for Britain
and the document was sent to London for a more imposing
signature, apparently with success.[72] The document (the word
'treaty' is a misnomer, for it was a 'declaration of intent', in
the words to me of one English Cabinet Minister) was handed
to Mollet on the morning of Friday 26 October.[73] Mollet sent
the document to Ben Gurion.[74] The die was cast.

By this time the British Cabinet had been brought fully into
the picture. It seems clear that Eden put the whole matter to a
meeting of the full Cabinet on 24 October.[75] The discussion
seems not then to have been conclusive and the meeting held
over to the 25th. It is therefore an illusion to suppose, as some
have argued,[76] that Eden acted without the backing of his

69. *The Times*, 24 October 1956.   70. Nutting, p. 104.
71. Peres, pp. 202–4.   72. From an Israeli account.
73. Evidence of a senior official.   74. Ely, p. 152.

75. Only Nutting speaks of this meeting and dates it 23 October (p.
104). Eden speaks of the meeting of 25 October (p. 523).

76. Contrary points of view were put by Paul Johnson (*The Suez War*,
p. 72), Randolph Churchill (*The Rise and Fall of Sir Anthony Eden*,
p. 277), Hugh Gaitskell (House of Commons, *Hansard*, vol. 602, col.
56–7), Harold Wilson in August 1966, and accepted by such students as
J. P. Mackintosh (*The British Cabinet*, p. 436) and Epstein (*British
Politics in the Suez Crisis*, p. 202). But see above, pp. 116–17, and below,
pp. 171–2.

Cabinet, though he is believed to have spoken with great passion and to have threatened to resign unless he got his way.

A Cabinet Minister present further explained that the Cabinet were explicitly told that 'the Jews had come up with an offer' to attack Egypt and so give Britain and France the chance at long last to launch Operation Musketeer. It seems likely that the possibility of an open alliance with Israel was raised but dropped. There can be little doubt that, justified or not, Dulles's behaviour on 2 October was the main factor in making up the Cabinet's mind to act independently of the US, not for those already resolved, who seized on the remark as a new pretext, but for the 'weak sisters', as Eden later called them. Eden now regarded Dulles as almost as much a personal enemy as he did Nasser. He was not alone in the Cabinet in wishing to prove England could still act independently of the US. No doubt too some Ministers were impressed (as I believe Butler was) by the sheer audacity of the plan, which had the advantage of apparently presenting the Government with the need for an immediate decision – so avoiding the need to consult with the US or the Opposition. Monckton only appears to have spoken against the plan.[77] The Israeli attack was a means of soothing sceptical members of the Cabinet and of getting round US and possible Soviet hostility. The Cabinet seem never quite to have looked on the proposed entanglement as 'the political alliance' that the Israelis saw it (it was so described by General Dayan in 1966 in *Le Monde*), only as a means of avoiding further postponement of Musketeer.

It will perhaps always remain a matter of controversy, even among those present, as to in what terms the 'offer' was made to appear. Eden probably made it seem that 'the Jews' were going to attack anyway; which in a sense was true, sooner or later, though the Anglo-French operation would determine at the least the form of the Israeli attack. All members of the Cabinet were aware of the angry tension on the borders of

77. Monckton said: 'I was the only member of the Cabinet who openly advised against the invasion though it was plain Mr Butler had doubts and I know that Mr Heathcoat Amory was troubled' (Birkenhead, *Walter Monckton*, p. 308).

Israel and of the fact that this might at any time become more acute. The precise role which Israel hoped the R.A.F. would play in destroying the Egyptian Air Force was perhaps not made clear to Eden; and all the military arrangements were kept by the Prime Minister, according to a colleague, 'very close to his chest'.[78] It is also unclear whether Britain's schemes with Nuri to overthrow the Syrian regime (in which she was acting jointly with the US, though not with the French) played any part in these discussions: though it is likely that at long last the plot was timed, like the Anglo-French-Israeli attack on Egypt, for the end of the month. Thus there were, no doubt, as one Minister put it, 'layers of knowledge',[79] and room for feeling afterwards, as another did, that Eden 'might have been a bit more frank'.[80] Eden often spoke elliptically and possibly he may have subconsciously welcomed the idea of an Israeli attack as a means of avoiding responsibility for the first blow. He doubtless preferred to re-enter the Canal Zone in the guise of a peace-keeper rather than in that of an imperialist reasserting British power in that place. Ministers not specifically occupied with military or foreign affairs were perhaps quite anxious not to know too much. Some Ministers seem to have gone away thinking in terms of a hypothesis: 'if the Jews go in, we shall do so and so.' It was for some a matter of 'if', rather than 'when', the Jews would act.[81]

Eden's own memoirs indeed tell more of the story than has sometimes been supposed. Thus in the passage which refers to events of 25 October, Eden says that a report came that Israel was about to mobilize ... 'I thought then, and I think now, that the Israelis had justification for their action.... We could not stand aside and watch events.... The chief peril to us lay not in the conflict but in its extension by the intervention of other Arab states. The best way to halt that was by intervening ourselves.'[82]

78. Evidence of a senior Cabinet Minister.
79. Evidence of a junior Minister.
80. Evidence of a junior member of the Cabinet.
81. Evidence of a Cabinet Minister.
82. Eden, p. 523. On 5 December 1956 Head told the Commons that it

So Eden asked the Cabinet to follow on the decision of the committee of Ministers on the 18th. They discussed 'the specific possibilities of conflict between Israel and Egypt and decided in principle how [they] ... would react'. The British and French would send an ultimatum which, if rejected, would set off 'Musketeer', nominally 'to separate the combatants'.[83] The leading Ministers now entered upon a secret mood of resolution which one prominent adviser referred to as 'a trauma from which all knowledge of the outside world was excluded'.[84] Such papers as did exist appear to have been burned.

On the substance of the discussions about Israel it was apparently decided that minutes would not be kept, to avoid having to circulate anything to civil servants.[85] One version of minutes was apparently prepared in long-hand for the Queen, who was thus fully informed and according to one account was worried.[86] Thus no question of unconstitutional procedure arises. But if at this stage the British Cabinet had indeed rejected the schemes of the Prime Minister, the whole alliance against Nasser would, of course, have collapsed, with unforeseeable consequences. With French and Israeli military preparations already so far under way as to be virtually irreversible, and British commitments already made, the British Cabinet was placed by the Prime Minister in a most unenviable position.

So far as can be seen only three civil servants were informed fully – the Head of the Foreign Office (Sir Ivone Kirkpatrick); the Secretary of the Cabinet (Sir Norman Brook); and the Deputy Under Secretary of State in the Foreign Office, Patrick

was on 26 October that he received 'true knowledge' of the pending Israeli attack on Egypt (*Hansard*, vol. 561, col. 1240).

83. Eden, p. 523. This may have been an error in the Eden memoirs. On the 25th the Cabinet seems simply to have proposed to call on the two sides to withdraw ten miles from the Canal, and would only have intervened if one side refused. On the 30th the ultimatum provided for Anglo-French action whatever happened.

84. Evidence of a senior Adviser.

85. Evidence of a senior official.

86. Evidence of an Adviser. See instructions to the Secretary of the Cabinet, 4 November 1919, in which it is said that a 'single copy' of Cabinet minutes would be kept where the Cabinet demands it.

Dean, who was responsible for most of the work. The decision as to 'whom to tell' in the Foreign Office was left to Kirkpatrick, who decided to tell no one, not even the Ambassadors to Egypt, Israel and France.[87] He was himself dubious about the proposed action even if hostile to Nasser. In France the secrecy was even more complete, the secretary-general of the Quai d'Orsay, Louis Joxe, being completely in the dark.

Churchill, unfortunately, had just had a slight cerebral spasm and was anyway in the South of France,[88] otherwise perhaps he might have given good advice: later he several times said that he would never have gone into Suez without US support. (For instance he said to Lord Ismay: 'I should have exerted all my strength and persuasion to win the Americans round to our point of view but if I had failed in this, I would never have gone forward alone.'[89]) Indeed, if he had been Prime Minister it is inconceivable on the basis of his entire political life that he would have gone ahead without the US. Selwyn Lloyd apparently suggested telling the Americans but he was dissuaded by both Eden and Macmillan – the latter explaining that he, after all, had seen Eisenhower in September and so knew better what the US reaction would be.[90]

As has been seen, Eden in his memoirs says that on 25 October the Cabinet discussed in detail the ultimatum which was, with one small change, delivered on 30 October. His arguments in 1956 that Britain had no time to inform the US or the Commonwealth were thus misleading. But how should Australia or Canada be told when only a few civil servants knew what was planned, and as yet no Ambassadors? The reason why the US was not consulted was of course that to tell the US meant to tell Dulles, who, as Mollet stated baldly in the Assembly on 20 December 1956, would certainly have once

87. Evidence of a Cabinet Minister.

88. Moran, *Churchill, The Struggle for Survival*, p. 706. Eden must be wrong in his memoirs in saying (p. 534) that Churchill lunched with him on a 'Sunday in October', for he was in France from 17 September till 28 October.

89. cf. also Moran, p. 710.

90. Evidence of a friend of Lloyd to whom he spoke in late 1956; and of an Adviser.

more applied his delaying tactic. That familiar sanctimonious voice would once again have sounded on the transatlantic telephone, morally insistent, boring, confused, but, no doubt, as the Cabinet feared, successful. Mollet put the matter perfectly frankly: 'We were convinced that if we told the Americans of the date of our decision, new delays, new conferences would be imposed on us and Israel during this time would risk disappearing ... I told them frankly: because you would have prevented us from acting because we could not wait any longer for you as we did from 1914 to 1917 or from 1939 to 1942.'[91] But in fact it seems possible that the British Secret Service (if they knew about it) hinted to the CIA what the Governments were planning, on some level high or low,[92] or, more likely, the CIA broke the British as well as the French and Israeli diplomatic codes.[93] It is also likely that photo-reconnaissance by U2 aircraft would have given the USA a clear idea of allied movements.

Meantime on the 24th the US had explicitly heard from Aldrich, their Ambassador in London, that Monckton's resignation had been due to his belief that force would be a great blunder – another hint.[94] One journalist in Tel Aviv wrote to his London paper: 'This is a tense weekend, potentially the most explosive since 1948. Here is the pattern ... Franco-British military action against Nasser; simultaneously Iraqi troops are expected to move into Jordan to provide one more

91. Speech in the National Assembly, 20 December 1956.

92. It would seem highly likely that this was one consequence of the 'Special Relationship'; to anyone who knows anything of British and US intelligence it is inconceivable that the one could have kept anything of this sort from the other, and as has been seen the CIA had already helped their Allies by providing aerial reconnaissance of Egypt by U2. So perhaps the British Secret Service improperly passed the secret to the CIA, who improperly kept it from Eisenhower.

93. This is believed to have been done at the cypher centre at Griffis Air Base, Rome (New York). See however the question put by George Wigg to the Prime Minister in the House of Commons on 29 November 1956 (*Hansard*, vol. 561, col. 574). cf. the claims by Allen Dulles in *The Craft of Intelligence*, p. 166, and Foster Dulles in Berding, *Dulles on Diplomacy*, p. 110.

94. Eisenhower, p. 64.

and pretty big headache for [Nasser] ... the Sabbath peace is likely to be rudely disturbed.'[95] But the article was dismissed by his London editor as too fantastic to be printed.

In Paris Mendès-France apparently about this time called on Mollet and begged for a summit conference on Suez.[96] But his voice, along with that of Jean Monnet, the father of Europe, was almost alone in France in favour of restraint and even he did not speak publicly in criticism. Another protester was the Foreign Minister of Australia, Casey, who got wind of what was now planned. He bearded Lloyd and Templer (the CIGS); they were uncomfortable and he warned of the bad results. Menzies however heard of this and sent a message to the British that they should pay no attention to Casey.[97] Another who apparently knew that the Suez crisis was by no means over was Bulganin who wrote a new letter to Eden on 23 October.[98]

Meantime, the preliminary preparations for launching Operation Musketeer were pushed diffidently onwards. Among the Allies, everything remained, however, even amongst the commanders, on a curiously hypothetical basis; thus the air task force commander, Air Marshal Barnett, found himself telling his commander-in-chief, Keightley, that, in the light of information about what he thought would soon be expected of him, he was now *without orders* going ahead to establish his communications centre at Akrotiri, the RAF base in Cyprus.[99] General Stockwell with his chief-of-staff Brigadier Darling met General Beaufre at the Villacoublay military airport on the 26th and Stockwell now gathered beyond doubt that 'the Israelis were about to launch an attack on Egypt'. He flew on to Malta and apparently on his own, though on Beaufre's urging, decided with the commander-in-chief of the British Mediterranean fleet, Admiral Grantham, to use the previously arranged and quite genuine operational exercise, Operation Boathook, 'as a cover plan to sail the assault fleet as soon as

95. As quoted by Philip Noel-Baker in the House of Commons, 13 November 1956 (*Hansard*, vol. 560, col. 869).

96. Alexander Werth, *The Strange Case of Pierre Mendès-France*, p. 391; cf. André Fontaine, *Le Monde*, 1 November 1966.

97. Evidence of an Adviser after discussion with Casey.

98. It was not answered.　　　　99. Evidence of a British commander.

we got the order to go'.[1] General Keightley obliquely refers to these dispositions in his official dispatch when he explains that having heard from 'intelligence sources' in 'Tel Aviv and elsewhere' during the last week of October of rumours of Israeli mobilization, 'certain precautions were taken as regards the preparedness of our forces'.[2]

The naval task force commander in fact set up combined headquarters in his flagship off Cyprus on 27 October,[3] and on French insistence (Abel Thomas again crossed to London to see Head),[4] Britain agreed that the slowest ships could leave Malta at night on 28 October – 'on exercises' – rather than, as had been previously insisted upon, only after the Anglo-French ultimatum, which would have meant that general disembarkation in Egypt would not occur till 9 November. Some loading began at Malta on 27 October and, on the morning of 28 October, general orders were given for 'a large-scale loading exercise as for war'.[5] The Anglo-French aircraft carriers under Admiral Manley Power sailed at dawn on the 27th eastward from Malta.[6] But in Cyprus the airborne troops, who had gone up into the mountains to look for EOKA, were only told at the last minute.[7] Twenty squadrons of Canberra and Valiant bombers had left East Anglia for Cyprus by 29 October.[8] Eisenhower, still in the dark (it would seem that if the CIA and Allen Dulles knew of Anglo-French plans, they did not pass them on to Eisenhower), tried by telegram to restrain Ben Gurion[9] from what the President seems still to have believed would be an attack on Jordan. (Ben Gurion had a temperature of 103°.[10]) Eisenhower then ordered the evacua-

---

1. Stockwell, *Sunday Telegraph*, 30 October 1966; Beaufre, p. 127.
2. Despatch, p. 5320.   3. Evidence of a task force commander.
4. Robertson, p. 164.
5. A. J. Barker, *Suez: The Six Day War*, p. 87. (Officers received instructions to attend an urgent conference on Sunday morning during the evening of 27 October.)
6. Stockwell, *Sunday Telegraph*, 30 October 1966.
7. Evidence of a commander.   8. See Appendix 1.
9. Eisenhower, p. 70.
10. Dayan, p. 73; Henriques, *100 Hours to Suez*, p. 57. Ben Gurion had caught a cold at Sèvres.

tion of US civilians from most Middle East countries.[11] The increase in communications noticed between Paris and Tel Aviv suggested to the Americans that plainly France at least was conniving at whatever was afoot.[12] The British Ambassador, Nicholls, spoke to Ben Gurion on the 27th and after the expected warning not to attack Jordan, warned him that if Israel attacked Egypt, Israel must expect British action against her under the Tripartite Declaration; Ben Gurion said: 'I think you will find your Government knows more about this than you do.' The last sentence of this telegram was cut from the circulated copies.[13]

Planning was much more organized in Israel. On returning from Paris to Tel Aviv on 25 October, Dayan noted in his diary: '(1) The Prime Minister ... has given approval in principle to the campaign and its aims. (2) Our forces will go into action at dusk on [Monday] 29 October.... (3) The decision on the campaign and its planning are based on the assumption that British and French forces are about to take action against Egypt.... (4) ... the Anglo-French forces propose to launch their operations on 31 October.'[14] Dayan told his General Staff that as far as the Anglo-French were concerned: 'We should behave like the cyclist who is riding uphill when a truck chances by and he grabs hold.'[15] In the directives which Dayan issued on 25 October, he described the 'Intention' of his Operation Kadesh as: '(1) *To create a military threat* [my italics] to the Suez Canal by seizing objectives in its proximity. (2) To capture the Straits of Tiran. (3) To confound the organization of the Egyptian forces in Sinai and bring about their collapse.'[16] The *prime* aim of Kadesh therefore was now part of an international ruse; not to *capture* the Suez Canal or Sinai, but merely to *threaten* the former. The other two aims were Ben Gurion's old objectives for over a year.

On Sunday, 28 October, at 10 a.m. the Israeli Cabinet approved the plan to attack Egypt. The final formation of an

11. Eisenhower, p. 72.   12. Eisenhower, p. 70.
13. Evidence of a senior officer. Nicholls's Jordan warning was made much of later in the Commons; e.g. Selwyn Lloyd on the 31st.
14. Dayan, p. 60.   15. Dayan, p. 64.   16. Dayan, p. 210.

Arab united command on 23 October had persuaded any doubters – though the Israeli Cabinet seem to have been in the dark until quite recently. A familiar call to the Israelis announced: 'Behold, He that keepeth Israel shall neither slumber nor sleep.'[17]

That Sunday night, in London, at a private dinner at the US Embassy, the US Ambassador, Aldrich, on specific instructions from Eisenhower by telephone, asked Selwyn Lloyd whether he knew of Israel's plans. Lloyd gave a negative answer.[18] But that day a number of British officials had been told; when they asked about the US and the Commonwealth, the answer they received was: 'It's all very awkward.'[19] Some were alarmed, and General Keightley, waiting (as he had done so often in these months) outside the Cabinet Room, expressed doubts as to how far French security would hold – a persistent anxiety on the part of British officials in those days: they were more preoccupied by the need for secrecy than for efficiency.[20] It was a bizarre situation for Keightley, since his deputy, Admiral Barjot, had another command over French assistance to Israel, and General Brohon, as well as being deputy to Air Marshal Barnett, was responsible for French aerial assistance to Israel. Twenty-four hours later, about 4 p.m. on 29 October, Israel attacked.

17. Dayan, p. 71.
18. Aldrich gave an account of this dinner in 'The Suez Crisis', in *Foreign Affairs*, April 1967, p. 545.
19. Evidence of a senior official (told at 11 a.m.) and of a senior Adviser (told in the evening). It is possible that *The Times* was also told.
20. Evidence of an Adviser.

A CORRIDOR FOR CAMELS

In the assurance therefore that in going abroad we shall
increase our power at home, let us set out on this voyage.
It will have a depressing effect on the arrogance of the Pelo-
ponnesians when they see that we despise the quiet life they
are living now and have taken on the expedition to Sicily.
At the same time we shall either as is quite likely become
the rulers of all Hellas by using what we gain in Sicily, or,
in any case, we shall do harm to the Syracusans. ... Our
security is guaranteed by our navy, so that we can either
stay there, if things go well, or come back again. ... Do not
be put off by Nicias's arguments for non-intervention.

Alcibiades's speech to the Athenians
before the expedition to Syracuse
(Thucydides, Book VI)

ON the afternoon of 29 October, 395 Israeli paratroops dropped
from sixteen Dakota transports, at Mitla Pass, thirty miles
east of Suez[1]; twelve Mystères patrolled the Suez Canal.[2] The
main border posts on the southern section of the Israeli-
Egyptian border were also quickly captured.[3] Thirty-six French
Air Force Mystères of the 2ième Escadre and 36 F84 Thunderstreaks, normally at St Dizier and Dijon as part of the French
NATO component, flew to Israel.[4] From Cyprus, French
Nordatlas transport planes dropped food and arms that night to
the Israelis by parachute, particularly those at Mitla.[5] These
missions of succour were carried out by the French air commander, Brohon, without the knowledge or approval of the
British air task commander, Air Marshal Barnett, Brohon's
nominal chief.[6] The British aerial watch on Egyptian airfields

1. Dayan, p. 77.   2. Dayan, p. 78.   3. Dayan, p. 78.
4. See *Air Pictorial*, August 1965. Some of these aircraft flew between
22 and 25 October.
5. Beaufre, p. 130. cf. Jean Planchais, *Le Monde*, 6, 7 and 8 December
1956; *Air Pictorial*, August 1965.
6. Evidence of a British commander.

also however began that night. In his memoirs, Eden explains a part of this:

> Late on the evening of the 29th I had a talk with the Minister of Defence [Head] and the Chief of Air Staff [Boyle]. I told them how important it was for us to have information upon which we could depend for certain as early as possible the next day. A dawn reconnaissance was ordered by four Canberras.... They would locate and, if possible, photograph the opposing forces. The Canberras carried out their instructions....[7]

The information obtained presumably passed to Israel via France. Meantime, the 10th Hussars at Akaba in Jordan stood in the way of any possible stab in the back by Jordan on the southernmost Israeli offensive.[8] (The Jordanians had at the time a small detachment of the Arab Legion some fifty miles north, at Ma'an.)

Eden heard the news of the Israeli attack at a dinner for the Prime Minister of Norway. A little meeting of those Ministers who were also guests was held and Eden also had a discussion with Robens, present as the Labour Party's spokesman on foreign affairs: Robens assumed that Eden would bring the Tripartite Declaration into effect and consult the US the next day, while Eden made great play with the need for national unity.[9] The Prime Minister was however now abandoning his recent reaffirmations of the Tripartite Declaration and his earlier firm statement: 'I know very few international instruments if any which carry so strong a commitment as that one'.

Next morning the British Cabinet considered the news of the Israeli attack. To none of them of course was it a surprise. But perhaps some of the Cabinet had assumed or persuaded

7. Eden, p. 524. He adds that all four were intercepted and fired on, suggesting that it must have been Russians in the Egyptians' MiGs.

8. Of course a Jordanian thrust was unlikely but, if there had been a long war, it would be expected by Egypt that a Jordanian force would try and reach Eilat. The Secretary of State for War (Hare) said later that the Israeli offensive had meant no special orders for the Hussars save that as a 'precautionary measure certain routine reliefs were deferred'.

9. Evidence of Lord Robens. The first official news of the Israeli attack came at 8.30 p.m. after an emergency telegram from Tel Aviv was deciphered (*Hansard*, vol. 561, col. 26).

themselves that an Israeli offensive had always been something of a hypothesis. Home, for instance, seemed to pale at the news when informed by a member of the secretariat at No. 10.[10] On the morning of 29 October one Minister still had thought that it was 'even money' whether the Israelis would attack or not: 'It was so terribly risky.' He had very much hoped they would not. Ben Gurion had after all only definitely decided on an attack on the 24th and the Israeli Cabinet had only given their formal approval on the 28th.

Eden told the Cabinet that 'Israeli troops ... had reached a point half way between their frontier and Ismailia. A second Israeli force was reported to be striking towards Suez.'[11] The Cabinet now 'acted as decided': to send an ultimatum to both sides calling on them to withdraw. Except for the one Israeli parachute battalion at Mitla Pass, the Israeli forces were, however, engaged near their own frontier. As Dayan put it: 'We are not within ten miles of the Canal and we have neither interest nor plan to come closer to it.'[12] Nevertheless his first communiqué as part of the ruse agreed at Sèvres implied that Israel was threatening the Canal.[13]

Eden, as conscious of the Rhineland and of the importance of guaranteeing oil supplies as he had been in July, swept the Cabinet along in accord with decisions which had already really been taken. The Ministers could only agree or get rid of him.[14] One Minister complained of the short time in which they had to make up their minds. Eden airily recalled that some of his colleagues had not served in a War Cabinet. Macleod said: 'We didn't know we were at war.'[15] There was still no question of giving information to the Americans. Eden and Lloyd had been 'the ones to talk about the US'[16] and if they said it was all right no one else was going to take up the cudgels for Dulles. Some Ministers comforted themselves with the belief that Eden's early letters to Eisenhower rendered any

10. Evidence of an Adviser.   11. Eden, p. 524.
12. Dayan, p. 97.   13. Israeli sources.
14. Evidence of a junior Minister, and of a senior Cabinet Minister.
15. Randolph Churchill, pp. 277–8; the name was later established.
16. Evidence of a Minister.

charge of deception out of the question.[17] It is somewhat unclear whether the news of the discovery of the Syrian exiles' plot and the arrest of some ringleaders in Damascus played any part in the Cabinet's deliberations. But at all events this set-back did not in any way give Eden pause.

The only Cabinet Minister who later did not keep up the story of 'separating the combatants' was Head who allowed himself to say on 8 November: 'The whole point of this is that the Canal cannot and must not be solely the concern of the Egyptian Government. That is what all this has been about.'[18]

Aldrich was meantime once again asked by Eisenhower to ask Lloyd what was up, and called at the Foreign Office in the morning, to be told that Britain was consulting France and would probably cite Israel as an aggressor before the Security Council.[19] In fact, Mollet and Pineau came over to lunch and afterwards at 3.20 p.m. and 3.30 p.m. respectively Kirkpatrick and Pineau gave ultimatums to the Egyptian and Israeli Ambassadors: these called on the two Governments to 'withdraw' to ten miles each side of the Canal and to allow the British and French to establish themselves along the Canal. Otherwise they would intervene in such strength as was necessary. The occupation would be 'temporary', a word used by Gladstone in 1882 as a preliminary to Britain's seventy-year previous presence in Egypt. At about 4.5 p.m. Eden told Gaitskell,[20] and the House of Commons at 4.30. Afterwards the US Ambassador, Aldrich, was told too.[21] Israel, not unnaturally, accepted her ultimatum, since its terms enabled her to advance on all fronts. Egypt as naturally refused it.

At the UN Sir Pierson Dixon and the British delegation meantime showed themselves 'completely unsympathetic' to any idea of condemning Israel for aggression. Eisenhower (persuaded to cancel his campaign trip to Texas) telegraphed amicably but firmly to Eden, expressing astonishment, for the

17. Comment of Gwilym Lloyd George, the Home Secretary.

18. *Hansard*, vol. 560, col. 262.

19. Evidence of a Cabinet Minister; Aldrich, in *Foreign Affairs*, April 1967.

20. Evidence of an Adviser.

21. Aldrich, in *Foreign Affairs*, April 1967.

British and French were bound by the Tripartite Pact to take joint action, including force within or without the UN, if the 1950 borders of Israel and the Arab countries were crossed. Eden's telegram describing the ultimatum crossed it. In New York, Britain and France used their veto at the UN for the first time in rejecting a Security Council resolution calling for all countries to refrain from force in the Middle East.

Gaitskell had never believed that Eden would use force over Suez without consulting him. He was furious. He and his lieutenants all guessed that the 'separation of the combatants' was a charade. Nor was this disbelief much staunched by the assurance of Lloyd on 31 October that 'there was no prior agreement between us about it ... we urged restraint upon the Israeli Government'.[22] But Eden was backed by 270 votes to 218, Anthony Nutting absenting himself from the division on grounds of ill-health. Mollet received a majority of 368 to 182 (including 149 Communists) when he put the same policy to the National Assembly.

The mood among some of the Cabinet appears to have been one of relief: Macmillan, for instance, seemed cockahoop: 'It was the young Macmillan of the thirties again, hat thrown in the air,' recalled one Cabinet colleague.[23] The Chancellor was overheard by an adviser saying to his son-in-law, Amery: 'I think Anthony's going to have a rough ride for the next few weeks. In fact I shouldn't be surprised if he lost his seat.'[24] This remark revealed only the truth. 'All the Cabinet knew that the next ten days were going to be hell', one of them later recalled.[25] Macmillan, mercurial as well as masterful, knew better than Eden perhaps that they were embarking on a great gamble and the chances of it coming off were, as he said to a colleague on 30 October itself, only '51 to 49'.[26] He knew, too, that if Nasser were successfully overthrown the succeeding regime could not be the same as in the old days: 'We mustn't

22. *Hansard*, vol. 558, col. 1569.
23. Evidence of a senior Cabinet Minister.
24. Evidence of an Adviser.
25. Evidence of a Minister.
26. Evidence of a junior Minister.

put back Mrs Hauksbee and the colonel in the Gezira Club.'[27]

As for Eden, one who worked with him reports him 'almost boyish, reminiscent of a young officer of the First World War, very calm, very polite, the captain of the first eleven in a critical match', who indeed looked on the dangerous endeavour upon which he had now embarked as a 'brilliant game of great importance', where loyalty among colleagues counted most and where the struggle once begun had to be seen through to the end however bitter.[28] It is difficult not to believe that in some respects he deceived himself about his responsibility for events. Thus he came into the passageway at No. 10 with the words: 'I say, we've had an absolutely splendid reply from the Israelis. Now we must wait for Egypt.'[29] Meantime two leading BBC officials, Harman Grisewood and Sir Norman Bottomley, were told by an official in the Ministry of Defence that the Government expected the BBC to re-establish a war-time system of controls and censorship.[30] Later, Grisewood learned through William Clark, Eden's press chief, that the Prime Minister had instructed the Lord Chancellor to prepare an instrument enabling the Government to take over the BBC completely.[31]

There were, however, still doubts: and the law officers, who were not in the Cabinet, insisted on placing on record the fact that they had not been consulted,[32] though this was, perhaps, in the case of the Attorney General, Manningham Buller, a matter of the traditional quarrel of law officers with the Lord Chancellor.[33]

It appears that the British Cabinet, even though two thirds of them had some military experience, were not all fully aware of

27. Evidence of a junior Minister.

28. Evidence of an assistant to Eden.   29. Evidence of an Adviser.

30. Grisewood, *One Thing at a Time*, p. 197.

31. Grisewood, p. 199. Eden allegedly relied on his old friendship with Sir Alexander Cadogan, the Chairman, to get this through. Some doubt, however, has been thrown on the authenticity of Grisewood's story by an article by F. R. MacKenzie, 'Eden, Suez and the BBC: a re-assessment' (*Listener*, 18 December 1969).

32. Evidence of a critically placed Minister.

33. Evidence of a Cabinet Minister. The Solicitor General, Hylton-Foster, however, was hostile to the Suez operation as a whole and later penned a letter of resignation.

the military implications of their decision of 29 October. For the result of the rejection of the ultimatum was not, of course, the immediate occupation of the Canal Zone but the setting in motion of Operation Musketeer. General Keightley having himself been instructed at 4.30 a.m. to occupy Port Said, Ismailia and Suez in order to 'bring about a cessation of hostilities' between Israel and Egypt [34] gave the order for action on 31 October at 5 a.m. [35] It was impossible to change the plan at short notice, for it now comprised an immense number of interlocking instructions and time-tables which together made up a volume about the size of a telephone directory, the bulk of which concerned carefully arranged back-to-front loading plans so that the right equipment came out on the quay in the right order. [36] One Cabinet Minister at least thought there could be 'some way of hurrying things up'. But there was not. Many units were already loaded, including the 6th Battalion of the Royal Tank Regiment which had begun to load tanks on to ships at 1 p.m. on the 30th, [37] while the assault fleet actually set off from Malta on that day at 10 p.m., or some hours before Keightley's final instructions and order. [38] 130 warships, over 100 freighters and landing craft lumbered forward across the, to British commanders, familiar Mediterranean. Others sailed from Algiers and Southampton. Bands, mess-kit, elaborate menus and batmen as ever smoothed the passage of officers setting out for war. (Professing Jews were allowed to remain behind on the assumption that action might be against Israel.) But the Malta armada was not due off Port Said until 6 November.

Despite appeals by Nutting and others on behalf of the 13,000 British subjects in Egypt, [39] Eden had insisted on not telling the Ambassador, Trevelyan, what was afoot. Trevelyan

34. Despatch, p. 5329.   35. Evidence of a task force commander.
36. Evidence of a French commander.
37. Statement by Secretary of State for War, *Hansard*, vol. 562, col. *138*.
38. *Hansard*, vol. 562, col. *82*.
39. Evidence of a critically placed Minister. Commander Noble (Nutting's successor, ironically, as Minister of State) later told the House of Commons that there were 13,000 British subjects, mostly Maltese or Cypriot, about 2,500 British by birth (*Hansard*, vol. 561, col. *30*).

heard of the ultimatum when somebody ran in to say that the news was 'coming through on the tape'.[40] Nasser, however, having received the ultimatum and given his reply via Trevelyan, thought that Eden was bluffing once again and sent his armoured brigade and other reinforcements against Israel in Sinai.[41]

Britain was expected to start bombing the Egyptian airfields when the ultimatum ran out, at 4.30 a.m. on 31 October, or thirty-six hours after the Israelis attacked Egypt.[42] There was an inexplicable delay. Ben Gurion, furious, desired to pull back his paratroops at the advanced post at Mitla, deeply worried lest his men were going to be cut off. He was dissuaded by Dayan. For these troops were the only Israelis who could then under any circumstances be said to be threatening the Canal and therefore to justify the great ruse upon which Israel's friends were embarking. And, despite the British delay, Israel had already established local command of the air in Sinai. Dayan later commented: 'even if the Anglo-French invasion were cancelled, I was confident that we would be able to proceed with our campaign.'[43] By dusk on 31 October the exposed paratroops at Mitla, who had been fighting hard all day,[44] had been joined by an armoured column which had raced across the desert. The Israeli Government's morale was high, since French fighters had established their defence umbrella over Israeli cities and French destroyers were providing the planned *ceinture maritime* on the coast (the *Kersaint, Bouvet*, and *Surcouf*, under Captain Guérin, not under the orders of 'Musketeer'). The frigate *Kersaint* of this squadron, under

40. Evidence of Sir Humphrey Trevelyan.

41. Nasser on BBC Television, 20 September 1966; *Sunday Times*, 24 June 1962.

42. *Air Pictorial*, August 1965; Dayan, p. 99, says 'This action started not twelve hours after the issue of the ultimatum – the time of the expiry – but twenty-five'.

43. Dayan, p. 96.

44. Dayan tells us the battle lasted from 13.00 till 20.00 (Israeli time), with 38 Israeli killed, 120 wounded; 150 Egyptian dead. The Israeli paratroops (202nd Paratroop Brigade) tried to capture Mitla Pass (and did) against orders. Their goal was not to get any nearer to Suez (Dayan, pp. 100–102).

Captain Roy, fired the first shot in the Allies' war on the Egyptian destroyer *Ibrahim el Awal*. Chafing at the delay, they fired an hour before the ultimatum had expired. Vice-Admiral Barjot telegraphed Paris: 'Have crippled Egyptian destroyer. But not entirely sure Egyptian. If this should prove a mistake it is not a deliberate attack ... on the [US] 6th Fleet.'[45]

The postponement of the first wave of bombing occurred because the air planners had arranged for the destruction of the airfields at night, not by day.[46] A later delay was caused because news was received in London that fifteen US transport planes were waiting to take off US civilians from the Cairo West airfield upon which the RAF were about to drop their bombs. A group of buses carrying US civilians was also on the Alexandria road which skirted this airfield. Eden told Head to delay the raid at all costs. Head got through to Keightley in Cyprus on the telex. Keightley said the bombers had already set off. Was he still in touch? Yes, Keightley thought he was. He was right. The bombers were recalled.[47] This could have been militarily fatal, for Cairo West was the main Ilyushin base in Egypt and so became for twelve hours a privileged sanctuary.[48] The Ilyushins could have been sent off to Cyprus or Israel with impunity. They were not, since the Egyptian pilots were mostly not yet trained for such action and because the Russian trainers and technicians had received orders from Moscow not to do so. In addition the original plan was that the first bomb should be dropped on Cairo Radio. Here too the Cabinet at the last minute hesitated since they wrongly supposed that Cairo Radio was in the capital of Egypt itself. In fact it was well out in the desert near Bilbeis, a fact that Fergusson pointed out forty-eight hours later.[49]

In the end the allied air offensive began at dusk on 31 Octo-

---

45. Tournoux, p. 159.   46. *Air Pictorial*, August 1965.

47. All this paragraph is evidence of a Minister; cf. Despatch, p. 5330, and Bernard Fergusson, *The Watery Maze* (history of combined operations), p. 395.

48. Azeau, p. 271.

49. Evidence of a general.

ber.[50] 200 Canberras, Venoms and Valiants, along with forty French Thunderstreaks, operating from aircraft carriers, from Malta and from Cyprus, swept from a 'discreet height of over 40,000 feet' over four Delta and eight Canal airfields for the next forty-eight hours.[51] Warning by radio and leaflets was previously given to Egyptians to keep away from the airfields. The size of the bombs was also limited to 500 lbs and 1,000 lbs[52] for humanitarian reasons, the bombing was extremely accurate, and the Egyptian casualties seem to have been few.[53] The plan was first to pock-mark the airfields with craters at night and then to destroy the aeroplanes by carrier-based aircraft at first light.[54]

There was also a minor engagement in the Gulf of Suez, where H M S *Newfoundland* sank an Egyptian frigate.

The bombing showed Nasser for the first time that Eden was not bluffing.[55] It forced Egypt into a major change of policy. On 31 October Israel had been held up quite well at Mitla and in the centre at Abu Aweiglia, where the Israelis used guided missiles for the first time in history in action (French Nord SS 10 anti-tank missiles).[56] Gaza had not yet been attacked. But if the British and French were about to arrive, maybe at Port Said, maybe (as Nasser still expected) at Alexandria, it was evidently foolish to keep half the Egyptian Army in Sinai. On the night of 31 October Egypt ordered a general withdrawal, to the Egyptian generals' annoyance. Nasser is believed to have had to offer his resignation to get his way.[57] Egyptian defences

50. 19.00 hours (Israeli time) (Dayan, p. 99).

51. *Air Pictorial*, August 1965. Evidence of a British commander.

52. *Air Pictorial*, August 1965.

53. Israeli sources say this limitation was a breach of the Sèvres understanding.

54. Evidence of a British commander.

55. Nasser said (on BBC TV, 20 September 1966) that until bombing began he had not believed Britain would actually attack. See also his account in *Sunday Times*, 24 June 1962.

56. *New York Herald Tribune*, 14 May 1957, *Air Pictorial*, August 1965; Dayan speaks of the 'great courage' of some of Abu Aweiglia's defenders (p. 105).

57. Azeau, p. 275; confirmed by Peter Mansfield, *Sunday Times* correspondent in the Middle East, after conversation with Nasser.

were then concentrated round Cairo, while in the Canal Zone workers were given a month's salary and told to prepare for guerrilla war.[58] All further air operations were cancelled, and such MiGs and Ilyushins as had escaped the first bombing were ordered to make their get-away to bases up the Nile, and even to other Arab States.[59] Egyptian pilots anyway seem to have preferred old Vampires and Meteors to MiGs. Orders were given to block the Canal by sinking ships in it filled with concrete; forty-seven were sunk within the next forty-eight hours.[60] Engineers of the Syrian Army, deprived on Egyptian orders of the dangerous pleasures of an attack on Israel, also blew up the three pumping stations on the Iraq pipe-line.[61] The Anglo-French ultimatum thus brought about what the two Governments sought to avoid – an interruption of the flow of oil.

The bombing was accompanied by the long-prepared aero-psychological attack. A million bloodthirsty leaflets were dropped, radio broadcasts from Cyprus told the Egyptian armed forces that they would be bombed wherever they were and assured the public that they had sinned by placing their faith in Nasser.[62] When Cairo Radio was finally put out of action (though only temporarily since only one transmitting mast was knocked down) on 1 November, 'the Voice of Britain' from Limassol became the only powerful station broadcasting in the Middle East. These activities were directed by Brigadier Bernard Fergusson, who had turned the until then successful commercial radio, Shark al Adna (previously financed by advertisements), into an organ of war. He was assisted by Ralph Murray, ex-Minister at the British Embassy in Cairo. (This station, requisitioned at 3 p.m. on 30 October, had been

58. Azeau, p. 273.

59. *Sunday Times*, 24 June 1962. Nasser confirmed this several times, e.g. on BBC TV, 20 September 1966.

60. R. A. Butler in the House of Commons, November 1956 (*Hansard*, vol. 560, col. 1942). Ultimately there seem to have been over fifty ships sunk.

61. The Syrian Cabinet could not at first believe that the Egyptians did not want them to attack (Seale, p. 262).

62. cf. pamphlet printed in *Hansard*, vol. 560, col. 945.

founded with government help in 1941 in Jerusalem and moved to Cyprus after the end of the Mandate. It had been for a long time a vehicle for clandestine British propaganda to the Arabs and had always been both anti-French and anti-Israeli.)

This aspect of the offensive appears to have been mistaken.[63] Propaganda that might be effective among tribesmen of the Persian Gulf did not work in a sophisticated city such as Cairo with middle-class leaders. Fergusson himself had no qualifications for the task, but merely chanced to be available (since he was commanding a Territorial Brigade which had just finished camp). This did not matter so much since Fergusson was gifted and intelligent. But he had only a small staff and he had difficulty in collecting it. The time he had for preparation was very short. None of his British staff had previous experience of the work, though some French officers had, in Algeria. Fluent Arabic speakers were difficult to find. The BBC had promised them in theory but withdrew the offer after 30 October. Fergusson had been promised an aircraft fitted with loud-hailer equipment for broadcasting from the air but this was then in Kenya being used against the Mau Mau. Owing to the need for secrecy, the RAF were not told for what the aeroplane was needed and the voice equipment was taken out at Nairobi. Finally the staff at Shark al Adna not only refused duty to Fergusson but broadcast to Egypt that they were on their side.[64]

Doubtless the broadcasting saved many Egyptian civilian lives since warnings were daily made to keep away from targets.[65] Nasser, with a semi-Churchillian speech and a well-publicized visit to a mosque, seemed to gain prestige under the attack.[66]

This prestige was sustained even when, after the withdrawal from Sinai, on the night of 31 October–1 November, the Israelis had things much their own way, capturing thousands of prisoners, taking Gaza by assault and pursuing the retreat-

63. The Commander-in-Chief, Keightley, later admitted that the aero-psychological warfare had been a mistake.
64. Private information and Nigel Birch in *Hansard*, vol. 562, col. 40.
65. Private information.   66. Azeau, p. 278.

ing Egyptians with venom and panache. The naval bombard-ment of Rafah on the Israeli's behalf by the French cruiser *Georges Leygues* (a part of Keightley's command), admittedly was not a great success.[67] But French fighters based in Israel attacked Nasser's armoured infantry after passing through Ismailia and French Thunderstreaks (based in Cyprus but actually operating, because of the distance, from Israel) de-stroyed twenty Egyptian bombers which had fled south to Luxor.[68] The air task commander did not know of this opera-tion until it was 'too late to do anything'.[69] Meantime the Malta armada of 100 ships was still 500 miles away and the airborne troops were waiting impatiently in Cyprus. The long delay before actual disembarkation caused the British and French to seem absurd as well as comical. 'I wouldn't go to sea for five days with a bad stomach,' was Churchill's comment later to Butler, referring to Eden's health.[70]

The British Government had hitherto survived all challenges at home, thanks partly to the almost total confusion as to what was actually happening – the rumour was so strong on the 30th that airborne troops were about to land that *The Times* and other newspapers the next day published quite false lead stories that paratroops were 'taking up key positions' on the Canal there and then; partly to the state of shock which made most people accept that Britain had in fact no prior agreement with Israel; and partly to the feeling of loyalty to the commanding

67. Escorted by two Israeli frigates, the cruiser delivered only 150 rounds of 155 mm fire. It was overflown by two swept-wing US aircraft (Tournoux, p. 161, who wrongly says 350 rounds were fired) and lasted half an hour from 2 a.m. to 2.30 a.m. on 1 November. Dayan speaks of the naval bombardment as a 'complete flop' though he does not explicitly identify the French as responsible. Nevertheless he makes it evident to any informed reader : 'We all expected that the pounding from the destroyers would be carried out on a European scale' (op. cit., pp. 132–3). Keightley apparently knew of this attack but did not wish to be informed officially (Bar-Zohar, p. 196).

68. *Air Pictorial*, September 1965 ; Bar-Zohar, p. 190, after an interview with a French superior officer. Evidence of a British commander.

69. Evidence of a British commander. Keightley's Despatch (p. 5330) mentions the bombing but not the base of the bombers.

70. Evidence of a senior Cabinet Minister.

officer, whatever he may do, which affects the Conservative Party and indeed much of the nation in times of trouble. The country had over the summer been conditioned to expect violence, while the boldness of the deceptions by the Government spokesmen swept most people along. Further, much of the country thought Nasser wrong and disliked Egyptians while many were quite pleased to see the Government flex its muscles, providing it was a success. From an analysis of the polls, however, it does not seem as if the Government ever had a clear majority for the use of force. On 1 and 2 November, to the question 'Do you think we were right or wrong to take military action in Egypt?', thirty-seven per cent of those questioned thought they were right, forty-four per cent wrong, and nineteen per cent did not know; about the same number pronounced themselves on that day dissatisfied with Eden's handling of the Middle East situation since Israel attacked Egypt. But on 10–11 November, a substantial majority of the population (fifty-three to thirty-two, with fifteen per cent not knowing) said that they were satisfied with Eden's conduct of Middle East affairs. This discrepancy might very well mean that as many were dissatisfied with the slowness of the arrival of the troops on 1–2 November as were satisfied with the cease-fire. So as usual polls are unsatisfactory guides.[71]

Criticism came mainly from the middle class, from Conservatives as well as old Labour supporters. The City and commercial circles were as sceptical as they had been in July, and indeed had there been a by-election in the City at the time it might very well have gone against the Government. There was hostility from nearly all the press, including the *Telegraph* and *Daily Mail*: the *Express* and *Sketch* were Eden's only real newspaper friends. *The Times* had crossed over. However on 30 October the *News Chronicle*, all unknowing, had said that after the Israeli attack 'the rapid deployment of British power in the Canal Zone might give us the opportunity of holding the conflicting forces apart'.

But abroad there were difficulties. Some could be held off by traditional arrogance: 'The U K is not accustomed to receiving

71. cf. Epstein, pp. 141–7.

advice from small Balkan countries,' Kirkpatrick told the Yugoslav Ambassador.[72] But despite the coming election Eisenhower was by no means 'lying doggo' as Macmillan had predicted. By not consulting him when Israel attacked, the President believed that his Allies had broken the Tripartite Declaration and therefore with him.[73] (The British explanation was that Egypt had dissociated herself from the Tripartite Declaration; but Egypt was not a party. France did not worry about this.[74]) Marshal of the Royal Air Force Sir John Slessor, an old friend of Eisenhower's, was the first Englishman to go to the White House after the ultimatum. The President seemed dazed; he said that the previous day had been the worst in his life. Eisenhower was not unnaturally furious to be double-crossed a week before the election, especially when he had agreed in 1955 to announce the date of the Summit Conference in time to assist Eden in his election.[75] Dulles was immediately convinced, on circumstantial evidence, that the Allies were acting in agreement with Israel (and told Washington correspondents so [76]), while Eisenhower's memoirs show that on 2 November the US heard from their Ambassador in Paris that Pineau had told him the 'whole history of French collusion', confirming British involvement.[77] Already on 30 October the US had introduced a resolution to the Security Council calling on all countries to refrain from force in the Middle East, thus getting in before the Russians. Britain and France vetoed it. Eisenhower's consequent language to Eden on the telephone

72. An account of this conversation was given at the time by a member of the Yugoslav Embassy to Paul Johnson, assistant editor of the *New Statesman*.

73. See Eisenhower, pp. 76–7.

74. Reply of D. Dodds-Parker (Joint Under-Secretary of State for Foreign Affairs) in November, *Hansard*, vol. 560, col. *105*. See too Eden in the House of Commons, 30 October.

75. Comment of a senior Adviser.

76. Dulles gave a long list of reasons for suspecting 'collusion', though he asked correspondents not to mention the absence of a British Ambassador in Washington as one; nor did he mention the warning sent by Dillon about France's war preparations on 19 October (evidence of Keith Kyle who was correspondent in Washington and the only non-US journalist present).   77. Eisenhower, p. 84.

was in barrack-room style.[78] Henceforth communications between the British and US Governments were almost nil; both
Butler and Lord Harcourt, the British Economic Minister in
Washington, remained privately in contact with the US Secretary of the Treasury (Harcourt saw Secretary Humphrey every
day, entering the Treasury by a back door), but the Foreign
Office ceased to send telegrams to Washington.[79] No one in
London seems yet seriously to have feared a run on the
pound.

The President called off his election campaign.[80] After two
days of manoeuvring at the UN, Dulles, determined to fore-
stall the Russians and as determined to prove to Eden that he
could not act independently of the US as Eden was determined
to prove that he could, introduced a resolution calling for a
Middle East cease-fire: Britain and France had knocked away
one of the two main legs of US diplomacy – the Alliance; the
US Administration at election time felt it had to lean specially
hard on the other one – the UN.[81] The cease-fire resolution was
approved by 64–5, Britain and France abstaining. Immediately
afterwards, Pearson, the Commonwealth leader most incensed
by British action (and informed by his able High Commissioner
in London, Norman Robertson), put forward a plan for a UN
peace force to occupy the Canal Zone in place of Britain and
France. This too was approved. Dulles was now anxious to
give Eden a political way-out. Pearson and Hammarskjöld
began to work on the arrangements for such a plan, while in
the early hours of 3 November Dulles, exhausted, went off to
hospital for an emergency operation for cancer.[82]

Meantime attacks on the main airfields of Egypt had continued at lower altitudes and therefore with more success than
on 31 October–1 November. The amount of air activity was
very great; aircraft were taking off and landing at Cyprus at the

78. The telephone was picked up at No. 10 by William Clark (see
Drummond and Coblentz, *Duel at the Brink*).

79. Evidence of a diplomat and of a senior Cabinet Minister.

80. Sherman Adams, p. 206.

81. Comment of a senior Adviser.

82. Lloyd had earlier suggested the idea to Eden who had spoken of it
in the House.

rate of one per minute and one every two or three minutes on the carriers.[83]

Faced with the menace of UN action, Pineau hurried over with General Challe to London at dusk on 1 November to press for some adjustment of the slow timetable of Operation Musketeer, as indeed had been persistently urged by the impatient French commanders on Cyprus. (Barjot and Beaufre had on the 31st urged strongly the adoption of their plan, 'Omelette', which would land airborne troops all the way down the Canal; on 2 November Barjot told Beaufre that Mollet and Bourgès thought airborne troops should and could be landed within two hours. Stockwell had refused to agree to this idea on the ground that the Allies were not yet in the position of 'no opposition' or 'all opposition can be ignored'.) Pineau now proposed that the paratroops should be dispatched there and then to the Canal, while the problem of their support for the three days before the expected arrival of the assault fleet would be solved by relying on Israel.[84] Ben Gurion, Dayan tells us in his memoirs, agreed to this, but Mollet would not go ahead without Britain.[85] Generals Ely and Challe attended a long meeting with their British colleagues on 2 November. But Mountbatten, who had always been hostile to the idea of an attack on Egypt, showed himself 'very reticent' on the possibility of hurrying the movement of the main expedition, while Templer was also unenthusiastic. In the end, the British Chiefs of Staff committee approved Ely's suggestion that the field commanders off Cyprus should be given greater licence to do what they thought best, but, given the dominance of the British commanders, this meant less than it seemed.[86] According to one account, Mountbatten became angry and spoke to the Queen, who apparently then presented Eden with the suggestion that, before he committed the nation to this extension of the battle, he should consult Gaitskell.[87] Eden did not desire to do this and the idea was scotched. Mollet would not agree without the

83. *Air Pictorial*, September 1965.
84. Azeau, p. 292; *The Times*, 5 November 1956.
85. Dayan, pp. 160–61.   86. Ely, pp. 164–5.
87. Bar-Zohar, pp. 204–5, on the testimony of Pineau.

British and (in Dayan's words) 'the British were not prepared under any circumstances to give up their "100 ship" plan ... and certainly not to maintain any military contact ... with Israel'. In the field, Keightley kept anxiously trying to keep to the rules of the ruse; the RAF even prevented the Israelis on 3 November with machine-gun fire from helping an English pilot who had baled out from a flaming aeroplane.[88] Ben Gurion kept to the ruse too; no Israelis were to be closer than ten miles to the Suez Canal, to avoid any possible excuse for the British to prove their impartiality by shooting at Israelis.[89] After further discussion however with Pineau and Challe, Eden dispatched the Minister of Defence, Antony Head, to Cyprus. He arrived just before dawn on 4 November to find that the British and French commanders had been arguing almost the entire previous day about possible changes. At one point, indeed, the French Chief of Staff, General Ely, had asked the French commanders in Cyprus to work out a plan for acting without Britain.[90]

Operation Musketeer was now at long last modified, at a conference between Head, the Commander-in-Chief and the task force commanders.[91] The airborne troops would drop the next morning, twenty-four hours before the arrival of the ships. (This scheme, long urged in one form or another by the French, was known as Operation Telescope.) To reduce Egyptian civilian casualties, the naval bombardment planned for the 6th would be cut to the minimum needed for safe landing. Any idea of 'turning right at Ismailia' for Cairo was dropped.[92] The plan was merely to capture the Canal Zone as quickly as possible. Keightley told Head that this would take forty-eight hours. And how long before the Canal would be reopened by the Naval clearing teams, who were following in the wake of the battleships? Fifteen days to two months. This

88. Dayan, p. 162.
89. See Jon Kimche in the BBC's 'Some Evidence of Collusion', Third Programme, 18 July 1966 (transcript, p. 12). 90 Azeau, p. 290.
91. See Head's speech in the House of Commons, December 1958 (*Hansard*, vol. 561, col. 1235). I am also grateful for the help here of a task force commander and of a French commander.
92. Beaufre, p. 143.

readjustment of the timetable was taken against the advice of the Naval task force commander, who knew that the good weather, in which the fleets were now making excellent progress, might not hold, and that there was a strong chance that he might not be able to land the main body of troops on 6 November. He would not be able to give close support to the paratroops by destroyers on 5 November, because the minesweepers were with the main fleet and were among the slower vessels.[93]

No sooner had these decisions been taken and Head was on his way back to London than another and more bizarre threat loomed up for the Anglo-French expedition. Thanks partly to the withdrawal of the Egyptians wherever possible and partly to their own resolution, speed and military prowess, Israel had, by 5 November, captured all her objectives. Gaza had fallen and, with the surrender at 9.30 a.m. on 5 November of Sharm-el-Sheikh and of the islands at the foot of the Gulf of Akaba, that waterway was free at last for Israeli shipping.[94] These victories had been accomplished for the loss of under 200 killed, against about 2,000 Egyptian deaths, mostly in the retreat (some at the hands of the Bedouin tribesmen). Israel now was willing, even anxious, to accept the UN cease-fire, providing that Egypt did so too.[95] Dayan recalls that at this Britain and France 'almost jumped out of their skins . . . Britain, therefore, asked France to use the full weight of her influence to persuade us to retract our announcement'.[96] Ben Gurion, though displeased at having to defy the UN for any more time, agreed and thought up some conditions to his acceptance of the cease-fire. But it was clear that the combatants whom Britain and France had nominally intervened to separate had now really ceased fighting and that Israel could not be counted on to keep up the scenario of strife much longer. Mrs Meir, the Israeli Foreign Minister, became one more bugbear for those in the British Government resolved to press ahead with operations.[97]

93. Evidence of a task force commander.
94. Dayan, pp. 187–200.　　95. Dayan, p. 181.
96. Dayan, p. 181.　　97. Evidence of a Minister.

Eden had already announced that if Egypt and Israel accepted a UN peace force he would not oppose a cease-fire, provided that Anglo-French forces remained along the Canal until they could hand over to the UN. Eden even bizarrely proposed that the British and French might constitute themselves the UN force. The likelihood of a UN force being got ready in a matter of days seemed remote, though the British from the start offered logistic support and though Hammarskjöld, aided by Pearson, worked hard. Despite her own compromising position in Hungary, Russia was calling for volunteers for Egypt. So was China. Eden was also being badgered by the Canadians to refrain from *all* military action until the UN had arranged Pearson's scheme for a peace force.

In Britain opposition to Operation Musketeer was growing that week-end. On 4 November, the resignation of Nutting was announced.[98] (Clark, the press officer at No. 10, was requested to give out that Nutting was going to resign anyway for private reasons – a piece of cynicism by the Whip's Office that constituted one more reason why Clark himself, who disliked tampering with truth, also resigned.[99]) A group of about fifteen Conservative MPs was organizing a protest under the leadership of Sir Alec Spearman ('the sheet anchor'[1] of those Conservatives opposed to Suez), Walter Elliot and the ex-Attorney-General, Heald. Eleven of these protesters signed a letter critically asking about the purpose of the policy of the Government, and Spearman was authorized by the signatories to deliver it to Eden on the 6th unless by then a cease-fire had been announced. (This letter had eleven signatures: Walter Elliot, Spearman, Boothby, Douglas Nairn, Sir Lionel Heald, Sir Keith Joseph, Peter Kirk, Nigel Nicolson, John Foster, Philip Bell and one who does not wish to be named. An earlier letter in more

98. *The Times*, 5 November 1956. *No End of a Lesson* (pp. 122–3) makes clear that Nutting in fact resigned on 31 October.

99. Evidence of an Adviser. In an interview to the *Sunday Telegraph*, 24 March 1968, Clark explained that another reason why he resigned was that he 'thought the Government were trying to use confidential relations with the press and the BBC to put forward a different version from what was actually happening'.

1. The phrase is that of a junior Minister.

explicit terms, demanding that the Government offer to place their troops under the immediate orders of the UN, had also been signed with the addition of J. J. Astor and without Foster, Elliott and Kirk, who were unwilling or unable to commit themselves so far.) Spearman showed the letter to the Chief Whip, Heath, on the 5th. Heath, who had never shown himself enthusiastic for the Government's policy, expressed concern, noted down the names and gave an understanding that Eden would immediately be informed.[2] Conservative opposition was also held up by a reluctance to come into the open while British troops were about to enter action.[3] The Solicitor-General, Hylton-Foster, meantime penned a letter of resignation though he did not send it.[4] In the Foreign Office a group of undersecretaries, the architects of the 'special relationship' over ten years, signed a round-robin criticizing the operations,[5] and the Foreign Office legal adviser, Fitzmaurice, circulated a memorandum criticizing the legal basis of the proposed action.[6] A few junior members of the Foreign Service resigned. The operation also raised the question of the Government's relations to the news media in an acute form. Thus the Government believed that Eden's broadcast of November was a ministerial broadcast of national importance to which the opposition had no right to reply. Gaitskell naturally dissented and the BBC gave him the verdict.[7] Thereafter a 'Foreign Office adviser' was dispatched

2. Evidence of a Conservative MP. The letter was never sent because the cease-fire did come on the 6th. Boyle was in touch with this group though Nutting was not.

3. See the comment of Nigel Nicolson, one of the protesters, in *People and Parliament*, p. 145.

4. Evidence of a junior Minister.

5. Evidence of a Foreign Office official. Hayter, Ambassador in Moscow, contemplated resignation when he heard of the ultimatum (see *The Kremlin and the Embassy*, p. 143).

6. Evidence of a Foreign Office official.

7. See the article by Stuart Hood reviewing Harman Grisewood's *One Thing at a Time* (*Listener*, 28 March 1968), and Grisewood, p. 202. Many would have disagreed that the BBC was hostile to the operation; see speech by Colonel Wigg in *Hansard*, vol. 560, col. 1055; and compare evidence presented by a future Solicitor-General, Peter Rawlinson, on 14 November (*Hansard*, vol. 560, col. 1023–31).

to attempt to keep news bulletins at least 'informed about' Government policy.[8] Eden continued to hanker for a take-over of the BBC by the Government, while the BBC determined to keep up their impartiality and broadcast adverse comment which might be heard by troops embarking on action.[9]

The Labour Party had violently attacked the Government throughout the week in the Commons, which was suspended (for the first time since 1924)[10] for half an hour on 1 November after disorder when it became clear that the now ashen-faced Prime Minister was unable to say whether the nation was at war or not, and if so whether the Geneva Convention applied.[11] The Ministers trooped into the Prime Minister's Room, and asked the Foreign Office legal adviser, Fitzmaurice, what the legal position was. He replied: 'We are in a state for which there is no legal precedent and into which I hope my country will never again be plunged.'[12]

It was on this occasion that Lady Eden and Mrs Gaitskell happened to sit next to each other in the gallery of the Commons. 'Can you stand it?' muttered Lady Eden. 'The boys must express themselves,' replied Mrs Gaitskell with grim humour. She was a more experienced politician and the veteran of many hustings. In contrast to their position in August, the Labour Party in Parliament was now united; even the seventeen Labour Jewish members stood by Gaitskell. Only one Labour MP, Stanley Evans (a self-made Birmingham business-man), voted against his party in sympathy with the Government. From his abstention in the vote on 30 October as well as sub-sequent statements in Singapore and Australia it is also clear that Emanuel Shinwell heartily backed Israel, though never really Eden. Another Jewish Labour MP, Harold Lever, was in much the same position.[13]

The Labour Party launched a campaign on the theme of 'Law not War', culminating in a large meeting in Trafalgar

8. cf. statement by Dodds-Parker in Commons, *Hansard*, vol. 562, col. *13*.

9. Grisewood, pp. 200–201.   10. Erskine May.

11. *Hansard*, vol. 558, col. 1625.   12. Evidence of an Adviser.

13. Epstein comments at length on the Jewish position (pp. 173–98).

Square on Sunday 4 November, followed by processions in the November gloom all over London calling for Eden's resignation ('Stop Eden's War'). Bevan made a brilliant and entertaining philippic, subtly showing however that he was well aware there was working-class support for Eden. The Cabinet, meeting in Downing Street, with Pineau and this time Bourgès-Maunoury present, were made aware by the noise of the crowds of the great division in the country over their policy. Bourgès-Maunoury is believed to have asked Eden: *'Mais où sont nos mitrailleuses?'* Small groups of professional men, lawyers and civil servants, met in London houses, wondering if they could do anything to end the conflict; doubtless if the war had lasted such groups would have become more formidable.

These pressures led Eden to waver and, worse, to begin to interfere in the detailed running of the planned operation. He told Keightley only on 4 November that the Allies could not count on the arrival of the 10th Armoured Division from Libya.[14] He asked Admiral Durnford-Slater, the Naval task force commander, if he could arrange the landing on the east side of the Canal: an impossibility at that stage with an immensely detailed plan.[15] He asked the commander-in-chief at 8.15 p.m. (10.15 Cyprus time) what was the latest time that a delay of twenty-four hours could be decided upon for the airborne landing [16] – an inquiry that reached the airborne brigade when actually on the tarmac with their parachutes on.[17] Keightley said 11 p.m. at the latest, and added that such a delay would have most serious consequences.[18] 'French command horrified,' he went on.[19] Though there was in fact no delay, the commanders cursed the speed of communications which made possible this kind of interference.[20] They cursed, too, Gaitskell's

14. Despatch, p. 5331.   15. Evidence of a task force commander.
16. See Keightley's Despatch.
17. Evidence of a commander.
18. Despatch, p. 5332.
19. Tournoux, p. 164. General Challe tells us that Eden had told him at three o'clock in the morning of 3 November, 'Eh bien, mon général, nous y sommes tout de même arrivés.' Challe replied with Laetitia Bonaparte's famous comment to her son: 'Pourvu que ça dure' (Challe, p. 31).
20. Evidence of a task force commander and a commander.

broadcast on the BBC which called on the Prime Minister to resign and which tried to persuade Conservative doubters to come over to him – an appeal which embarrassed these Conservatives as much as the general tenor of his broadcast angered men about to land on Egypt in the next day or two. Such are the inconveniences of entering on war during nominal conditions of peace and without national unity.

The inconveniences for Britain of acting without her most powerful ally were also becoming evident: the US 6th Fleet, helping to evacuate US civilians from Alexandria, was standing in the middle of the British carrier zone. The British task force commander, Admiral Durnford-Slater, asked the US admiral to move. He refused, though telegraphed back to Washington: 'Whose side am I on?' The US ships were operating with lights on at night, so the British put theirs on too, so that the Egyptian bombers, if they came, were given as good a chance to hit US ships as British.[21] Vice-Admiral Brown of the 6th Fleet later denied that he had specially manoeuvred to get in the way of the Allies, but added 'it was necessary to disperse my forces to assure the best protection of ships and aircraft engaged in operations of evacuation against an attack or even some misadventure'.[22]

At dawn on 5 November, at long last the landing began, when 600 British and 487 French paratroops were dropped outside Port Said. Complete command of the air afforded by aircraft carriers offshore gave these men effective support. Few of the British had any combat experience, save some who had crossed the Rhine in 1945. Their equipment was old; and all three radio sets dropped at Gamil airport were smashed.[23] But the battalion anti-tank gun missing in July had been supplied by the US NATO bazooka.[24] These drops were accomplished with great success: only one Englishman killed and no aircraft shot down.

21. Evidence of a task force commander.
22. *US News and World Report*, 14 December 1956.
23. A. J. Barker, *Suez: The Six Day War*; cf. Despatch, pp. 5332–3.
24. See Colonel Wigg's speech in February 1957 (*Hansard*, vol. 564, col. 338).

The French, mostly veterans of many drops in Indo-China or Algeria, were helped by the technically brilliant Nordatlas aerial command post in which General Gilles circled 1,000 feet up and directed the battle.

A second wave of landings was made at 1.45 p.m. One centre of resistance, the Coastguard Barracks, was demolished by an accurate air strike by Wyverns and Sea Hawks operating from carriers.[25] Surrounded and cut off from reinforcements and from the waterworks (captured by the French), the Egyptian commander, El Moguy, agreed to discuss terms of surrender in the early afternoon. This was reported back by the British airborne commander, Brigadier Butler, with the caveat that he doubted whether much would come of this.[26] The caveat appears to have been lost *en route* (communications from Port Said to headquarters were poor), and the Commons treated the news as if Nasser himself had surrendered. Conservatives cheered and waved order papers in a scene which seemed like a bizarre reenactment of famous debates of 1938;[27] thus J. J. Astor, a Conservative heretic, remained seated and the infuriated Colonial Secretary Lennox-Boyd shouted at him to stand up.[28]

But Nasser would not allow El Moguy to give in. Port Said was rallied by loud-speaker vans touring the city with the comforting news that the Third World War had begun and that London and Paris had been attacked by missiles.[29] The astute Russian consul general in Port Said helped to supervise the distribution of rifles to civilians.[30] Nevertheless Port Fuad effectively fell to the French. In the evening Bulganin sent Notes of great violence to Eden, Mollet and Ben Gurion saying that Russia was ready to crush them, by use of 'every kind of modern destructive weapon'. The Note to Israel put 'a question mark against the very existence of Israel as a state'. This action was apparently taken on the recommendation of the Syrian President, Shukri el Kuwatly, who was in Moscow on a state

25. Despatch, p. 5332.   26. Evidence of a commander.
27. Evidence of several eye-witnesses.
28. Evidence of a Conservative M P.
29. Despatch, p. 5332.   30. Despatch, p. 5332.

visit.[31] A fourth Note reached Eisenhower with the suggestion that Russia and the US should jointly intervene in the Middle East, presumably by once again 'separating the combatants'.

Thus Russia, preoccupied by Hungary, had taken six days to realize that the US were really hostile to the Anglo-French action. Eisenhower turned down this proposal [32] but a mood of semi-panic swept over parts of Washington, now on election eve: 'We must stop this before we are all burned to a crisp,' wailed someone in the State Department.[33] These apprehensions (with Dulles absent and Eisenhower driving US foreign policy chiefly by himself, with the help of the Bostonian Lodge at the UN and the somewhat inexperienced Herbert Hoover in the State Department) probably had an effect on US policy the next day. Eden and Mollet, on the other hand, though agreed that the Russian missile threat was false [34] (as it certainly was, given the then structure of Soviet missile forces [35]) did not quite discount the possibility of some sort of Soviet intervention (for example by volunteers).[36] According to one French account, Dillon called at midnight on Mollet with a message saying 'If you continue with your culpable attitude do not count on us', while President Eisenhower is himself understood to have told Hervé Alphand, the French Ambassador in Washington, that he was at the end of his tether, that he would stick to the UN Charter to the end and that he wished to present himself before his creator with clean hands.[37]

In this confused international situation, the first ships of the great Anglo-French armada at long last but punctually arrived off Port Said, followed at a discreet distance by two US sub-

31. Nasser in the *Sunday Times*, 24 June 1962. Eden in the House of Commons on 6 November read the Note to Britain; Dayan publishes that to Israel (pp. 184–5).

32. Eisenhower, p. 90.

33. Murphy, p. 476. This was a 'high-ranking official of the State Department ... not a career Foreign Service officer'. Mr Murphy explicitly denied any panic at the White House in his broadcast on BBC TV, 21 September 1966, and in his book specifically excluded Eisenhower.

34. Evidence of a Cabinet Minister; Eden, p. 555.

35. See the article by John Erickson in *Listener*, 4 August 1966.

36. Evidence of a Cabinet Minister.

37. Tournoux, p. 166.

marines of the 6th Fleet, the *Cutlass* and the *Hardhead*. At dawn on 6 November the naval bombardment of Port Said by destroyers began, carefully limited to those targets which might prove a genuine hindrance to the landing.[38] The great guns of the heavier ships, such as those of the one battleship, the *Jean Bart*, were silent. For two hours before the assault 'the Voice of Britain' on Cyprus broadcast continuously, warning people in Port Said to take cover. But when they were told by the paratroops that the beaches were mined, these obstacles were 'drenched with fire', and all the Egyptian fireposts were knocked out. At 4.50 a.m. the British commandos went on shore. Tanks followed. The waterfront captured, the commandos moved swiftly through the squares of modern Port Said in collaboration with the tanks. The French landed at 6.45 at Port Fuad, while their airborne troops, which had landed the day before, held off any Egyptian reinforcement.[39] It would appear, however, that the nature of the resistance the previous day caused General Stockwell to reject finally any plan of a parachute drop at Kantara and at Ismailia such as the French airborne General Massu still argued for.[40]

At 11 a.m. came yet another false surrender: Generals Stockwell and Beaufre, with Admiral Durnford-Slater and Air Marshal Barnett, went out in a small boat to receive surrender at the splendid Canal Company building. When they were about to land, a bullet from an upper window passed between Stockwell and the Admiral and the distinguished quartet realized that they had been about to disembark at a building which had not yet given in, and therefore had been within an ace of capture.[41] They beat a hasty retreat, and the battle continued,

38. Evidence of a task force commander (cf. Despatch, p. 5333). It is hard therefore to know what to make of Eden's two denials in the House of Commons on 6 and 7 November that *any* naval bombardment had been carried out.

39. The best general detailed account of the fighting in Port Said is in A. J. Barker; see also Azeau.

40. See Brigadier C. N. Barclay, 'Operation "Musketeer" ', in *Brassey's Annual*, 1957, p. 80.

41. Evidence of a French commander, and of a task force commander. cf. Despatch, p. 5334, and Beaufre, p. 168.

marked by a good deal of sporadic shooting in 'Arab Town' and 'Shanty Town', and the poignant destruction by the Fleet Air Arm of the well-defended Navy House, the great stone headquarters of the Royal Navy during the years of British occupation.[42] 400 men of 45 Commando Battalion were landed from HMS *Ocean* and *Theseus* by helicopter – the main military innovation of the campaign though the helicopters had been supplied by the US under the Offshore Agreement.[43] The final surrender of Port Said came in the late afternoon. Immediately afterwards an armoured column, with Brigadier Butler in the leading tank, set off south to Suez. British patrols had already reached as far as Fayid, south of Lake Timsah, and only twenty-five miles short of Suez.[44] But during the evening the Brigadier heard the news (on the BBC first) [45] that the Government had ordered a cease-fire at midnight, by which time he and his column had not reached much further than the village of El Cap, twenty-five miles south of Port Said and only just across the causeway. Suez remained elusive, seventy-five miles away from the main force. The British had lost twenty killed, the French ten,[46] and the Egyptians probably between 650 and 1,000.[47] Ten allied aircraft were lost, four in accidents, against 260 Egyptian aircraft destroyed.[48]

The British Cabinet decided to accept the UN call for a cease-fire for a number of reasons, and it is not now quite clear which was decisive. The fact that Israel and Egypt had ceased to fight meant that the overt reason for Anglo-French military intervention no longer existed. Eden himself saw the force of this argument, and, hoist with his own petard, states, in

42. Despatch, p. 5334.

43. Evidence of a commander. cf. too George Wigg in the House of Commons in February 1957 (*Hansard*, vol. 564, col. 338).

44. Despatch, p. 5334.

45. Evidence of a commander and of a task force commander.

46. Keightley, Despatch; A. J. Barker.

47. Sir Edwin Herbert, President of the Law Society, has 650 in his Report (p. 27), but even on his own evidence that seems a bit low: see his discussion with the Italian Consul (pp. 15–16) and Eisenhower's estimate (p. 95).

48. *Air Pictorial*, September 1965; A. J. Barker; Keightley, Despatch.

his memoirs, that this consideration weighed most in his mind.[49] (This argument counted with Lloyd and with Butler,[50] who had earlier, on 3 November, said to a colleague: 'We've got to make this respectable',[51] though he had earlier attended all the decisive meetings of the Cabinet.[52]) Then Mrs Meir, the Israeli Foreign Minister, the new threat to the tougher members of the British Cabinet and to all the French cabinet, was anxious to have her country obey the UN.[53] Fear of Russian intervention seems to have been secondary, though throughout 6 November there were ugly and far from baseless rumours of Russian jets flying to Syria over Turkey.[54] Eden's health was also important: the calm with which he had met the challenges of the first days after the ultimatum had waned and it was clear by 6 November that, weary from interrupted nights, troubled by the crumbling of alliances all around him, conscious of the division in the country and even in the Conservative Party, perhaps doubtful in his heart whether he was acting correctly, he was close to exhaustion. Political opposition in Britain was certainly not the main cause of the Government's decision; but the Cabinet must have known that if there were not a cease-fire they would be faced by much more trouble at home and possibly more resignations from the Cabinet, Government and civil service also. Iain Macleod apparently 'seriously considered resignation' on 4 November[55] and it would seem likely that within a few days other members of the Cabinet would have made some protest.

Finally a new danger was brought forward by the Chancellor of the Exchequer, Macmillan. Selling of sterling had been heavy in New York since the ultimatum, though this fact had been hidden from the world by support from the Bank of England, so that *The Times* on the morning of 6 November gave very

49. Eden, p. 557.   50. Private information.
51. Evidence of a junior Minister.
52. Checked with a member of the Cabinet secretariat.
53. Evidence of a Minister.
54. See Tournoux, pp. 147–50, where the implication is left that they were fabricated by the USA; Eisenhower, p. 91.
55. Randolph Churchill, p. 287.

comforting news. Calling in at the Treasury, where his young Economic Secretary, Boyle, had just resigned, Macmillan was told that the gold reserves had fallen by £100 million in the last week, that in New York sterling was being offered for sale in £1 million blocks and that the US Treasury was opposing the request of Britain to withdraw capital from the IMF.[56] (The IMF Board of Directors has to approve any withdrawal and, since voting is weighted according to the size of the deposit, the US Director was decisively influential.[57]) Macmillan appeared at the Cabinet a chastened man. He does not seem to have thought of this possibility beforehand, although Sir Alec Spearman at least had raised it at a meeting of the 1922 Committee in September.[58] It seemed as if Macmillan's emotional need for action was now purged and that, coming out of what a senior adviser has referred to as his 'trauma', he was able to forget both his earlier proud insistence that Britain should not become another Netherlands and his desire to keep 'the lawns of England green' for his grandchildren,[59] and so to announce in doleful and obviously earnest terms that he could 'not any more be responsible for Her Majesty's Exchequer' unless there was a cease-fire.[60] Macmillan was the strong man of this Cabinet by now and it seems to have been really his advice as a man not as a Minister that brought the fighting to an end. Had Macmillan still been Foreign Secretary and Butler Chancellor, the financial arguments would have, perhaps, weighed less. At all events Macmillan now became the leader of those who wished to halt the operation, leading also what was basically a rebellion against Eden's leadership; according to one reliable source, Macmillan now felt that Eden was 'playing ducks and drakes' with the country and had to be halted – even perhaps overthrown.

Head, Thorneycroft and Lennox-Boyd argued for continu-

56. Eden, p. 556. Macmillan gave the figures for sterling on 4 December 1956 (*Hansard*, vol. 561, col. 1050). See Randolph Churchill, p. 287.

57. Evidence of a diplomat.

58. Evidence of a Conservative MP.

59. Evidence of a senior official; the remark was made to at least two people.

60. Evidence of a Minister.

ing to the end of the Canal[61] though they do not seem to have used the one argument that might have helped their case: that if the Allies held the whole Canal, they could at least clear it before handing it over to the UN.[62] Nor is it clear how long the Chiefs of Staff were prepared to estimate it would take to get to Suez: Eden's memoirs say his advice was at least five days more and Head in December said that the military appreciation was 'about seven days',[63] but no one on the spot thought it could have been more than forty-eight hours at most and probably less; this view was also expressed by the French Government.[64] Lennox-Boyd, with, as Colonial Secretary, a direct line to Cyprus, seems to have so argued at the time. (Head in 1958 said it would have been 'a few days'.[65]) The explanation for this discrepancy is that it was one thing to reach Suez with an advanced detachment, quite another to become established all the way along the Canal without fear of communications or water supply being cut off. No one quite knew whether Egypt would fight before Ismailia or not; anyway the political assumption was that the Anglo-French forces would head for Cairo from Ismailia.[66] Finally Macmillan received word that the US would back an IMF loan of £300 million to hold the pound if there were a cease-fire by midnight.[67] Thus the US Administration, perhaps more worried

61. Evidence of a Minister, which I have accepted despite another Cabinet Minister saying he does not remember it like that and the fact that Eden in his memoirs (p. 557) says that 'no suggestion was made by any of my colleagues, either then or in the hours which elapsed before my announcement in the House that evening, that we and the French should continue our intervention'. On the other hand, Head stated in the House of Commons in December 1958: 'In my view the tragedy is that the operation stopped' (*Hansard*, vol. 597, col. 1076).

62. Evidence of a Cabinet Minister.　　　63. *Hansard*, vol. 561, col. 1235.

64. Evidence of a commander, a task force commander and a French commander. Fergusson in *The Watery Maze* (p. 401) says there was nobody in Port Said from force commanders downward who was not convinced that Ismailia would fall that night and Suez the next day. The French view that it would have been only forty-eight hours was given by Bourgès-Maunoury in the debate in the Chamber on 8 December 1956.

65. *Hansard*, vol. 597, col. 1075.　　　66. Despatch, p. 5330.

67. Evidence of a junior Minister.

than any European power by the possibility of the extension of the war by Russia, and with Dulles ill, seemed to hold Britain to ransom.[68] Eisenhower had said that if France and Britain were attacked by Russia, the USA would fulfil her NATO obligations, but it was not clear whether this applied to Anglo-French action outside Europe. (On 13 November General Gruenther explained that if Russia had attacked Britain or France with missiles, Russia would have been destroyed in reply 'as night follows day'.[69]) At a meeting in the White House at that moment, the President was approving about twenty separate measures to achieve 'an advanced state of readiness' for war.[70]

The British Cabinet finally agreed to a cease-fire, apparently without consulting the Chiefs of Staff,[71] though there was an interruption at Downing Street when Ministers had to go off to observe the splendid if then inappropriate ritual of the opening of Parliament by the Queen. Eden's pain at this turn of events was obvious. Did the idea really flit across his mind of accepting the resignation of Macmillan and those keen for cease-fire, and of forming a government of under-secretaries, with Head, Lennox-Boyd, Sandys and a few others? Or did he perhaps comfort himself with the belief that this was merely a truce and no armistice? One day doubtless the full story of this Cabinet will be told.

Eden telephoned Mollet just before lunch (Adenauer had arrived in Mollet's office), presented him with a *fait accompli* and then hung up. Pineau has recalled that he has never forgotten the dramatic intensity of this conversation.[72] Mollet,

68. Evidence of a diplomat.   69. Tournoux, p. 167.
70. Eisenhower, p. 91.   71. Evidence of a senior officer.
72. Evidence of an Adviser. A French source has a bizarre account of Eden's remarks on this occasion: 'Je suis acculé. Je ne peux plus tenir. Tout le monde me lâche. Mon fidèle collaborateur Nutling [*sic*] a démissioné de son ministère d'État. Je ne puis même pas m'appuyer sur les conservateurs unanimes. L'archevêque de Canterbury, l'Église, les pétroliers, tout le monde est contre moi ! Le Commonwealth est menacé d'éclatement. Nehru veut rompre les liens. ... Je ne puis être le fossoyeur de la Couronne. Et puis, comprenez-moi, comprenez-moi bien, le président Eisenhower m'a téléphoné. Je ne peux pas faire cavalier seul sans les États Unis' (Tournoux, p. 169).

anxious, like his entire Cabinet, to continue, with the franc still hale and hearty, and for some time unable to get in touch with Eden, refused to go on with the struggle without Britain.[73]

Pineau, who had earlier been far less keen on the whole adventure than Mollet, was now more anxious to go on to the end and tried ineffectively to persuade Mollet.[74] He and Bourgès-Maunoury tried to work out a way of continuing in alliance with the Israelis who, of course, were poised along the east of the Canal and would have been able to fall easily on both Suez and Ismailia.[75] Various ideas were proposed, and General Dayan even offered to take these cities in French uniforms.[76] Had it not been for the key commands held by the British commanders, the French might indeed have gone on, though only three Ministers in the French Cabinet actually wished to do so without Britain: Pineau, Bourgès-Maunoury and the Minister of War, Max Lejeune.[77]

But not only did the integration of commands make it diffi-cult to continue alone. The bridge connecting the French in Port Fuad with the road along the Canal on its east bank had been destroyed. So any advance would have to be on the west bank. But there British tanks were at the head of the column. The road is narrow and no deviation is possible in the swamp. It is indeed, as *The Times* might have put it, 'a corridor for camels'. The British would presumably not have let the French past, though the matter was not tested.[78] Although a patrolling French armoured car did apparently get to within a few miles of Suez and back in the course of the afternoon of the 6th,[79] the French commanders, with a reluctance shared fully by their British colleagues, accepted the cease-fire.[80] 'I examined the possibility of disobedience', General Beaufre wrote ten years

73. Pineau, *Le Monde*, 4 November 1966. Evidence of an Adviser.
74. Evidence of a French Minister.
75. Pineau, *Le Monde*, 4 November 1966.
76. Evidence of an Israeli commander.
77. Evidence of a French Minister.
78. Evidence of a French commander.
79. Evidence of a task force commander. The British got to Fayid.
80. Evidence of General Beaufre.

later.[81] Next day the weather changed, and the admirals comforted themselves with the reflection that they would not have been able to land anyway on the 7th.[82]

Afterwards, once more, as Eden believed, came the 'long drawling tides of surrender': 'Myopia' he calls it in his memoirs.[83] The cease-fire was permanent, not a temporary truce. No time since the 1780s has been quite so humiliating as the weeks following Suez during which, inch by inch, Britain was forced to withdraw by remorseless US pressure and threats to cut her off from oil.[84] Despite this, Eden's popularity, according to the polls, steadily grew throughout November.[85] The British and French handed over to a UN force and Israel withdrew to her old frontiers, though the UN thereafter ran Gaza and held open the Gulf of Akaba. There was petrol rationing in Britain in December and a long balance of payments crisis, overcome by the offer of a 3-*tranche* IMF loan (for $561·5 million); by a pledge from the Import-Export Bank (for $738 million and $1,000 million against British government dollar securities); and by a delay in repaying the instalment due on the 1948 US loan.[86] Eden's health was ruined and, after false encouragement given by a holiday in Jamaica, soon with great reluctance he retired on medical advice, having shown, at a meeting of the 1922 Committee on 18 December, that he was anyway only half the man that he had once been.[87] Butler, responsible while Eden was away in Jamaica for the

81. Beaufre, p. 261.　　82. Evidence of a task force commander.

83. The last chapter title in *Full Circle*.

84. Evidence of a senior Cabinet Minister. Mr Selwyn Lloyd was cheered in New York. But it is difficult to think of any occasion since the 1780s when Britain was thwarted in a major design of this sort. cf. Sherman Adams, p. 212.

85. cf. Epstein, *British Politics in the Suez Crisis*, pp. 161–2.

86. The details of these arrangements were explained later by the Chancellor of the Exchequer in the House of Commons but the diplomat (involved with these negotiations) with whom I discussed them referred to them as 'a bisque' – they were stand by agreements which could be taken up when needed. As it turned out the size of the loan so mobilized altered the situation of the pound so that it did not have to be used (cf. Walker-Smith, *Hansard*, vol. 562, col. 215).

87. See note on this meeting, in Appendix 8, pp. 224–6.

evacuation of troops whose use he regretted, was saddled with blame for this final 'scuttle' and so lost what chance he had of succeeding Eden. Monckton visited Port Said to estimate Egyptian casualties in the assault which he had helped to plan but which he had always disliked. Eight Conservatives only abstained in voting for the Government in the critical vote of 8 November; they included Nicolson, Astor and Boothby, of Spearman's group; the others were Anthony Nutting, who did not go back to the Commons after his resignation, Boyle, William Yates, Sir Frank Medlicott, and Colonel Banks.[88] Selwyn Lloyd, visiting Dulles in hospital in November, received a final blow, almost comic in its incongruity: 'Why did you stop?' Dulles asked.[89]

The allied occupation of Port Said lasted till December and was enlivened by the offers of dirty pictures and of good laundry service that had marked the previous rather longer British stay in Egypt.[90] The French looted the stores,[91] and on their return to Cyprus some embittered paratroops gave away their weapons to EOKA. The British conducted themselves better and looted little, though one officer of my acquaintance stole from the flat in which he was billeted a little wooden carved duck decoy,[92] perhaps the only prize brought back from the last great amphibious expedition in British imperial history.

88. Their political fates are explored in detail in Epstein, *British Politics in the Suez Crisis*, pp. 98–122. Spearman, Keith Joseph and some others voted for the Government on this occasion after an undertaking by Heath that the Government were the next day going to announce they would hand over to the UN unconditionally.

89. Evidence of a Cabinet minister, confirmed by Selwyn Lloyd in *Sunday Telegraph*, 30 April 1967. Murphy apparently said the same in 1958 (Tournoux, p. 151) and in his memoirs says he was amazed that Britain and France stopped (p. 477).

90. Evidence of a commander and of an officer.

91. Evidence of an officer.   92. Evidence of an officer.

EPILOGUE

The Cost

SUEZ cost rather less than the £500 million mentioned by the Chancellor to Murphy as being set aside in late July; Eden spoke of £100 million,[1] unlikely to be an underestimate, but the Labour Party worked out a figure of £328 million, to take into account loss of exports and increase in costs of imports directly attributable to the expedition to Egypt[2]; the precise costs cannot be determined now. The British lost a total of twenty-two killed, the French ten, the Israelis 200, and the Egyptians probably between 2,650 and 3,000. Among the British deaths was that of the unfortunate Lieutenant Moorhouse, who was smothered, probably by accident, during the occupation of Port Said.[3] Ten allied aircraft were lost, four in accidents, against 260 Egyptian aircraft destroyed.[4]

The Strategy

The British and French Governments decided in early August 1956 that they had to persuade or force Egypt to accept their minimum demands achieved at the first London conference. By the time that the force their advisers judged necessary was assembled (in early September), it had become obvious anyway that the Egyptian Government would not voluntarily accept these demands.

The two Governments sought to get a joint Western or UN decision to use the assembled forces, but were prevailed upon to delay by a change in the mood of public opinion in the world

1. Eden, p. 556.
2. Labour Party 1959 Speakers' Handbook (see Appendix 10).
3. Evidence of an officer, who looked for him.
4. *Air Pictorial*, September 1965.

and especially by their US allies, who devised several schemes of prevarication in order to postpone any action at least until after the US elections of 6 November. Partly for military reasons (such as the fear of a change in the weather) this postponement was unacceptable to Britain and France, who thereupon decided (reluctantly, in the British case) to use the long-established Israeli desire for a preventive war as a 'trigger' for their own action. Thus what the Israeli Chief of Staff later described as 'a political alliance' was concluded between the three countries. The Israeli and Anglo-French battle plans, Operation Kadesh and Operation Musketeer, were timed to fit in with one another and the agreement confirmed at Sèvres by a 'declaration of intent'.

The separation of the combatants was a stage prop, though one which nevertheless became increasingly important in its own right, so that the fact that the combatants had ceased fighting before allied troops reached Port Said became a real factor in the British Cabinet's willingness to accept a cease-fire.

The Anglo-French plan was to secure their oil supplies and give some sort of real international status to the Suez Canal. But it is frankly doubtful if the two Governments would have gone ahead first either to contemplate the assembly of a force or then to use it, had it not been for a series of emotional arguments which, starting as supporting arguments for the main international economic ones, seem to have become dominant: in Britain, the superficial political argument, that an already rather shaky Government could not afford to appear weak, and the deeper psychological one, that the Prime Minister genuinely saw in the nationalization of the Canal Company a new Rhineland which had to be dealt with firmly (as the Rhineland Crisis of 1936 had not been, during Eden's first time as Foreign Secretary). Britain had already quarrelled with Nasser before the nationalization and France regarded Nasser as the source of her difficulties in Algeria. Both Governments allowed their policies to be too greatly influenced by these secondary arguments, none of which was firmly based: Nasser was not the only or even the main force for dissension either in Algeria or in the rest of the Middle East, he was not a new Hitler nor was he completely in the hands of Russia, and he was much more popular in Egypt than the Western Governments believed. Further, the ambiguous policies of Britain, France and also the USA throughout the Middle East since 1945 had themselves been disruptive: the desire to weld as many countries of the area as possible into an anti-Communist defence pact was evidence of a mistaken view of the nature of Communism, of the Communist threat, and of Middle East nationalism. In the Tripartite Declaration of 1950, the three countries had taken on a series of responsibilities which they did not have the will to make real.

It was doubtless true, as Mr Selwyn Lloyd told the House of Commons on 31 October 1956, that the Government had not incited Israel to attack.[5] For the Foreign Secretary to say that 'there was no prior agreement between us about it'[6] appears, in the light of evidence summarized here, to be a lie, as does Eden's statement in the House of Commons on 20 December 1956 that there was 'not foreknowledge that Israel would attack Egypt'.[7] Equally mendacious, by commission or omission, seem to be speeches of other Ministers when speaking on this theme at this time. Of course, these were lies of state, devised with the highest motives as a joint enterprise in the interests of the people and to avoid ill-effects on the rest of the Arab world.

The delicate question of 'how much the Cabinet knew' has been touched upon from time to time in this account. It would seem that they were clearly told of an Israeli 'offer' to attack

5. The evidence presented on p. 92 above suggests that the French Ministry of Defence cannot be exempted from this charge.

6. The Foreign Secretary on this occasion stated in full: 'The right hon. Gentleman asked whether there had been collusion with regard to this matter. . . . It is quite wrong to state that Israel was incited to this action by Her Majesty's Government. There was no prior agreement between us about it.' There may perhaps be room for speculation about what the words 'about it' may indicate but in the context it can surely only reasonably be held to refer to 'this action' and not the 'incitement' alone. *Hansard*, vol. 558, col. 1569.

7. *Hansard*, vol. 562, col. 1518. See Appendix 7, p. 223.

Egypt at some time in the future, though it is doubtful if the date was known to them very long before. An almost irreversible decision was probably taken on 18 October by a committee of Ministers before the whole Cabinet had been consulted. But they were told and agreed on 23–4 October. The Cabinet as a whole perhaps did not know the extent to which the French and Israelis were working together; the *ceinture maritime*, the bombardment of Rafah by the *Georges Leygues*, the assistance to the paratroops at Mitla, even perhaps the French fighter defence of Israeli cities, were probably unknown to them, and so perhaps was the role which the Israelis hoped the RAF would play in destroying the Egyptian air force. All these were 'technical military matters' which Eden 'kept very close to his chest'.

The policy once decided, the operational order was finally given by the Anglo-French command at 5 a.m. on 31 October 1956 and carried through for 6 days 18 hours until halted at midnight on 6–7 November partly by a run on the pound, partly by the desire of some prominent Ministers to take the pretext seriously; both these pressures were evidence of the opposition of world public opinion directed by the estranged Government of the USA. For the first time, as General Dayan put it, Britain had to bring a war to an end at a time and place not of her own choosing. This was not really the first moment when the power of Britain faltered but, more important, when it was shown to have done so.

The Consequences and Implications

The consequences of Suez were different from the predictions of both those who backed the operation and those who condemned it. Thus instead of the American alliance being broken, the British have never since ventured on a foreign policy independent of the USA. It was the Entente Cordiale that broke, which thus died, as it was born, over Egypt. Suez was partly responsible both for Gaullist diplomacy and for the end of the Fourth Republic. At the same time, Suez failed both to give the UN military substance, as the Conservatives claimed desperately in the closing hours of the military action to be at least one lasting achievement, and to destroy it, as Labour predicted. The Commonwealth undoubtedly took a harsh blow from the lack of consultation, and it would doubtless not be the same again in the event of another world war; but it has staggered on, changed more by other things. A 'Suez reflex' may have affected Labour ministers over Rhodesia in 1965, just as a 'Munich reflex' affected their predecessors in 1956.

Nor did Suez prove that Britain was unable to take any military action without the USA: only that she could not do so while maintaining a reserve currency and needing to rely on the USA both for oil and for ultimate protection against Russia. Further, even if the USA were to launch an attack on, say, Panama, international opinion would constitute a serious menace to the US Administration if the campaign were to be begun by a slow sail across the Caribbean. No monetary difficulties held back Mollet. Hence doubtless one reason why France has insisted that Britain jettison sterling as a reserve currency before entering the Common Market.

The USA's exclamations of righteous indignation make curious reading against a background of other adventures in Cuba, Santo Domingo, Vietnam and even (as Eden himself bitterly remarked) Guatemala. Eisenhower's letters to Eden could have been sent with advantage, and only a few names changed, on several occasions by English Prime Ministers to Presidents Kennedy or Johnson. Actually Eisenhower might reluctantly have lain 'doggo' if the Anglo-French action had been delayed till after the election. It was the timing and, as so often in this affair, the manners of their allies which drove the USA to condemn them outright at the UN: Britain and France seemed publicly to knock down the main plank of US foreign policy just before a presidential election. Eden, the most perfect gentleman in English politics since 1918, thus caused a major crisis by seeming ill-bred. More serious was the damage afforded by Suez to the previously growing reputation of Britain as the most progressive and reasonable of the nations of the developed world.

Britain and France made two major mistakes so far as the

USA was concerned; they thought that Eisenhower, old friend from the Grand Alliance, could be separated from Dulles; and that Eisenhower would be rendered inactive over the election partly because of the Jewish vote in New York. Eden seems to have believed that he had received a certain freedom of action in the Middle East from Eisenhower during his visit in January 1956, and Eisenhower perhaps, through his innate politeness and vagueness of language, may very well have left that impression. Dulles has sometimes been saddled with the whole blame for Suez, and it is certainly hard to believe, taking into account the fact of two major affronts (those of 13 September and 2 October), that he was merely unconsciously rude. With a remarkable capacity for convincing himself that whatever he did was morally justified, the evidence suggests that he really believed that a certain brutality would be in the long run the kindest policy towards Britain. His conduct over Suez too was only the last straw following ten years during which British politicians, officers and diplomats had been 'irritated almost beyond measure' by what one senior officer described 'as the unhelpful and sometimes . . . inimical attitude of the State Department . . . in the Middle East . . . based on their extraordinary sentimental outdated and . . . hypocritical obsession with the evils of British colonialism'. This mood of resentment was later reflected in the signature of the famous anti-American motion in the Commons by 127 Conservative MPs.[8]

The scenario of separating the combatants, the pretext by which, for so many motives, Britain and France ultimately launched their expedition, acquired during the operation, as has been seen, a substance of its own. Indeed, the Anglo-French invasion of Egypt at that point was the one act of international policy which was able to give victories to both Egypt and Israel: Egypt got the Canal and a victory over 'imperialism'; Israel freed the Gulf of Akaba, destroyed the *fedayun* bases in Gaza and ruined Egyptian military prestige. It was a fitting

8. Only 118 at any one time. They said the USA was 'gravely endangering the Atlantic Alliance.' Twenty-six Conservatives, including most of Spearman's group, signed a counter motion urging restoration of full co-operation.

conclusion, for both Nasser and Ben Gurion had outplayed the statesmen of old Europe in guile and resolution. Nasser, unlike Russia, understood (doubtless through the agency of the US ambassador, Byroade) that US policy and Anglo-French policy were not the same. A major war between Egypt and Israel, on the cards early in 1956, was thus staved off, at the cost of not much more than 3,000 lives. The scenario thus had a certain point after all, though of course it was not the one which had been specifically sought by Britain and France (however much Mollet has since understandably striven to show that he saved a sister socialist republic from destruction, as Léon Blum failed to do over Spain in 1936; this was *a* French motive, not the main one).

Suez had a greater effect on the politics of Europe than of the Middle East (though the Russian missile threat was in many places believed to have been the main reason why the Allies halted, so damaging Western prestige seriously). As well as driving Britain to abandon any attempt to act independently of the USA, Suez began a period of disillusion with Conservatism in the English middle class which took some years to be overcome, although this disillusion was masked in the election of 1959 when there was so powerful a swing of the country as a whole towards Macmillan. Russia did not do so well out of Suez as might have been expected, and it was possibly a dispute over the implications of the crisis that led to the fall, in early 1957, of the Russian Foreign Minister, Shepilov. In the Middle East, though Suez hardly delayed the doubtless inevitable fall of Nuri, British and French prestige recovered rather faster than could have been expected. Nasser ten years later seemed further than ever from uniting the Arabs.

Apart from the unhappy aero-psychological activity, the military side of the Suez operation was remarkably successful. (The lesson of the aero-psychological side was that such complicated operations cannot be hastily set up on a shoe-string.) The amphibious assault was most efficiently carried out. No doubt, too, the display of overwhelming air power by Britain and France and Fergusson's warnings from Cyprus did cut down casualties, both those of the Allies and Egypt's. (The warnings were partly designed to win a big listening audience.) But the crisis revealed British unpreparedness for this sort of limited war, shown in the shortage of all sorts of equipment, from waterproofing material to transport aircraft; the curious political-military mishandling in the week before 29 October (which ensured that there was really no military 'collusion', whatever might have occurred politically) is surely without parallel in British annals; while the variation of Operation Musketeer actually used with whatever humane motives broke an essential rule of war: an assault must be both swift and violent. Further, Cyprus proved inadequate as a substitute for a base in the Canal Zone, though its efficacy in case of need was the main strategic justification for the British withdrawal from Suez in 1954.

It can be argued, of course, that the sheer size of the force assembled might, along with other techniques, have ensured that there would be 'no opposition' or that 'all opposition can be ignored', so there would be no fighting, and hence no war. But, as might have been expected, this did not turn out to be the case.

In defence of the military planners, it may be said that they did apparently at some stage before the event prepare a note which presented what turned out to be a fairly accurate account of what transpired: US and UN opposition and action, pressure on the pound and ignominious withdrawal. (Eden is understood to have had copies of this called in and destroyed.[9]) Whatever may be now said about the plans and the quality of the expedition, it is quite evident that, judged purely as a military operation, two serious mistakes were made: first, to place such faith in aerial means, particularly aero-psychological means, was mistaken; and second, more important still, the timing of the moment to begin the operation was so delayed as to lose all chance of swift victory.

The Anglo-French overestimated the military strength of Egypt. But if the assault force had been smaller it could not have got from Malta any faster and it is possible that the Czech and Russian technicians would actually have used their MiGs

9. Evidence of a senior officer.

and Ilyushins. The Anglo-French integrated command worked well in action, though perhaps less so at headquarters, where the international clash of temperament between Eden and Dulles was reflected by another between the intuitive Stockwell and the intellectual Beaufre. On 5–6 November the extent of political interference was an object lesson in the evils of swift communication: 'Nelson would never have won a single victory if there'd been a telex,' an admiral remarked in 1966. If, as seems to be the case, the Chiefs of Staff were indeed not consulted on 6 November about the cease-fire, the British Government could have brought about the serious embarrassment of their troops.

The operation actually proved the importance of aircraft carriers in limited war: their aircraft were responsible for the destruction of the Egyptian air force on the airfields, for the support of the paratroops on 5 November and for the helicopter-borne second wave of paratroops on 6 November; but the main military consequence was, because of Bulganin's last letter, to confirm in the mind of both the British and French Governments the need to pursue a new illusion: the absolutely independent nuclear deterrent and the *force de frappe*.

Suez was a good example of how a single individual can affect events. It showed the almost limitless power of a Prime Minister in modern circumstances, particularly when supported by a powerful group of Ministers. Probably Eden, a good Foreign Secretary (with a blind spot over Europe shared by his countrymen), should never have been encouraged by Churchill to be his heir. Even in diplomacy he never understood Middle East nationalism. But then few Western politicians of that time did. It seems clear anyway that Eden in 1956 was driven to follow policies alien to his nature and experience. From this ambivalence in Eden's mind followed the various mistakes: the failure to consult Gaitskell (Gaitskell was left in September to get information, like the rest of the population, from the official spokesman or the inspired leak); the failure to consult Eisenhower and the Foreign Service, for they might have argued too persuasively; hence the failure to make the political and diplomatic preparation for war which all nineteenth-century statesmen would automatically have ensured. There seems too to have been a failure to think through all the political and strategic consequences of action: could the Canal ever be held without occupying Egypt, was it really practicable to contemplate occupation, and, as a British commander put it, 'where was the second eleven to run Egypt?' If the answer was really Nahas Pasha and his friends, it can hardly be that the Government was planning for a very long-lasting settlement. The same British commander described Eden as behaving in this crisis as one who had 'obstinately decided like a girl to scratch out the eyes of his opponent but hadn't quite thought of what would happen afterwards'. Doubtless in the long run Eden was seeking some sort of new order in the Middle East, based on an international settlement of the Canal and a new Egyptian Government which would have been nationalistic though pro-British. But, surely, such plans were based upon dreams, not substantial things. A new deal in the Middle East in the 1950s had to take into account the USA and Arab nationalism could not be by-passed.

The biggest mistake however was to commit the country to war with what, in the light of the evidence now available, must be seen as a deliberate deception of the people. It is inexcusable to send troops into battle and to make appeals for national unity on a false premise. General Sir Hugh Stockwell has made the same point when explaining that 'the lack of a clear political aim' bedevilled the expedition, so that no one in the forces had a 'full and clear idea as to what they were being sent to do and why'.[10]

It is clear, however, that the Government were, as Bevan put it at the time, unskilled in skulduggery. Eden was a statesman whose politics, if sometimes debatable, had been always characterized by honesty. Neither he nor his Ministers could bring themselves to believe that they had left that familiar territory; once away, they remained there as short a time as possible (like Lloyd at Sèvres), and came back hardly able to believe, and not to admit even to themselves, that they had ever been away from home. If they deceived their country, they

10. *Sunday Telegraph*, 13 November 1966.

also seem to have deceived themselves. No British military plans were made which took into account the relationship with Israel. Britain did not thus reap the advantages which she might have done from a secret alliance with Israel. Israel's contiguous land frontier was allowed to mean nothing to the British planners. The '100 ship plan' went on. The scenario (separation of the combatants) was even allowed to dictate the timing of military moves. Thus ships were generally not allowed to leave Malta till shortly before the expiry of the ultimatum. Again, General Stockwell has now made clear that 'had we been given the information about the intention of the Israelis' (which the Cabinet knew) he would have launched an airborne operation, even though he could not have linked up with his troops immediately.[11]

The British as well as British leaders were doubtless sated by so many years of power and victory that the thwarting of their designs by the USA, particularly in the Middle East, was previously unthinkable. Eden was thus in a way a sacrificial figure for the nation's illusions. Eden seems to have been instinctively aware that ten years after 1945 the nation was ready for a spot of adventure: the hero of John Osborne's *Look Back in Anger*, produced that spring, and the Prime Minister were thus on the same level. Eden knew too that the country would welcome some daring stroke of foreign policy independent of the USA and that there was a case for riding roughshod over the mandarins of the civil service. He picked indeed the right horses; but not, unfortunately, the right race. Would matters have been different if Parliament had been persistently sitting throughout the crisis? It is an open question. The most curious aspect of this whole affair is that Eden himself who, at the time, seemed to some likely to go down in history as unscrupulous and Machiavellian beyond parallel in English history, has since attained in the public mind the name of one who, however foolhardy his policies and however ineptly they were carried out, has 'lost everything save honour'. It is obviously a tragedy that he should have ended his political life in this manner.

The truth of the 'declaration of intent' exchanged with Israel

11. ibid.

was bound to leak out eventually: too many people were in the secret or became aware of it; it is curious that Eden or Macmillan could not at some time afterwards have brought themselves to make a clean breast of things, rather in the same manner as the USA did after the Bay of Pigs. It is true that such a confession might have risked British lives and property in the Middle East; but less surely than the actual operation itself did. The secrecy with which the Sèvres Agreement was concluded has no doubt magnified its importance and perhaps too much can be made of its unprecedented nature; its parallels are those secret treaties during the First World War promising Constantinople to Russia, or Southern Tyrol to Italy: or the Sykes–Picot agreement carving up Turkey in 1916.

The inter-relation of the crisis in Suez and Hungary is beyond the scope of this study, but such evidence as there is suggests that Russia would have intervened in Hungary whatever might have happened in Egypt.[12] But the internal pressure in the USA for action over Hungary would have been more difficult for the President to withstand; in this sense, Suez was a lucky windfall for the US Administration. Whether even the moral pressure of a united West would have given the Russians pause over Hungary is, however, dubious. But Suez was undoubtedly, as Sir William Hayter put it in his memoir, a 'Godsend' to Russia too, diverting the possible hostility of the Asiatic and 'Third World' to Russia over Hungary.[13]

A settlement of Anglo-French difficulties over the Suez Canal might have just been reached on the basis of Selwyn Lloyd's six principles agreed in New York. Such a settlement would have been a far better one for Britain than that which was actually achieved, though the Conservative Party, in its Llandudno mood, would have regarded the six principles as a surrender. Lloyd apparently wanted to go on negotiating in October. But to persuade the Conservatives to accept a surrender would have demanded a leader more artful and more compelling and in a way less honest than Eden actually was: a de Gaulle. Using hindsight, it is clear that this might have been

12. cf. John Erickson, *Listener*, 4 August 1966.
13. Hayter, *The Kremlin and the Embassy*, p. 154.

done by means of some dramatic gesture over Europe, so saving the Fourth Republic and enabling Britain to enter the Common Market when she could have dictated its future shape.

Eden's health does not seem to have had a decisive effect on events. A leading doctor who knew Eden well thinks he would not have acted very differently in the Suez crisis if he had been in robust health. But doubtless the bile, traditional spring of odd tempers, had had an earlier effect on Eden's whole personality. It is also possible that from 5 October onwards Eden was really ill and that his doctors should then have recommended his resignation. Perhaps something would be explained if a full medical history of the events of 5 to 8 October were to become available. But Eden's doctor, Sir Horace Evans, died before his patient and was apparently no Moran.

Personal hatreds seem to have played a major part in events more than health. In 1956 Eden could turn only to Butler (who, though sceptical at the end was in the beginning rather more in favour of force than is sometimes supposed, and was also both in poor health and in poor spirits) or to Macmillan, who seems to have derived an almost aesthetic satisfaction from danger and risks. Macmillan, too, shared Eden's false historical analogies and saw Egypt through a forest of Flanders poppies and gleaming jackboots. Neither Butler nor Macmillan admired Eden; the latter found him too feminine, the former too un-intellectual. And beyond Macmillan there was Mollet, desperate and persuasive, who, with the eagle eye of an ex-Resistance chief of Arras, saw Nasser as Hitler more plainly than anyone. Finally, Lady Eden is believed to have complained that the Suez Canal was running through her drawing-room; but she was probably not a calming influence on her husband.

The bizarre aspect of this whole affair is that with a few exceptions nearly all the British Ministers seem to have been hostile or dubious about the use of force by the end of October; but they were caught up in a whirlpool, partly of their own making, and, transfixed by Eden's superior reputation, were unable to act. Throughout the summer and early autumn they remained, as if spellbound, in the mood of *The Times*'s early leaders. They also knew from Llandudno how the feeling ran in their Party. The pressure on them to act 'loyally' was tremendous. One Minister voiced a complaint; and 'they' replied with the devastating rejoinder 'A—, you're yellow.' The crisis was long: over three months of persistent strain. Nevertheless, those Ministers who did not resign and who did disapprove of Eden's action showed a lack of moral courage: as Lord Salisbury's grandfather, the great Prime Minister, put it: 'Those who have the absolute power of preventing lamentable events, and, knowing what is taking place, refuse to exercise that power, are responsible for what happens.'[14] Butler has explained his conduct, not unsympathetically, against the background of the rest of his career: 'If I am wanted I am there ready to serve ... you can't alter your own nature.'[15] Perhaps for the others, the best epitaph was spoken by that Minister who later recalled: 'We were offered the poisoned chalice, we had the choice of draining it to the bitter dregs or dashing it from our lips.'[16] They drained it.

To embark on an offensive of this size without bringing in the normal civil service made many British officials, particularly abroad, look foolish or dishonest, and damaged the Government machine when it was most needed. For Jebb, the Ambassador in Paris, to pick up a version (inaccurate, so it transpired) of what was afoot from a casual conversation with the French Minister of Defence, for Trevelyan, the Ambassador in Cairo, to know nothing till the news of the ultimatum came over the tapes, for Hayter in Moscow to have to wonder whether he had drunk too much at a party in the Kremlin when he heard of the ultimatum, and for Dixon, the permanent Representative at the UN, apparently to hear of it from his Soviet opposite number, were bizarre rewards to these officials after years of faithful service, much of it to Eden, hardly compensated for by the knowledge that French officials were being similarly treated by their chiefs.

Churchill once remarked of Suez to Head: 'I am not sure I

14. Quoted in W. S. Blunt, *Diaries*, vol. 2, p. 472.
15. *Listener*, 28 July 1966.
16. Another version of this remark is: 'The cup was presented to us; we had the choice of dashing it from our lips or draining it to the dregs.'

should have dared to start; but I am sure I should not have dared to stop.' The Canal, in fact, whatever was said in Whitehall, might have been conquered within twenty-four hours (there were under eighty miles to go, and Egyptian defences were concentrated on Cairo). Probably there would have been neither world war nor devaluation if the Allies had continued for this time and, having got so far, the morale of the Army and the Entente Cordiale, that incomparable friendship, would certainly have been better served by going on to Suez. But the risk was imponderable, and the two old Empires would have had probably to withdraw as quickly as they had to do anyway, still before even the Canal was clear.

Twelve years on, it is hard to avoid seeing the macabre humour of the events described here : the spectacle of over one hundred thousand men setting off for a war which lasted barely a day and then returning has few parallels in the long gallery of military imbecility. The 'grand old Duke of York' at least got to the top of the hill.

It is nevertheless tragic to see great imperial countries (especially our own) ending their pretensions in comic style; and the general point at issue was serious enough. Arab nationalism, and particularly Egyptian nationalism, was certain to be inimical to Britain in the short run. The question was whether this enmity should have been met by seeking to extirpate it by force, or by a policy of magnanimous friendship, in the hope that in the long run a reasonable *modus vivendi* might have been achieved.

Eden, it is true, attempted friendship to begin with, but that fell short of magnanimity. Thereafter he chose force, as Mollet and his predecessors had chosen force in Algeria. In making these choices Eden and Mollet assumed policies which had not been theirs before they had either of them gained supreme power. Events showed that under their leadership neither Britain nor France was strong enough, economically or militarily, nor resolute nor clever enough to carry through this policy even in the short term. Had they not fumbled things in a number of ways, they might, it is true, have very well succeeded in the limited matter of occupying the Canal Zone; even 'turning right at Ismailia', they might have established at Cairo a provisional government sympathetic to them. A successful *coup d'état* at Damascus could doubtless also have been arranged.

But it is impossible to believe that, even if the benevolent connivance of the USA had been ensured beforehand, any re-establishment of Anglo-French power could have been permanently achieved in the Middle East by the use of force. The faith that Britain seems to have had in Nahas Pasha and in Nuri es-Said are evidence of a certain unreality, or romanticism, in their approach to these matters. In simple terms of *realpolitik*, the situation would have been different if we had had the physical power. But we did not. If the only settlement of the problems of the Middle East which was acceptable to the Governments of Britain and France meant that the armed forces of these countries would have to reoccupy parts of Egypt, if there had followed longer periods of rule by Western puppets, then hatreds in the region would obviously have swollen; Russia would really have been 'let into Africa'; Israel's fate would have been even more unpredictable; and the British and French peoples would surely have had to face a prolonged time of sabotage of their oil supplies, thrusting them completely into the hands of the USA to maintain their economies at all. Other economic difficulties would perhaps have brought impoverishment.

Of course, the Suez expedition was popular at home among many people for a time; so was Alcibiades's expedition to Sicily, before it left Athens. Of course the French, having embarked upon a policy of repression in Algeria, had everything to gain from drawing Britain into their debilitating conflict. But it is impossible to believe that France could eventually have avoided conceding the independence of Algeria. For all these reasons the whole idea of a 'great expedition', to restore national pride as well as to internationalize the Canal, appears, again like that of Alcibiades, to have been doomed from the start.

Map II

THE BATTLEFIELD
October–November 1956

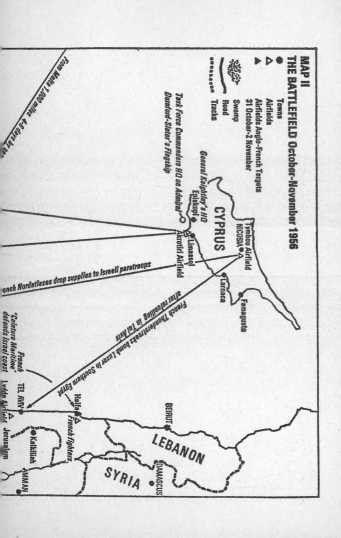

MAP II
THE BATTLEFIELD October–November 1956

● Towns
△ Airfields
▲ Airfields Anglo-French Targets
Airfields 31 October–2 November
Swamp
Road
Tracks

From Malta 1,000 miles 4–6 days by sea

French Nordatlases drop supplies to Israeli paratroops

Task Force Commanders HQ on Admiral
Durnford-Slater's Flagship

General Keightley's HQ
Episkopi ●
○ Akrotiri Airfield
● Limassol

CYPRUS

Tymbou Airfield
NICOSIA ●△

● Larnaca

● Famagusta

French Thunderstreaks bomb Luxor in Southern Egypt

French Thunderstreaks after refuelling in Tel Aviv

French Mystères after refuelling in Tel Aviv

'Ceinture Maritime' defends Israeli coast

Haifa ● △ French Fighters
TEL AVIV ● △
Lydda Airfield

BEIRUT ●

● Jerusalem

LEBANON

● Kalkiliah

● DAMASCUS

SYRIA

AMMAN ●

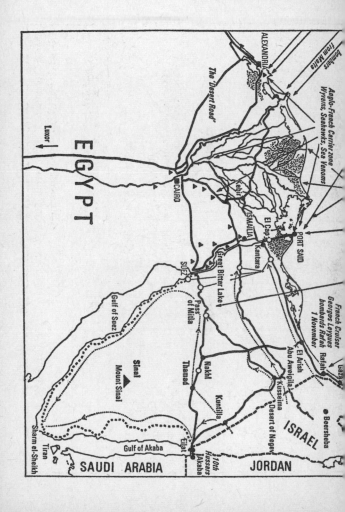

bombers (from Malta)

ALEXANDRIA

The 'Desert Road'

Luxor

E G Y P T

Anglo-French Carrier zone
Wyverns, Seahawks, Sea Venoms

CAIRO

Kabrit

ISMAILIA

El Cap.

Kantara

PORT SAID

SUEZ

Great Bitter Lake

French Cruiser
Georges Leygues
bombards Rafah
1 November

Gulf of Suez

Pass
of Mitla

El Arish

Abu Aweigila

Rafah

Gaza

Sinai
Mount Sinai

Thamad

Nakhl

Kusseima

Kuntilla

Desert of Negev

ISRAEL

Beersheba

Sharm el-Sheikh

Tiran

Gulf of Akaba

Eilat

Akaba

10th
Hussars

SAUDI ARABIA

JORDAN

APPENDIX 1

Aerial Units Involved in the Suez Operation

(Reproduced by kind permission of *Air Pictorial* from their issue of August 1965)

Royal Air Force

Squadron	Type of Aircraft	Usual Base	Date of Leaving	Base of Operations	Returned to UK
Bomber					
9	Canberra 6	Binbrook	Oct. 56	Luqa, Hal Far	Nov. 56
10	Canberra 2	Honington	26/10/56	Nicosia	9/11/56
12	Canberra 6	Binbrook	Sep. 56	Hal Far	1/12/56
15	Canberra 2	Honington	Oct. 56	Nicosia, Luqa	Jan. 57
18	Canberra 2	Upwood	Oct. 56	Nicosia	Dec. 56
27	Canberra 2	Waddington	Oct. 56	Nicosia	Dec. 56
35	Canberra 2	Upwood	Oct. 56	Nicosia	Nov. 56
44	Canberra 2	Honington	Oct. 56	Nicosia	Nov. 56
57	Canberra	Honington	Oct. 56	Nicosia	Nov. 56
	(Pilots only)				
61	Canberra 2	Honington	Oct. 56	Nicosia	Nov. 56
101	Canberra 2	Upwood	Oct. 56	Nicosia	Jan. 57
109	Canberra 6	Binbrook	Oct. 56	Luqa	Dec. 56
115	Canberra 6	Binbrook	Sep. 56	Luqa	Jan. 57
115	Canberra 2	Marham	Oct. 56	Nicosia	Nov. 56
138	Valiant	Wittering	Oct. 56	Luqa	Nov. 56

Royal Air Force – continued

		Aircraft	Base	Date	Base	Date
	139	Canberra 6	Binbrook	Oct. 56	Luqa	Nov. 56
	148	Valiant	Marham	Oct. 56	Luqa	Nov. 56
	207	Valiant	Marham	Oct. 56	Luqa	Nov. 56
	214	Valiant	Marham	Sep. 56	Luqa	Dec. 56
Fighter	1	Hunter 5	Tangmere	Oct. 56	Nicosia	Nov. 56
	6	Venom 4	Akrotiri	—	Akrotiri	—
	8	Venom 4	Akrotiri	—	Akrotiri	—
	32	Venom 4	Akrotiri	—	Akrotiri	—
	34	Hunter 5	Tangmere	Oct. 56	Akrotiri	Nov. 56
	39	Meteor 13	Luqa	Oct. 56	Akrotiri	Nov. 56
	249	Venom 4	Akrotiri	—	Akrotiri	—
P.R., etc.	13	Canberra 7	Akrotiri	—	Akrotiri	—
	37	Shackleton 2	Luqa	—	Luqa	—
	1903 Flt.	Auster 6	Nicosia	—	Akrotiri	—
Transport	30	Valetta 1	Dishforth	Oct. 56	Nicosia	Nov. 56
	70	Hastings 1	Nicosia	—	Nicosia	—
	84	Valetta 1	Nicosia	—	Nicosia	—
	99	Hastings 1/2	Lyneham	Oct. 56	Nicosia	—
	114	Valetta 1	Khormaksar	Oct. 56	Nicosia	Nov. 56
	216	Comet 2	Lyneham	Nov. 56	Nicosia	Nov. 56
	511	Hastings 1/2	Lyneham	Nov. 56	Nicosia	Nov. 56
	JEHU	Sycamore, Whirlwind	Middle Wallop	—	HMS Ocean	—

French Air Force

	Squadron	Type of Aircraft	Usual Base	Date of Leaving	Base of Operations	Date of Return
Fighter	1 Escadre	F-84F	St Dizier	23/10/56	Lydda	Dec. 56
	2 Escadre	Mystère IVA	Dijon	23/10/56	Haifa	Dec. 56
	3 Escadre	F-84F	Rheims	Oct. 56	Akrotiri	Nov. 56
P.R.	33 Escadre	RF-84F	Cognac	Oct. 56	Akrotiri	Nov. 56
Transport	61 Escadre	Nordatlas	Algeria	Oct. 56	Tymbou	Nov. 56
	63 Escadre	Nordatlas, Dakota	Orleans	Oct. 56	Tymbou	Nov. 56
	64 Escadre	Nordatlas		Oct. 56	Haifa	Nov. 56

Royal Navy

	Squadron	Type of Aircraft	Usual Base	Date of Leaving	Base of Operations	Date of Return
Strike	800	Sea Hawk 4	Eagle	—	Albion	—
	802	Sea Hawk 3	Ark Royal	—	Albion	—
	804	Sea Hawk 4	Ark Royal	—	Bulwark	—
	809	Sea Venom 22	Albion	—	Albion	—
	810	Sea Hawk 6	Albion	—	Albion	—
	830	Wyvern 4	Eagle	—	Eagle	—
	831	Wyvern 4	Eagle	—	Eagle	—

	Squadron	Aircraft				
	891	Sea Venom 21	Eagle	—	Eagle	—
	893	Sea Venom 21	Ark Royal	—	Eagle	—
	894	Sea Venom 21	Albion	—	Albion	—
	895	Sea Venom 21	Albion	—	Albion	—
	897	Sea Hawk 4	Bulwark	—	Bulwark	—
	899	Sea Hawk 4	Eagle	—	Eagle	—
P.R., etc.	'A' Flt. 849	Skyraider 1	Eagle	—	Eagle	—
	'B' Flt. 849	Skyraider 1	Albion	—	Albion	—
Transport	845	Whirlwind 22	Theseus	—	Theseus	—

French Navy

	Squadron	Aircraft				
Fighter	14F	Corsair	Arromanches	—	Arromanches	—
	15F	Corsair	Arromanches	—	Arromanches	—
Strike	9F	Avenger	Lafayette	—	Lafayette	—

APPENDIX 2

A Leader from The Times, 27 August 1956

Escapers' Club

THIS brief breathing space in the Canal crisis, between the end of the London conference and the outcome of the approach to the Egyptian dictator, is a good moment to consider some of the public reactions to it. They prompt reflections that carry us far beyond Suez. When the news of Nasser's seizure of the Canal burst upon the world there was an immediate response of indignation and a determination that it should not be successful. The Government were firm and made the issues clear. They were also admirably put by Mr Gaitskell in a balanced speech in the House of Commons (ever since, some of his colleagues have been using the balance to quote only those qualifying clauses which suit them). The seizure, said Mr Gaitskell, 'was done suddenly, without negotiation, without discussion, by force'; the episode, moreover, had to be recognized as part of the struggle for the mastery of the Middle East.

That is something which I do not feel that we can ignore. One may ask, 'Why does it involve the rest of the Middle East?' It is because of the prestige issues which are involved here. I said something about prestige when I spoke in the Middle East debate some months ago, and I must refer to it now, because prestige has quite considerable effects. If Colonel Nasser's prestige is put up sufficiently and ours is put down sufficiently, the effects of that in that part of the world will be that our friends desert us because they think we are lost, and go over to Egypt.

Mr Herbert Morrison was equally forthright. Colonel Nasser – 'this pocket dictator in Cairo' –

is not a person to be praised because he has asserted the rights of his country against this Canal, which is owned in a certain way. He is a person to be condemned because he has acted contrary to the law of nations, of international good faith.

Mr Morrison went on to express his worry at the way in which some people, having spent many years in denouncing jingoism and imperialism in respect of Britain, and having enjoyed its advantages,

are now spending their spare time in praising countries like Egypt, which are doing the very thing that Britain and other imperialist countries were doing a hundred years ago.

It is indeed strange, and stranger still is the way in which this catch – it is hardly enough to be called a chorus – has continued to be heard since then.

'What aggression did Nasser commit? Where did he use any force? Was he not perfectly within his rights? What is the illegality of what he has done? Are not Britain and the other Powers to blame for their past administration of the Canal? If we do anything shall we not inflame the whole of the Arab world and antagonize the east?' So it goes on, till one might almost believe it is Nasser who has been taken by surprise and is heroically resisting an act of western aggression. Moreover, all this is symptomatic of a certain stratum of political thinking. Nearly eighty years have gone by since Disraeli castigated those 'cosmopolitan critics, men who are the friends of every country save their own'. They are still with us, and unfortunately they appeal to a certain masochistic strain in our present national conscience. To these people any trouble-maker anywhere is bound automatically to have right on his side. We are asked to sanctify a Makarios; to believe that British soldiers and administrators trying to preserve law and order in any turbulent area are instinctively cruel and oppressive. Democracy undoubtedly demands vigilance. It must be sure that the men who are acting for it do not degrade its good name. Any irregularities by them must be denounced and punished. But it does not demand that *prima facie* they shall be believed always to be in the wrong. We may be a good people grown careless; we are not a bad people grown hardened. The truth is that it is easier to blame ourselves than anyone else. After all, there is no direct come-back in that case. It is the same mood that urges for the sake of peace and quiet we should be prepared to pour more and more millions into the maw of Mr Mintoff.

Another strange thing is the way these people define 'colonialism'. It is all a matter of water. Let Russia or China or any other Power overrun, capture, dictate to, or even destroy any of its neighbouring countries and apparently all is well. The most elementary freedoms can be exterminated, the most outrageous excesses committed. There is silence. But let Britain seek to keep law and order in some territory she is bringing along to self-government, let her say it is in the interests of the people of that territory that they should walk before they run, and at once the cry of colonialism goes up. It is true we were once a great imperial Power; it is also true that few Powers in history have exercised their tutelage with a greater degree of beneficence and restraint. The day for great empires may have gone, unless they are Communist ones. But Britain's was a deliberate act of liquidation, and there is something ludicrous in the spectacle of some back-bench Labour M P arraigning Mr Lennox-Boyd as if he were Burke indicting Warren Hastings.

All this is part of a deplorable flight from responsibility which has sapped so much of the effectiveness both of our national life and our international position. Other nations do not realize it is easiest for us to blame ourselves, and that while we are generally masters of understatement this does not apply where our conscience is concerned. They take these self-accusations at their face value. There is a similar flight from responsibility in the constant parrot cries that everything difficult or unpleasant be referred to the United Nations. Of course, Britain believes in the United Nations. She wants to make it strong. It does no good to force it into a position where it will merely be ineffective. And so far as Suez is concerned it will presumably have first to get Nasser to obey its five-year-old resolution about Israeli shipping before it can have any confidence in going on to one about the canal as a whole. Then there are the advocates of 'playing the crisis slowly'. They refer to Abadan. If the crisis can be *successfully* settled in that way, well and good. But Suez is not Abadan. It will be a long haul in more ways than one. And workers who have not so far understood the need to make any temporary sacrifice in their living standards to save the economy are hardly likely to be persuaded to suffer any long privation to prevent another dictator controlling a faraway strip of water about which they know little.

The last strand of irresponsibility is that which is beginning to ask whether we will, in fact, suffer in any way, whatever happens. Does the canal really matter? Cannot we believe either that this act of Nasser's portends nothing serious, or that if it does we can sidestep all the consequences? It is part of the same thinking which produced the debilitating slogan 'Don't worry, it may never happen'. But it has happened and, as Mr Gaitskell saw, yet more will happen. Already the first tremors have been felt in Morocco. There is the blow to confidence at a moment when the underdeveloped countries are crying out for investment, and half-threatening to bring us down in their ruin if they do not get it. There is the fact that Russia is now a Middle Eastern Power.

It may seem to be taking these various surface waves of criticism too seriously to deal with them thus. Public opinion, despite what the dissidents angrily say, is remarkably firm. Of course, it wants to avoid the use of force. So does everyone and we hope no one does so more than the British Government. But that is a far cry from saying that because there seems little we can do about it the best thing is to find excuses for, and forget the whole business. Nations live by the vigorous defence of their interests. Even Mr Nehru, who so conscientiously sermonizes the rest of the world, does not let a trick go in Kashmir. As G. M. Trevelyan reminded us many years ago, the sun of Venice set because of the double event of the Turkish blocking of the caravan routes and the discovery of the Cape route and America. A pleasure-loving people more interested in their revels than in their responsibilities did the rest.

During the eighteenth century the material decline of Venice was complete, accompanied by a degeneracy in public spirit that made her a by-word even in the Europe of the *ancien régime*. Atrophy was not, however, followed by dissolution. The corpse lived on.

Doubtless it is good to have a flourishing tourist trade, to win Test matches, and to be regaled by photographs of Miss Diana Dors being pushed into a swimming pool. But nations do not live by circuses alone. The people, in their silent way, know this better than the critics. They still want Britain great.

APPENDIX 3

Speech by Mr Hugh Gaitskell, 2 August 1956, in the House of Commons

MR HUGH GAITSKELL (Leeds, South): While the House will, of course, be a little disappointed that the Prime Minister was unable to tell us about the outcome of the talks now taking place, I am sure that we all appreciate and accept the reasons why he could not do so. I think, too, that we are all grateful to him for the statement he has made about the attitude of Her Majesty's Government to Colonel Nasser's action.

For a long time, the Opposition has been critical of the Government's policy in the Middle East. We carried those criticisms so far as to divide the House on the Adjournment on 7 March, and I must say, at the start, that we do not feel that in the months that have elapsed since then there has been any great improvement in the Government's policy. We have criticized from time to time the attitude of the Government on the question of the balance of arms in the Middle East, and I think that many of us feel that in the matter of the Aswan Dam the vacillations that have taken place are certainly a subject for criticism.

But I do not propose today to develop these criticisms of the Government. Maybe, in the future, in a calmer situation, a further examination, a post-mortem, should take place, but I am sure that today what the country wants to hear about is the implication of Colonel Nasser's action and what should be done about it. Moreover, while I have not hesitated to express my disagreement with the Government in their policy in the past, I must make it abundantly plain that anything that they have done or not done in no way excuses Colonel Nasser's action in seizing the Canal.

I think that it is worth spending a moment or two on the

question of why we do take such strong exception to this action. I know that some hon. Members may say, 'It is quite simple; it is an arbitrary act, a sudden act, something that involves various dangers for us,' but we have to recognize that the Egyptians are putting their point of view and that this point of view is being listened to elsewhere in the world. It is extremely important that the exact reasons why we resent and object to this action should be made clear at the start.

The Egyptian argument is perfectly clear. It is that this is an Egyptian company and that as the Government of Egypt they are perfectly entitled to nationalize any company they wish to nationalize, provided that they pay compensation; as regards the right of transit through the Canal they have given assurances that they regard it as necessary to observe the 1888 Convention. I should like to give my answers, as I see it, to that case put forward by the Egyptian Government.

First, so far as my hon. and right hon. Friends are concerned at any rate, we certainly do not say that the act of nationalization in itself is wrong. Nor would we say that the act of nationalizing a foreign-owned company was necessarily wrong, provided that the compensation was reasonable and fair. I must say, in passing, that I think we can have reasonable doubts about whether, in fact, the Egyptian Government, in this instance, will be in a position to pay compensation. I think that some objection might be taken to the termination of the concession prematurely. I do not know whether or not this is illegal – I am not a lawyer, and I offer no opinion – but I certainly would not even stress that as the main point to which we object, provided again that proper compensation is paid.

The real objections, it seems to me, are three. In the first place, as the Prime Minister has rightly emphasized, this is not an ordinary Company, conducting ordinary activities. It is a Company controlling an international waterway of immense importance to the whole of the rest of the world. It is, therefore, bound to be a matter of international concern when it changes hands. Hitherto, it has been under the control and ownership very largely of the States using it, of the maritime

Powers, and it is quite true, as the Prime Minister has said, also, that while I think that the interests of Egypt have been considered and taken into account, and, as Colonel Nasser has recently said, relations between the Company and the Egyptian Government have been amicable, nevertheless the Company has certainly taken care of the interests of the user countries.

Now the ownership and control of the Company is to be transferred to a single Power, to the hands of one State controlling it and, therefore, in a position even more than before to decide how the Canal shall be run. It may be said there is no need for anxiety because we have had these assurances about the 1888 Convention. I am bound to say that it seems to me the strongest reason for having doubts in our minds as to whether we can accept these assurances has been the behaviour of the Egyptian Government in stopping Israeli ships from going through, and equally important – indeed, even more important – the clear defiance of the Resolution of the United Nations condemning this action, passed in September 1951.

The second reason why I think we must take strong exception to this is that any confidence we might have had in an action of this kind was profoundly shaken by the manner in which it was carried out. It was done suddenly, without negotiation, without discussion, by force, and it was done on the excuse that this was the way to finance the Aswan Dam project. Colonel Nasser himself, at the conclusion of his speech a week ago, said :

Thus, you will see that our wealth has been restored to us and that we shall not look forward to the Anglo-American financial aid amounting to 75 million dollars because we shall henceforth get from the profits of the Suez Canal the sum of 100 million dollars every year and in five years we shall secure 500 million dollars.

That, in effect, means that he is proposing to take the whole of the gross revenues of the Canal – almost all of them transit dues – and divert them for the purpose of the Aswan Dam. Yet ho has promised compensation. How can he at one and the same time both keep the Canal going, spend the necessary money on the repairs, extensions and reconstruction, pay the compensation or service the compensation loan to the shareholders, and also find money for the Aswan Dam?

Like the Prime Minister, I have tried to work out the finances of this, and I would only say that so far as I can see, looking at the figures, the most that Colonel Nasser could do, and even then at the expense of diverting reserves which ought to be used for the Canal, might amount to about £5 million a year – at any rate, quite inadequate and absurd in relation to the cost of the Dam. But there is, of course, one way out for Colonel Nasser, and that is that he can put the charges up. He can increase the transit dues. So the whole implication of his speech is precisely that, that he intends to make the users pay more than they have been paying before.

I do not think one can deny that this action is, first, to some extent a threat to access to the Canal in the light of what the Egyptians have done about the Israeli ships; secondly, a warning that he may not maintain the Canal adequately; and, thirdly, a very definite implication that higher charges will be levied. As the Prime Minister has said, this is serious not only for us but for every maritime nation in the world; East and West, all are involved.

My third reason for thinking that we must object to this is that we cannot ignore – and this is a matter that the Prime Minister did not touch upon, no doubt for good reasons – the political background and the repercussions of the whole of this episode in the Middle East. We cannot forget that Colonel Nasser has repeatedly boasted of his intention to create an Arab empire from the Atlantic to the Persian Gulf. The French Prime Minister, M. Mollet, the other day quoted a speech of Colonel Nasser's and rightly said that it could remind us only of one thing – of the speeches of Hitler before the war.

Colonel Nasser has certainly made a number of inflammatory speeches against us and his Government have continually attempted subversion in Jordan and other Arab States; he has persistently threatened the State of Israel and made it plain from time to time that it is his purpose and intention to destroy Israel if he possibly can. That, if ever there was one, is a clear enough notice of aggression to come.

The fact is that this episode must be recognized as part of the struggle for the mastery of the Middle East. That is something which I do not feel that we can ignore. One may ask, 'Why does it involve the rest of the Middle East?' It is because of the prestige issues which are involved here. I said something about prestige when I spoke in the Middle East debate some months ago, and I must refer to it now, because prestige has quite considerable effects. If Colonel Nasser's prestige is put up sufficiently and ours is put down sufficiently, the effects of that in that part of the world will be that our friends desert us because they think we are lost, and go over to Egypt.

I have no doubt myself that the reason why Colonel Nasser acted in the way that he did, aggressively, brusquely, suddenly, was precisely because he wanted to raise his prestige in the rest of the Middle East. He wanted to show the rest of the Arab world – 'See what I can do'. He wanted to challenge the West and to win. He wanted to assert his strength. He wanted to make a big impression. Quiet negotiation, discussion around a table about nationalizing the Company would not produce this effect.

It is all very familiar. It is exactly the same as that we encountered from Mussolini and Hitler in those years before the war. We must not underestimate the danger of the effect which this may have on the other Arab States. Indeed, I would venture to say that this is probably the most important immediate effect that it may have, and I am thinking particularly of Iraq, whose King is, I think, still a visitor in this country, and which is, of course, an ally of this country. I am thinking of Jordan and Saudi Arabia.

It has been said in many quarters that this may lead other Arab States to nationalize the oil concerns. I personally do not regard that as the major danger. As far as we are concerned, we are getting our oil chiefly from Persia and Kuwait. I do not think that there is much danger of action in Persia, and, as for Kuwait, it seems to me that, equally, an arbitrary act by the Sheikh is not a thing that we have seriously to worry about.

The danger is much more of a political kind. The danger is that a Government which is friendly to us in Iraq, and can be relied on to a very large extent to exercise restraint in the Middle East, may well be replaced by a Government of a very different complexion. I also think that in the long run this action must involve a greatly increased threat to Israel; and I must again remind hon. Members that we are pledged under the Tripartite Declaration to go to the assistance of whichever State is attacked – Israel or her Arab neighbours.

It seems to me, summing up the position, that this is really where we stand. Colonel Nasser wanted to get a loan for the Aswan Dam. Many of us have sympathy – indeed, I would go much further: I think that all of us would wish to see economic development in Egypt and energetic steps taken to raise the appallingly low standard of living in that part of the world. For what it is worth, we are told – and I am bound to say that I think there is force in this – that Colonel Nasser has pledged the cotton exports of his country to pay for arms, that because he has done that he is in great financial difficulties, and, without going into the merits of the handling of the question, the loan for the Dam was rejected and turned down on those grounds.

I do not think I can have much sympathy with a man who, however much one may want to help his country, as we do, spends far more than he can afford on arms which, admittedly, are for aggressive war, and then, when he is told that because of the economic situation he cannot have a loan, says to the rest of the world, 'I am seizing the Canal and I am going to make you pay for the Dam in that way'. I am satisfied, for these reasons, that if the Western democracies and, indeed, other countries in the world, had simply accepted this and done nothing about it, highly dangerous consequences would have followed.

I turn now to consider what kind of action should be taken. I emphasize again what I have said in other speeches, namely, that this is not our affair alone. It would be ridiculous to treat ourselves as though we were the only Power involved. It is essentially a matter for all the maritime Powers of the world, and we must act in concert with other nations. I warmly welcomed at the time the action of the Government in inviting the French and American Governments to discuss the matter.

I mention, in passing, that the United States herself depends for about fifteen per cent of her imports of oil upon the Suez Canal. All Europe is involved in this, involved in the Middle East as a whole, and involved in the Canal. India and South-East Asia are equally heavily concerned.

There has been much talk in the press about a conference, and I myself hope that that is what these talks are going to produce. The first step is to call a conference of the nations principally concerned. The signatories of the 1888 Convention form one possible group of nations concerned. The list does, in some respects, seem to be a little out of date, including, for instance, Austria-Hungary; but, as a basis, it is a good start. I would say, at any rate, in the light of comment in the newspapers, that in my opinion it would be the most foolish step not to invite Soviet Russia to take part in this conference.

After the Prime Minister's talks with the Russian leaders and his obvious attempts to improve relations with them, I should be surprised indeed if he were to be party to a decision to exclude them from such an important conference. I would remind the right hon. Gentleman that Russia herself, in 1946, declared that in her opinion the Suez Canal necessitated an international control with the participation of the Powers most concerned. That is, I think, a statement of which the Russians might perhaps be reminded.

I should like any control commission which may be set up as a result of this conference to be a United Nations agency. I am myself sure that, from the point of view of world peace and development, it is far better that it should be done under the United Nations than in some independent way. The first thing is to get the conference and prepare a plan for international control. I would say, too, in case there is any doubt about the matter, that it would, of course, be obvious common sense to invite Egypt to this conference as an ultimate signatory of the 1888 Convention.

There remains the question of what other steps can be taken. In the circumstances, and until we have, as I hope we shall have, a settlement, the economic measures taken by the Government are fully justified. I would just add one other point about them. The Prime Minister has told us – and it has been confirmed today – that all shipments of arms or war material from this country to Egypt have been suspended. But there is, of course, the possibility that arms may be going from this country to other States unfriendly to us in that part of the world. Indeed, I am told that at this moment a ship is being loaded at Liverpool with arms for the Lebanon. I would ask the Prime Minister to consider seriously whether Syria and the Lebanon, at any rate, had better be covered by the same arms embargo.

Another step which I think should be taken, and ought seriously to be considered, is to investigate what routes alternative to the Canal may be available. Here, I make a specific suggestion to the right hon. Gentleman. There has been talk of constructing a canal from the Gulf of Akaba to Haifa. The objection has been put – I think a fairly strong objection – that this will take a very long time and involve very heavy capital expenditure. But there is something else which could be done along that line. It would be possible, I believe, to lay a pipe-line from Akaba to Haifa, the distance being about 250 miles, and I am told that this would take a matter of months, not years, to complete.

I should have thought that that might have been well worth considering and might be a very helpful move in all sorts of ways at the present time. The Government should, I think, also consider seriously giving assistance to ship owners to encourage them to build larger tankers which can go round the Cape. Further, though I do not want to make a great deal of this, and I am well aware of the difficulties, I do feel that the Government must once again give serious consideration to the question of arms for Israel.

Last of all, I come to a matter which cannot be ignored at this moment just before the Recess. There has been much talk in the press about the use of force in these circumstances. First, I would say that we need to be very careful what we say on this subject. It is unwise to discuss hypothetical situations in present conditions. Obviously, there are circumstances in which we might be compelled to use force, in self-defence or as part of some collective defence measures. I do not myself object to the precautionary steps announced by the Prime Minister today; I think that any Government would have to do that, as we had to do it during the Persian crisis.

I must, however, remind the House that we are members of the United Nations, that we are signatories to the United Nations Charter, and that for many years in British policy we have steadfastly avoided any international action which would be in breach of international law or, indeed, contrary to the public opinion of the world. We must not, therefore, allow ourselves to get into a position where we might be denounced in the Security Council as aggressors, or where the majority of the Assembly were against us.

If Colonel Nasser has done things which are wrong in the legal sense, then, of course, the right step is to take him to the International Court. Force is justified in certain events. Indeed, if there were anything which he had done which would justify force at the moment, it is, quite frankly, the one thing on which we have never used force, namely, the stopping of the Israeli ships. We have not done that; and it would, I think, be difficult to find – I must say this – in anything else he has done any legal justification for the use of force. What he may do in the future is another matter.

I come, therefore, to this conclusion. I believe that we were right to react sharply to this move. If nothing at all were done, it would have very serious consequences for all of us, especially for the Western Powers. It is important that what we do should be done in the fullest possible co-operation with the other nations affected. We should try to settle this matter peacefully on the lines of an international commission, as has been hinted. While force cannot be excluded, we must be sure that the circumstances justify it and that it is, if used, consistent with our belief in, and our pledges to, the Charter of the United Nations and not in conflict with them.

APPENDIX 4

*Exchange of Letters between Marshal Bulganin
and Sir Anthony Eden*

Bulganin's Letter to Sir Anthony Eden of 11 September 1956

MR PRIME MINISTER,

I would like to draw your attention to the gravity of the situation which has developed in connexion with the Suez Canal question and, in view of this, to express some considerations as to how my colleagues and I assess this situation.

First of all we must not forget the existence of the United Nations, created by the joint efforts of Britain, the United States and the Soviet Union, the founders of this organization, which were also joined by France. The United Nations was set up to prevent another war, to ensure a peaceful life to the peoples. Its direct duty is to examine conflicts and frictions which might arise in relations between states, in order to prevent such a development of events as could bring about a breach of the peace. It has also the task of developing peaceful co-operation between states and strengthening friendly relations between them.

The United Nations Charter directly forbids the employment of force against any state except in cases of self-defence, when a state is subjected to armed attack or the threat of force, and obliges its member-countries to seek for peaceful ways of settling disputes or situations which might arise between states.

The Charter, naturally, also provides for the possibility of using force, sanctions, in extreme cases when it is necessary to rebuff an aggressor and ensure the maintenance or restoration of peace. But the question of employing force is decided not at the discretion of one country or another, or of a group of countries, guided by their narrow interests, but in conformity with a decision of the Security Council, which has the respective powers.

I thought it necessary, Mr Prime Minister, to draw your attention to this because in connexion with the Suez Canal question attempts are being made to ignore the United Nations and the principles solemnly endorsed, among other member-states of the United Nations, by Great Britain as well.

Indeed, what is happening today? Britain is demonstratively concentrating her troops in Cyprus, in the neighbourhood of the Suez Canal area. French military formations, too, have been landed on Cyprus. Other military measures have also been taken, aggravating the tension. All this is accompanied by public official declarations of the readiness of Britain and France, on the pretext of defending their interests, to land their forces on Egyptian territory and infringe Egypt's territorial integrity and inviolability. Statements are made about readiness to begin hostilities against Egypt if she refuses to place the Canal under foreign administration.

Can all these actions by Britain and France be regarded as compatible with their participation in the United Nations? It is clear that they cannot.

The British and French Governments evidently intend to seize the Suez Canal, which passes across the territory of Egypt and is under Egyptian sovereignty. But, Mr Prime Minister, I beg you to consider what this could end in. There can hardly be any doubt that such an action would lead to tremendous destruction on the Canal itself. No less destruction would be caused to oilfields located in the countries of the Arab East and to pipelines passing through the territory of these countries.

In that case all the Arab people would rise for a sacred struggle against foreign invasion. This would mean that the material losses, particularly for Britain and France, and for the whole of Europe as well, would assume tremendous proportions. Needless to say, the delivery of oil to the European countries from the Near and Middle East area would be completely disrupted. One can imagine what losses Britain, as an island power, would sustain in such a situation as a result of aggressive actions against Egypt.

The truth must be faced squarely, Mr Prime Minister. In the event of foreign invasion into Egypt, such actions, besides having the aforementioned material consequences, would undoubtedly arouse the deep hatred of the African and Asian peoples for the countries which took the path of aggression. It would hardly be an exaggeration if I say that this hatred would make itself felt throughout the lifetime of many generations.

My colleagues and I, Mr Prime Minister, are convinced that now, when the United Nations exists, when there is a great upsurge of the Eastern peoples who have embarked on the road of independent development and national regeneration, in the age of atomic weapons, one must not threaten to use arms or brandish arms. In our times it is no longer possible to act as during the age of colonial oppression, when the colonial system was imposed on the Asian and African peoples by blood and iron.

Since the times have changed and the Asian and African peoples have become different, any military measures directed against the sovereignty and territorial integrity of Egypt, in the given case, can end only in failure.

Is it not clear, Mr Prime Minister, that France – which lost the war in Viet Nam, where it tried to preserve the colonial system, and is now waging a similar war in Algeria – is trying to involve Britain in dangerous military plans around the Suez Canal, counting on remedying her affairs in Algeria with the help of Britain. If the situation is soberly assessed, it must be admitted to be a gamble. Neither Egypt nor Algeria can be subjugated. Attempts to do so are inevitably doomed to failure. Is this not demonstrated by the experience of France, which shows that, notwithstanding the army of close on half a million men in Algeria, the situation there continues to grow more tense.

Nor can the fact be ignored that although the United States expresses itself in favour of a peaceful settlement of the question, it does not protest against the concentration of troops and the threat of using them, which clearly encourages in Britain and France the proponents of employing force against Egypt.

I think you will agree with me that today, just as in the past, small wars can turn into big wars, with all the grave consequences for states and peoples following therefrom.

All these are such serious questions, Mr Prime Minister, that we want to put them before you frankly and without any diplomatic evasions.

It is said sometimes that the Russians are inciting Egypt. But such statements are utterly groundless and do not merit serious attention. The absurdity of such statements is seen if only from the fact that we learned about Egypt's nationalization of the Suez Canal from radio reports and the press. Moreover, is it not clear from what USSR Foreign Minister D. T. Shepilov said in London about the Soviet Government's stand on the Suez Canal question, from what was said in the Soviet Government's statement of 9 August, this year, and from my present message to you, that far from inciting anyone, we are striving to promote a peaceful settlement of this question, taking into account all the interested states and naturally with full respect for the sovereignty of Egypt? We speak about this to the Egyptians as well.

How can the Soviet Union support an unjust cause, measures of pressure and threats against Egypt? How can the Soviet Union fail to regard Egypt's position favourably if she is defending her sovereignty, her national territory and her inalienable right to that territory – which, by the way, no one disputes. The fact is that it is not Egypt that is concentrating forces and threatening anyone with hostilities, but it is Britain and France which are concentrating forces and threatening Egypt with the employment of armed forces against her. Under such circumstances, how can one fail to be on the side of Egypt, if one is guided by the noble principles of the United Nations? We are proceeding from the principles of the United Nations, we have been and are consistent enemies of colonialism.

This does not in the least mean that we underrate the interests of Britain and France as maritime powers. We fully understand your interests and have stated this more than once. But we proceed from the indisputable premise that recognition of these interests must not prejudice the sovereignty of the Egyptian state.

Furthermore, we are ready to co-operate in ensuring freedom of navigation in the Suez Canal, which is fully feasible in view of Egypt's similar striving. But this can be attained through agreement between the states concerned and by no means through military measures or threats against Egypt.

It is evident that both in Britain and France there are certain circles which are instigating hostilities against Egypt. They are instigating one-sided actions by Britain and France, the imposition on Egypt of a settlement of the Suez Canal question by force of arms. But we would not want to believe that these circles could gain the upper hand, taking into account the dangerous path on to which they are impelling their own countries.

I must tell you, Mr Prime Minister, that the Soviet Union, as a great power interested in the maintenance of peace, cannot hold aloof from this question.

I have thought it necessary to present these considerations with the utmost frankness, taking advantage of the fact that my colleagues and I have established good personal contacts with you, which we value highly. We want to warn you in a friendly way of the dangerous development of events which might follow if the necessary prudence is not displayed. We believe that your experience and the experience of your colleagues will be used, just as it has been more than once in the past, to achieve by joint efforts a just and peaceful settlement of the Suez question.

With respect,
N. BULGANIN

Sochi, 11 September 1956

APPENDIX 5

*Exchange of Notes between the Secretary-General of the
United Nations and the Egyptian Minister of Foreign
Affairs concerning the Suez Canal, 24 October and
2 November 1956*

24 October 1956

DEAR DR FAWZI,

You will remember that at the end of the private talks on
Suez, trying to sum up what I understood as being the sense of
the discussion, I covered not only the 'requirements', later
approved by the Security Council, but also in a summary form
arrangements that had been discussed as possible means of
meeting those requirements. However, time then proved in-
sufficient for a satisfactory exploration of those arrangements.

Before you left New York I raised with you the question of
time and place for a resumption of the exploratory talks, in
case the three Governments directly concerned would find that
such further talks should be tried. As a follow up to these
observations to which, so far, I have had no reactions either
from you or from Mr Selwyn Lloyd or M. Pineau, I would
for my own sake, wish to put on paper how I envisage the
situation that would have to be studied at resumed exploratory
talks, if they were to come about.

Again, what I do is not to put out any proposals on my own,
nor try to formulate proposals made by you or any of the
others. Just as I did at the end of the private talks in New
York, I just wish, in my own words, to try and spell out what
are my conclusions from the – entirely noncommittal – observations made in the course of the private talks, interpolating
on some points in the light of my interpretation of the sense
of the talks where they did not fully cover the ground. Whether
you approve of my phrasing or not, I feel that it would be

valuable to know if, in your view, I have correctly interpreted the conclusions from the tentative thinking which would provide the background for further explorations.

1. From the discussions I understood that the legal reaffirmation of all the obligations under the Constantinople Convention should not present any difficulty; this is a question of form, not of substance. I further understood that it would not present any difficulties to widen the obligations under the Convention to cover the questions of maximum of tolls (as at present); maintenance and development; reporting to the United Nations.

2. Nor should, if I understood the sense of the discussions correctly, the questions of the Canal Code and the regulations present any difficulties of substance, as I understood the situation to be that no revision of the Code or the regulations was envisaged which would lead to rules less adequate than the present Rules. I further understood that revisions would be subject to consultation.

3. Nor, in my understanding, should the question of tolls and charges present any difficulties, as, according to what emerged in the discussions, the manner of fixing tolls and charges would be subject to agreement, and as also the reservation of a certain part of the dues for development purposes would be subject to agreement.

4. Nor, in my understanding, should the principle of organized co-operation between an Egyptian Authority and the users give rise to any differences of views, while, on the other hand, it obviously represents a field where the arrangements to be made call for careful exploration in order to make sure that they would meet the three first requirements approved by the Security Council. The following points in the summing up of my understanding of the sense of the discussions refer to this question of implementation of an organized co-operation:

A. The co-operation requires obviously an organ on the Egyptian side (the authority in charge of the operation of the Canal), and a representation of the Users, recognized by the Canal Authority (and the Egyptian Government) and entitled to speak for the Users.

B. Provisions should be made for joint meetings between the

Authority and the representation to all the extent necessary to effect the agreed co-operation.

C. Within the framework of the co-operation, the representation should be entitled to raise all matters affecting the Users' rights or interests, for discussion and consultation or by way of complaint. The representation should, on the other hand, of course not, in exercising its functions, do this in such a way as to interfere with the administrative functions of the operating organ.

D. The co-operation which would develop on the basis of points A–C would not give satisfaction to the three first requirements approved by the Security Council unless completed with arrangements for fact-finding, reconciliation, recourse to appropriate juridical settlement of possible disputes and guarantees for execution of the results of reconciliation or juridical settlements of disputes.

E. (*a*) Fact-finding can be provided for by direct access for the Party concerned to a checking of relevant facts, or by a Standing (Joint) Organ, with appropriate representation for both Parties;

(*b*) A Standing (Joint) Organ might also be considered for reconciliation;

(*c*) In case of unresolved differences, as to facts or other relevant questions, not resolved by the arrangements so far mentioned, recourse should be possible – as the case may be – to a Standing Local Organ for arbitration, set up in accordance with common practices, or to whatever other arbitration organ found necessary in the light of a further study of the character of the conflicts that may arise, or to the International Court of Justice (whose jurisdiction in this case of course should be mandatory), or to the Security Council (or whatever other Organ of the United Nations that may be established under the rules of the Charter);

(*d*) Concerning the implementation of findings by a United Nations Organ, normal rules should apply. In respect of the implementation of awards made by a Standing Organ for Arbitration, or by whatever other organ may be established for similar purposes, the parties should undertake to recognize the awards as binding, when rendered, and undertake to carry them out in good faith. In case of a complaint because of alleged non-compliance with an award, the same arbitration organ which gave the award should register the fact of non-compliance. Such a 'constatation' would give the complaining party access to all normal forms of redress, but also the right to certain steps in self-protection, the possible scope of which would be subject to an agreement in principle; both sides, thus, in a case of a 'constatation' should be entitled to certain limited 'police action', even without recourse to further juridical procedures.

5. It was, finally, my understanding that the question covered by the requirement in Point 6 of the Security Council Resolution would not give rise to special difficulties, as the subject seems fairly well covered by the formulation of the principles itself.

Whether or not a set of arrangements will meet the first three requirements approved by the Security Council, will, according to my understanding of the situation, depend on the reply to the questions under Point 4 above. That is true not only with an arrangement starting from the assumption of operation of the Canal by an Egyptian Authority, but also on the assumption that the operation of the Canal (in the narrow sense of the word) is organized in another way. If I have rightly interpreted the sense of the discussions as concerns specifically the questions of verification, recourse and enforcement (Point 4, (e)), and if, thus, no objection in principle is made *a priori* against arrangements as set down above, I would, from a legal and technical point of view – without raising here the political considerations which come into play – consider the framework sufficiently wide to make a further exploration of a possible basis for negotiations along the lines indicated worth trying.

I am sure you appreciate that whatever clarification you may give of your reaction to this interpretation of mine of the possibilities, would be helpful for me in contacts with other parties – of the reactions of which I likewise need a more complete picture – and might smooth the way to progress beyond the point reached in the private talks.

(Signed) Yours sincerely,
DAG HAMMARSKJÖLD

Egyptian Mission to the United Nations
New York, 2 November 1956

EXCELLENCY,

I have the honour to transmit to you the following communication which I have just received from Dr Mahmoud Fawzi:

'Dear Mr Hammarskjöld,

'I have the honour to refer to your letter of 25 October 1956. You will recall that on 29 October, I informed you through the Permanent Representative of Egypt, Ambassador Omar Loutfi, that it was under careful consideration and that I shall convey to you the result as soon as possible.

'I am doing this; and am pleased to be able to tell you that, with the exception of the latter part of "*d*" of subparagraph "E" of Paragraph 4, we share with you the view that the framework you have outlined in your letter is sufficiently wide to make a further exploration for a possible basis for negotiation along the lines indicated in it worth trying. Mahmoud Fawzi.'

Please accept, Your Excellency, the assurances of my highest consideration,

(Signed) OMAR LOUTFI
Permanent Representative of
Egypt to the United Nations

H.E. Mr Dag Hammarskjöld
Secretary-General of the United Nations

APPENDIX 6

Statement by Sir Anthony Eden, 30 October 1956,
in the House of Commons

WITH your permission, Mr Speaker, and that of the House, I will make a statement.

As the House will know, for some time past the tension on the frontiers of Israel has been increasing. The growing military strength of Egypt has given rise to renewed apprehension, which the statements and action of the Egyptian Government have further aggravated. The establishment of a Joint Military Command between Egypt, Jordan and Syria, the renewed raids by guerrillas, culminating in the incursion of Egyptian commandos on Sunday night, had all produced a very dangerous situation.

Five days ago news was received that the Israel Government were taking certain measures of mobilization. Her Majesty's Government at once instructed Her Majesty's Ambassador at Tel Aviv to make inquiries of the Israel Minister for Foreign Affairs and to urge restraint.

Meanwhile, President Eisenhower called for an immediate tripartite discussion between representatives of the United Kingdom, France and the United States. A meeting was held on 28 October, in Washington, and a second meeting took place on 29 October.

While these discussions were proceeding, news was received last night that Israel forces had crossed the frontier and had penetrated deep into Egyptian territory. Later, further reports were received indicating that paratroops had been dropped. It appears that the Israel spearhead was not far from the banks of the Suez Canal. From recent reports it also appeared that air forces are in action in the neighbourhood of the Canal.

During the last few weeks Her Majesty's Government have thought it their duty, having regard to the obligations under the Anglo-Jordan Treaty, to give assurances, both public and private, of their intention to honour these obligations. Her Majesty's Ambassador in Tel Aviv late last night received an assurance that Israel would not attack Jordan.

My right hon. and learned Friend the Foreign Secretary discussed the situation with the United States Ambassador early this morning. The French Prime Minister and Foreign Minister have come over to London at short notice at the invitation of Her Majesty's Government to deliberate with us on these events.

I must tell the House that very grave issues are at stake, and that unless hostilities can quickly be stopped free passage through the Canal will be jeopardized. Moreover, any fighting on the banks of the Canal would endanger the ships actually on passage. The number of crews and passengers involved totals many hundreds, and the value of the ships which are likely to be on passage is about £50 million, excluding the value of the cargoes.

Her Majesty's Government and the French Government have accordingly agreed that everything possible should be done to bring hostilities to an end as soon as possible. Their representatives in New York have, therefore, been instructed to join the United States representative in seeking an immediate meeting of the Security Council. This began at 4 p.m.

In the meantime, as a result of the consultations held in London today, the United Kingdom and French Governments have now addressed urgent communications to the Governments of Egypt and Israel. In these we have called upon both sides to stop all warlike action by land, sea and air forthwith and to withdraw their military forces to a distance of 10 miles from the Canal. Further, in order to separate the belligerents and to guarantee freedom of transit through the Canal by the ships of all nations, we have asked the Egyptian Government to agree that Anglo-French forces should move temporarily – I repeat, temporarily – into key positions at Port Said, Ismailia and Suez.

The Governments of Egypt and Israel have been asked to answer this communication within twelve hours. It has been made clear to them that, if at the expiration of that time one or both have not undertaken to comply with these requirements, British and French forces will intervene in whatever strength may be necessary to secure compliance.

I will continue to keep the House informed of the situation.

APPENDIX 7

*Two Statements by Sir Anthony Eden, 20 December
1956, in the House of Commons*

I

I SHOULD like to speak at once on this matter.

First of all, regarding the last observation of the right hon.
Gentleman about whether I agreed with what M. Mollet has
said about the United States, naturally, I suppose, the House
has not entirely in its mind what I myself said at the beginning
of the whole of this business, on this very subject, on 31
October. I am sorry to have to quote myself, but I did say
this which, as I think the House will see, is not, shall we say,
irrelevant to what M. Mollet said the other day. I was referring
to the United States economy not being dependent upon the
Canal. I said that was true and that their position was different
from ours. I went on to say :

If anyone says that on that account we should have held up action
until agreement could be reached with the United States as to what
to do, I can only say that this would have been to ignore what
everyone here and in the United States knows to have been different
approaches to some of these vital Middle Eastern questions. They
know it. We know it. Of course, we deplore it –

And here is the point –

but I do not think it can carry with it this corollary, that we must
in all circumstances secure agreement from our American ally before
we can act ourselves in what we know to be our own vital interests. –
[OFFICIAL REPORT, 31 October 1956; Vol. 558, c. 1453.]

I am bound to say to the House that the list of charges has
changed in character. [HON. MEMBERS: 'Hear, hear.'] I want
the House to note that. I want to try to tick off those charges
which are not, shall I say, now made. Some may say that they

were never made. They have not been made by the right hon. Gentleman the Leader of the Opposition, but at any rate they were made by others. There is no charge of incitement – [HON. MEMBERS: 'There never was.'] That is very interesting. I am merely readjusting the list. Nor is there a charge of any prior agreement with Israel or foreknowledge. [HON. MEMBERS: 'Yes.'] I do not know about that. Last weekend the hon. Gentleman himself said that we had a 'shrewd idea'. That is quite a different matter from 'collusion' or 'incitement'. To have a 'shrewd idea' of what may happen in the Middle East seems to me the minimum which could be expected of a Government – the very minimum. To have a shrewd idea of what is likely to happen is quite a different thing from 'collusion'.

I want to come to the last question, which is, 'Did we have plans with the French, and discussions about plans with them?' Most certainly we had discussions about plans with the French. We have had them, roughly, from the beginning of August in one form or another – military discussions of some kind. They had been going on in various forms also in the tripartite discussions. What was different from the beginning of August and any earlier time was that we were moving out reinforcements to the Eastern Mediterranean, and so were the French. We both had forces there and, as a result, it was only proper – it would have been mad if we had not – to have some form of discussion with each other.

The right hon. Gentleman made a previous reference to Jordan and wrote that off quite quickly. I think he will understand, and I think I am entitled to say to the House, that although it is quite easy to write that one off quickly now, that was, in fact, by far and away the greatest anxiety we had at that period – by far and away – because it seemed to us – [HON. MEMBERS: 'Why?']. I will say that it seemed to us, particularly when the staff talks were made between Egypt and the two Arab States of Jordan and Syria that – and Israel could see it – it·was tightening the noose round Israel's neck. That being so, which of the three countries – supposing Israel reacted at all – was she most likely to react against?

MR DENIS HEALEY (Leeds, East) *rose* –

THE PRIME MINISTER: I cannot give way. I am trying not to trespass upon the time of the House. I think that I am entitled to put this view. Looking at the matter from a military point of view, it seemed possible, to put it no higher – I would put it higher than that, and say probable – that, feeling the noose tightening –

AN HON. MEMBER: It is all in order now.

MR DEPUTY-SPEAKER: Order. An hon. Member said, 'It is all in order now'. The Prime Minister is answering questions which the Leader of the Opposition put to him. That is why I am allowing him to continue.

THE PRIME MINISTER: If anybody had been in Tel Aviv at that time, and if they were concerned with what had happened, they would have known that Israel would strike out before she was strangled. Jordan was a possibility upon the list, and a possibility in a different category from Egypt, from our point of view, because we had a treaty with Jordan. Not only had we a treaty with her, but nobody else had. If there is anybody in the House who thinks that France or the United States would have acted in a military sense if Israel had taken military action there they are entitled to their belief; it is a belief about which I would have some doubts.

The position is more difficult than that, because we had the only air arm and armour in Jordan. I can tell the House that there was an occasion, in one of these raids, when it seemed that we would actually be called upon to put the Royal Air Force into operation, because it was thought that Israeli aeroplanes were in action. If they had been, it would have been a very grave matter indeed. If we had put the Royal Air Force into action against Israel's air force it would have been a matter of the utmost gravity. I do not know what it would have led to. We should have been involved in the actual fighting. [AN HON. MEMBER: 'We all agree about that '] All I am saying is that this fact cannot be left out of our discussion.

The right hon. Gentleman said that I told the House recently – in fact, we told the country publicly at the time – that we issued warning after warning. I give that as one example of the matters which we raised. I do not deny that this was a matter which we discussed with our allies. I do not deny that it was a matter about which we warned Israel. There were no plans got together to attack Egypt; there were military discussions of various kinds and finally the decision was taken on that day.

I am not going to say what our military plans were, but I say that we were right to make those preparations. Otherwise, I cannot conceive the point of having troops in the Eastern Mediterranean at all. The decision to put them into operation was taken here on the day I gave.

II

I should like first to deal with the questions asked by the hon. Member for Orkney and Shetland (Mr Grimond) about dates and knowledge in respect of Tel Aviv. In a sense, they will meet also the point raised by the hon. Member for Dudley (Mr Wigg). Whatever may or may not have been said in supplementaries in sharp quick answers, the facts are these. They have been said, and I want to make them absolutely clear in relation to dates.

On 26 October, we heard from our representatives in Tel Aviv that Israel was mobilizing. It was not then known whether it was a partial or total mobilization. We sent instructions on the next day, 27 October, to our Ambassador at Tel Aviv to make representations to Israel on the matter. It is quite true that he pointed out once again, not for the first time, that if there were an Israeli attack on Jordan, the United Kingdom would be bound to intervene in accordance with the Anglo-Jordan Treaty. That is quite true.

Our ambassador also urged restraint on Israel in other directions, amongst other reasons because it was quite obvious that if Israel attacked any of the other Arab countries, whichever it might be, there was the possibility of Jordan becoming involved and a difficult situation being created for the United Kingdom. That was quite apart –

MR S. SILVERMAN *rose* –

HON. MEMBERS: Sit down.

THE PRIME MINISTER: I am answering the hon. Gentleman behind the hon. Member, who put some specific questions to me. I have looked out these dates very carefully to make sure that I am getting the matter right. The hon. Member was not even in the House when this was going on.

MR SILVERMAN: Yes, I was.

THE PRIME MINISTER: I beg the hon. Member's pardon. That representation was quite apart from the risk of a general war which could have resulted from any such attack.

On 29 October, our Minister in Tel Aviv saw the Israeli Minister for Foreign Affairs and she assured him that no further hostile move was intended against Jordan – [*Interruption*] – that was in the morning. She also said that Israel was not seeking military adventures, and she explained the mobilization on the ground that Israel had to be prepared against possible attack. That was the position on 29 October.

I want to answer –

MR PHILIP NOEL-BAKER (Derby, South) *rose* –

HON. MEMBERS: Sit down.

THE PRIME MINISTER: I want to answer that before I give way. I do not know how long Mr Speaker will allow this debate to continue. I want to answer these questions, which were asked some time ago. I wish to make it clear that there was no joint decision in advance of hostilities about the use of a veto. There was no joint decision about the use of the French Air Force in advance of hostilities.

MR CROSSMAN *rose* –

THE PRIME MINISTER: Let me finish my sentence. I want to say this on the question of foreknowledge, and to say it quite bluntly to the House, that there was not foreknowledge that Israel would attack Egypt – there was not. But there was something else. There was – we knew it perfectly well – a risk of it, and in the event of the risk of it certain discussions and conversations took place, as, I think, was absolutely right, and as, I think, anybody would do. So far from this being an act of retribution, I would be compelled – and I think my colleagues would agree – if I had the same very disagreeable decisions to take again, to repeat them. [HON. MEMBERS: 'Hear, hear.']

APPENDIX 8

Meeting of the 1922 Committee, 18 December 1956

(Notes on two statements by Sir Anthony Eden)

These notes were made immediately after the meeting in question by a Conservative MP who had been present.

EDEN: I thank those of you who were loyal to the Government. I was most reluctant to accept the advice to go abroad, to go away was the shortest way back.

We feared an Israeli–Jordan war all summer. A fantastically false picture to imagine that UNO could deal with the situation. The noose was tightening round Israel. 'We did everything we could by warning.' My main fear was of the other Arabs joining in.

As long as I live, I shall never apologize for what we did (*loud cheers*).

Why did we not go on? Because, according to the estimate we were given, it would have taken six days to get to Suez.

The Cabinet were united on the decision to halt.

One of the main charges against us is that we have constantly changed our ground. Of course we have; as events unfolded, new statements had to be made. For example, we knew before about Russian infiltration into Egypt, but not the extent of it, which only our action revealed.

America. We have been patient with the US over a long time. We might have expected something in return. Now we must rebuild the Atlantic alliance, a real partnership.

France. A Renaissance. Much impressed by the young men in Mollet's cabinet.

Defence. Fewer men, better equipment.

Home. Suez an undoubted set-back to our economy.

Conclusion. I am not one of those who think that the next General Election is lost. Our Suez action was supported by a great mass of ordinary men and women. On our unity all depends. We are the better party and only disunity can cause us to fail.

Later, NIGEL NICOLSON *spoke*, as one of those 'who were disloyal to the Prime Minister'. He complained that the operation was not only inexpedient, but wrong in principle. 'It was undertaken in such a way as to force honourable men, including the Prime Minister himself, to make use of methods which were at variance with our Party's principles and pledges, and of arguments which were in themselves dishonourable. I have been shocked by the series of half-truths which we have been obliged to tell to justify our action. I needn't specify them because they are nearly all familiar. Iremonger raised one of them just now – the charge of collusion. Why did the Prime Minister not give him a more direct denial? Then there is the difference between the French and the British explanations of why we did not tell the Americans. And the legend that we have "helped the UN". Let me add a fourth. What did the Prime Minister mean when he said just now that "we did everything we could by warning" to stop the Israel–Arab war? Whom did we warn of what? . . .

'This is the sort of thing I mean by "half-truths". . . . They are out of character with the tradition of our Party, and (if I may say so) with the personality and record of the Prime Minister himself. I felt that it could not be to the discredit of the Party, if at least one of us on the backbenches rose up and said so.'

EDEN *replied* : 'Much obliged to Mr Nicolson. I would certainly not complain of any "disloyalty". We have always been proud in our Party that everyone should feel free to express what he thinks.

'Of course there was something unpleasant about our action. Surely you don't imagine that M. Mollet and I enjoyed going behind the back of the Americans and United Nations? But what was the alternative? To let the war spread, while UNO debated for three months what to do? I can understand what Mr Nicolson means by "half-truths". Some – and if they existed at all, they were not serious or many in number – were necessary, and always are, in this sort of operation which demands extreme secrecy in its operation.'

NICOLSON then said that he had not wished to 'leave it to UNO but to invoke the Tripartite Declaration, which had been devised for exactly this type of situation, and if the Americans refused to join us, as they said they would (*shouts of* Oh No, they wouldn't), then we should have implemented it alone with the French.'

EDEN: 'I will have to look up your point about the Americans and the Tripartite Declaration. I haven't got it in my head.'

[The last admission was one which suggested to some present that Eden was no longer able to carry out the business of being Prime Minister.]

APPENDIX 9

Ben Gurion speaks to Malcolm Muggeridge

(*Listener*, 2 May 1968, p. 569)

MUGGERIDGE: When the next war with the Arabs came up, this was connected with the Suez operation.

BEN GURION: Well, about Suez I can tell nothing for the time being.

MUGGERIDGE: And yet you know in England people have told so much.

BEN GURION: I know they know everything, but not from me. Although I am not under obligation – neither to what's his name, Eden, nor to anybody else – because Eden didn't behave like a gentleman. I know they know everything. I have four volumes of what happened before the war, but I gave them an order not to publish it, and I have it here in this room and it wasn't published.

MUGGERIDGE: One day perhaps?

BEN GURION: Yes, of course, one day. When they will not be alive – Eden, Selwyn Lloyd and the others. But even then it took us only seven days to defeat them in Sinai.

APPENDIX 10

The Labour Party's Estimated 'Bill for Suez'

(Extract from 1959 Speakers' Handbook, Foreign Affairs Section, page 3)

ACCEPTING the Government's own figures for the value of the installations and ignoring the loss of gold and dollar reserves incurred during the financially disastrous period from October to December 1956 (£234 million) and the fall in production and employment in Britain, the total bill looks something like this:

	£
Extra expenditure by:	
Army	52,476,000
Navy	3,800,000
RAF	850,000
Value of Suez base:	
Stores and installations	64,000,000
Inadequate compensation for property taken over by Egypt, estimated at	50,000,000
Loss of oil revenue to British Petroleum	9,000,000
Loss of trade with Egypt (decline in exports over 1955)	
1956	6,000,000
1957	26,000,000
1958	16,000,000
Increase in cost of imports due to Suez crisis, estimated at	100,000,000
(Correct to nearest £ million)	£328,000,000

BIBLIOGRAPHY

APART from the Despatch by General Sir Charles Keightley (*Operations in Egypt*; a supplement to the *London Gazette*, 10 September 1957), there are no Government papers generally available though, as has been seen, possibly the British papers will yield few secrets; they are bound to have some, however, and the French and Israeli documents may be more complete. US papers will become available in a few years: Dulles's are already; but it is doubtful whether the State Department papers at least will throw much new light on what has already become known.

As for memoirs, there are now, on the English side: Eden's (first) volume of memoirs, *Full Circle* (Cassell, 1960), naturally of great interest, but an apologia and purely official and diplomatic. There is nothing about the Israeli friendship, but no denial of it. The only other Cabinet Minister of that time who has yet written a memoir is the Earl of Kilmuir, with his *Political Adventure* (Weidenfeld & Nicolson, 1964). Anthony Nutting's *No End of a Lesson* (Constable, 1967) is a study of great interest. Harold Macmillan's account of this crisis is awaited with keen interest. Mr Selwyn Lloyd's review of the first edition of this book (*Sunday Telegraph*, 30 April 1967) is of interest. Kirkpatrick wrote his memoirs, *Inner Circle* (Macmillan, 1959), but decided not to discuss Suez. Two British executants of policy have contributed some memories: Sir William Hayter, the ambassador in Moscow, in Chapter 2 of his *The Kremlin and the Embassy* (Hodder, 1966), and General Sir Hugh Stockwell has written an honest account from his point of view in the *Sunday Telegraph*, 30 October, 6 November, and 13 November 1966. The relations between Government and press during the Suez crisis are discussed in Harman Grisewood's *One Thing at a Time* (Hutchinson, 1968).

On the French side, Pineau, Mollet and Bourgès-Maunoury have given some sort of account to Terence Robertson (see below) and Pineau also spoke to Peter Calvocoressi on the BBC (19 July 1966). Pineau wrote an article about his part in the affair in *Le Monde* (4 November 1966) and again contributed some interesting views in the *Daily Telegraph*, 6 June 1967. General Beaufre wrote first an article in *Le Figaro* (8 November 1966) and then a brilliant military study, *L'Expedition de Suez* (Grasset, Paris, 1967). There is a short but revealing passage about Suez in the memoirs of General Maurice Challe (*Notre Révolte*, Presses de la Cité, Paris, 1968) and a long and even more interesting one in Volume II of the memoirs of General Paul Ely (*Mémoirs*, II, *Suez ... le 13 mai*, Pion, Paris, 1969). The Israelis are represented by General Moshe Dayan with *Diary of the Sinai Campaign* (Weidenfeld & Nicolson, 1966), and *David's Sling* by Shimon Peres (Weidenfeld & Nicolson, 1970). The diaries of Tsur (*Prélude à Suez*, Presses de la Cité, Paris, 1968) are of interest. Iraqi policy is illuminated by Waldemar Gallman, *Iraq under General Nuri; my recollections of Nuri al-Said* (Baltimore, 1964).

The US have now Eisenhower's second volume of memoirs, *Waging Peace* (Heinemann, 1966), of considerable interest (the appendixes especially), and Robert Murphy's *Diplomat among Warriors* (Collins, 1964). Memoirs by Emmet Hughes (*Ordeal of Power*, London, 1963) and Sherman Adams (*First Hand Report*, London, 1963) have some relevant passages. See also the article by W. Aldrich, the then US Ambassador, in *Foreign Affairs*, April 1967, and Cary Joynt, *John Foster Dulles and the Suez Crisis*, which makes use of the Dulles papers, in Gerald N. Greb (editor), *Statesmen and Statecraft of the Modern West: Essays in Honour of Dwight E. Lee and H. Donaldson Jordan* (Barre, Mass., 1967). For Egypt, Nasser has given occasionally interesting interviews (e.g. *Sunday Times*, 17 June, 24 June and 1 July 1962).

The Times and other newspapers of the time are of incomparable value as is *Hansard*. An important debate was that in the House of Lords on 1 June 1967.

The most general secondary books are: Henri Azeau, *La Piège de Suez* (Laffont, Paris, 1964), a brilliant book written from the French point of view, very suggestive but not always fair or accurate where the British are concerned; Michel Bar-Zohar, *Suez: ultra-secret* (Fayard, Paris, 1965), is an account of Franco-Israeli friendships. Terence Robertson, *Crisis* (Hutchinson, 1965), is a book of great interest but open to doubt as to the exact accuracy of some of the conversations. He is most reliable where Canadians are concerned. Herman Finer's *Dulles over Suez* (London, 1964) is a passionate attack on Dulles, with the accusation that Dulles acted out of fear of Russia and against Eisenhower, who is accused of panic. Leon David Epstein's *British Politics in the Suez Crisis* (London, 1964) is a scholarly treatment of internal party politics and public opinion. The various pieces of testimony by actors of the time to the BBC programmes in 1966 were brought together by the BBC in *Suez Ten Years After* edited by Anthony Moncrieff (BBC, 1967).

On special subjects, there is A. J. Barker's excellent account of the military operations, *Suez: The Six Day War* (Faber, 1964), and Edgar O'Ballance's *The Sinai Campaign* (Faber, 1959), written from the Israeli viewpoint. There is also S. L. A. Marshall's *Sinai Victory* and Sholmo Bauer's *The Weekend War.* A contrast is Erskine Childers' apologia for Egyptian nationalism, *The Road to Suez* (MacGibbon & Kee, 1960). Sir Anthony Eden emerges much the worse for wear from Randolph Churchill's *The Rise and Fall of Sir Anthony Eden* (MacGibbon & Kee, 1959), which has new material in it. (See also the debates in the House of Commons in December 1958 deriving from a serialization of it.) Merry and Serge Bromberger gave a famous account in *Les Secrets de Suez* (Editions des 4 fils Aymon, Paris, 1957), deriving from the French Ministry of Defence for whom it is an apologia; much of it is true, even the conversation. Paul Johnson's *The Suez War* (MacGibbon & Kee, 1957) is an exciting account of the background, though on the details events turned out to have been even more unusual than he thought. The two volumes of the *Survey of International Affairs* published by Chatham House (1955–6 and 1956–8) are as usual a useful general guide to both background and events. Patrick Seale's *The Struggle for Syria* (Oxford University Press, 1965) is most illuminating both for the general background and for Anglo-Iraqi activity against Syria.

A novel, *No. 10* by William Clark, Eden's press officer, though not a *roman à clef*, provides some keys.

The reviews of both the first edition of this book and of Anthony Nutting's *No End of a Lesson* contain interesting material.

Among interesting articles on Suez are:

André Fontaine, 'Il y a dix ans la Guerre de Suez' (*Le Monde*, 30–31 October, 1 November 1966).

O. M. Smolansky, 'Moscow and the Suez Crisis 1956; a Reappraisal' (*Political Science Quarterly*, December 1965).

Brigadier C. N. Barclay, 'Anglo-French Operations against Port Said' (*The Army Quarterly*, April 1957).

V. Flintham, 'Suez 1956: A Lesson in Air Power' (*Air Pictorial*, August and September 1965).

Captain Cyril Falls, 'Operation "Musketeer" ' (*Brassey's Annual*, 1957).

Captain C. J. Smith, 'Suez and the Commando Carrier Concept' (*RUSI Journal*, February 1963).

J. E. Dougherty, 'The Aswan Decision in Perspective' (*Political Science Quarterly*, vol. 74 (March 1959), pp. 21–45).

M. S. Venicataramani, 'Oil and US Foreign Policy during the Suez Crisis' (*International Studies*, vol. 2, No. 2, October 1960).

Two articles (by A. L. Goodhart, 'Some Legal Aspects of the Suez Situation', and Clyde Eagleton, 'The UN and the Suez Crisis') in Philip W. Thayer, *Tensions in the Middle East* (Baltimore, 1958).

Percy Corbett, 'Power and Law at Suez' (*International Journal*, vol. 12, No. 1, Winter 1956–7).

Peter Calvocoressi, BBC Broadcasts July–August 1966, together with articles in the *Listener* (14 July–4 August 1966).

A. H. Hourani, 'The Middle East and the Crisis of 1956', in *St Antony's Papers* No. 4, Middle East Affairs No. 1 (London, 1958).

Watt, Donald, *The High Dam at Aswan and the Politics of Control*, in W. M. Warren and Neville Rubin, *Dams in Africa* (Frank Cass, London, 1969).

To those who wish to investigate the connexion between statecraft and liver failure, there is the 'Neuropsychiatric Syndrome Associated with Hepatic Cirrhosis and an extensive Portal Collateral Circulation' by W. H. J. Summerskill *et al.* (*Quarterly Journal of Medicine*, New Series, vol. XXV, No. 98, April 1956).

INDEX

MORE ABOUT PENGUINS
AND PELICANS

Penguinews, which appears every month, contains details of all the new books issued by Penguins as they are published. From time to time it is supplemented by *Penguins in Print*, which is a complete list of all books published by Penguins which are in print. (There are well over three thousand of these.)

A specimen copy of *Penguinews* will be sent to you free on request, and you can become a subscriber for the price of the postage. For a year's issues (including the complete lists) please send 4s. if you live in the United Kingdom, or 8s. if you live elsewhere. Just write to Dept EP, Penguin Books Ltd, Harmondsworth, Middlesex, enclosing a cheque or postal order, and your name will be added to the mailing list.

Another book by Hugh Thomas is described on the following page.

Note: *Penguinews* and *Penguins in Print* are not available in the U.S.A. or Canada

Also in Penguins by Hugh Thomas

THE SPANISH CIVIL WAR

New and Revised Edition

'A prodigy of a book. With boundless, incredible industry and sustained intelligence the author has assembled and studied all the available facts about the most heroic and pitiful story of this century' – Michael Foot in *Tribune*

A whole generation has grown up since the Spanish Civil War and it is still a subject of intense controversy. What was it that roused left-wing sympathizers from all over the world to fight for a cause for which their governments would not give active support? In this completely revised edition of his famous history Hugh Thomas presents an objective analysis of the issues of the first major explosion in the international conflict between Fascism and democracy.

'I have read it from cover to cover with enthralling interest ... he has the historian's most important quality, a tremendous appetite for detail and a grasp of the essential.... Almost no aspect of the Civil War, however painful or unpopular, escapes him in this splendid book' – Cyril Connolly in the *Sunday Times*